STALIN'S LIQUIDATION GAME

Ukrainian Research Institute
Harvard University

Harvard Series in Ukrainian Studies 86

Cambridge, Massachusetts

FILIP SLAVESKI AND YURII SHAPOVAL

STALIN'S LIQUIDATION GAME

THE UNLIKELY CASE OF OLEKSANDR SHUMS´KYI, HIS SURVIVAL IN SOVIET PRISON, AND HIS SUBSEQUENT ARCANE ASSASSINATION

50 years ■ 1973–2023

Distributed by Harvard University Press
for the Ukrainian Research Institute
Harvard University

The Harvard Ukrainian Research Institute was established in 1973 as an integral part of Harvard University. It supports research associates and visiting scholars who are engaged in projects concerned with all aspects of Ukrainian studies. The Institute also works in close cooperation with the Committee on Ukrainian Studies, which supervises and coordinates the teaching of Ukrainian history, language, and literature at Harvard University.

Printed in India on acid-free paper

ISBN 9780674291591 (hardcover), 9780674292550 (paperback), 9780674292567 (epub), 9780674292642 (PDF)

Library of Congress Control Number: 2024944167
LC record available at https://lccn.loc.gov/2024944167

Cover art by Anya Styopina, https://zemla.studio
Book design by Andrii Kravchuk

Publication of this book has been made possible by the generous support of publications in Ukrainian studies at Harvard University by the following benefactors or funds endowed in their name:

Ostap and Ursula Balaban
Jaroslaw and Olha Duzey
Vladimir Jurkowsky
Myroslav and Irene Koltunik
Damian Korduba Family
Peter and Emily Kulyk
Irena Lubchak
Dr. Evhen Omelsky
Eugene and Nila Steckiw
Dr. Omeljan and Iryna Wolynec
Wasyl and Natalia Yerega

CONTENTS

EDITORIAL NOTE

In the text and bibliographic references of this book, the full Library of Congress system (ligatures omitted) is used to transliterate Ukrainian and other East Slavic personal names and toponyms, including diacritics and the soft sign (ь) and, in masculine surnames, the final "й" (thus, for example, Shums′kyi, Manuïl′s′kyi, Khvyl′ovyi, and Hrushevs′kyi, not Shumsky, Manuilsky, Khvylovy, and Hrushevsky). As a rule, personal names are given in forms characteristic of the cultural traditions to which the given person belonged. The exception to this is the transliteration of well-known personal names such as Joseph Stalin (not Iosif Stalin), Leon Trotsky (not Leon Trostkii), Lavrentii Beria (not Lavrentii Beriia), Lazar Kaganovich (not Lazar′ Kaganovich), Nikolai Yezhov (not Nikolai Ezhov), and others that appear here in spellings widely adopted in English-language texts, while the spelling of several other names of living authors follows their own preference.

Toponyms are either transliterated (diacritics omitted) from the language of the country in which the designated places are currently located, or spellings widely adopted in English are used (thus Moscow, not Moskva; Munich, not München, and so on). For the Ukrainian capital, the spelling Kyiv is consistently used in the text and in bibliographic references.

In the twentieth century, the Julian calendar (abbreviated OS for Old Style) used by the Eastern Slavs until 1918 lagged by thirteen days behind the Gregorian calendar used in Western Europe.

LIST OF ABBREVIATIONS

ACP(b)	All-Union Communist Party (of Bolsheviks)
Cheka (VChK)	All-Russian Extraordinary Commission
Comintern	Communist International
CP(b)U	Communist Party (of Bolsheviks) of Ukraine
CPP	Communist Party of Poland
CPSU	Communist Party of the Soviet Union
DAZhO	State Archives of Zhytomyr Oblast
DVU	Government Publishing House of Ukraine
GARF	State Archive of the Russian Federation
GPU	State Political Directorate
GUGB	Main Directorate of State Security in the NKVD
HDA SBU	Sectoral State Archive of the Security Services of Ukraine
KPK	[Communist] Party Control Commission
MGB	Ministry of State Security (known as the NKGB until 1946)
MVD	Ministry for Internal Affairs (known as the NKVD until 1946)
NEP	New Economic Policy
NKGB	People's Commissariat of State Security
NKVD	People's Commissariat for Internal Affairs
OGPU	Joint State Political Directorate of the USSR
OUN	Organization of Ukrainian Nationalists
RCP(b)	Russian Communist Party (of Bolsheviks)
RSDLP	Russian Social Democratic Labor Party
RSFSR	Russian Soviet Federative Socialist Republic

RUP	Revolutionary Ukrainian Party
Selrob	Ukrainian Peasants' and Workers' Socialist Alliance
Sovnarkom	Council of People's Commissars
SVU	Union for the Liberation of Ukraine
TsA FSB	Central Archive of the Federal Security Service (Russia)
TsDAHOU	Central State Archive of Public Organizations and Ukrainica of Ukraine
UAOC	Ukrainian Autocephalous Orthodox Church
UCP(b)	Ukrainian Communist Party (of Borotbysts)
UHVR	Ukrainian Supreme Liberation Council
UkrSSR	Ukrainian Soviet Socialist Republic
UMO	Ukrainian Military Organization
UPA	Ukrainian Insurgent Army
UPR	Ukrainian People's Republic
UPSR	Ukrainian Party of Socialist-Revolutionaries
USDRP	Ukrainian Social Democratic Workers Party
USSR	Union of Soviet Socialist Republics
VAPLITE	Free Academy of Proletarian Literature (Ukraine)
VUAN	All-Ukrainian Academy of Sciences
VUTsVK	All-Ukrainian Central Executive Committee
ZP UHVR	External Representation of the Ukrainian Supreme Liberation Council

ACKNOWLEDGMENTS

We would like to thank everyone who contributed to our research and to the development of this book. We address our gratitude, first of all, to colleagues in the Ukrainian historical archives: Andrii Kohut, Director of the Sectoral State Archive of the Security Service of Ukraine (Haluzevyi derzhavnyi arkhiv Sluzhby Bezpeky Ukraïny, HDA SBU), Olʹha Bazhan, Director of the Central State Archive of Public Organisations of Ukraine (Tsentralʹnyi derzhavnyi arkhiv hromadsʹkykh ob’iednanʹ Ukraïny, TsDAHOU), Larysa Batrak, employee of this archive, and Nataliia Makovsʹka, former Director of the Central State Archive of Supreme Bodies of Power and Government of Ukraine (Tsentralʹnyi derzhavnyi arkhiv vyshchykh orhaniv vlady ta upravlinnia Ukraïny, TsDAVOU).

Our research assistants, Liudmyla Druzenko and Antonina Berezovenko, also contributed to the development of this book. So did members of the Harvard Ukrainian Research Institute (HURI), particularly Serhii Plokhii and Oleh Kotsyuba, who have long appreciated both the historical and contemporary importance of our subject. We are deeply grateful to editors Michelle Viise (HURI), Jessica Hinds-Bond, and Claire Rosenson for their tireless work on improving the manuscript of this book in more ways than we can describe here.

Research for this book was partially funded by the Australian Government through the Australian Research Council (ARC).

Filip Slaveski was the recipient of an ARC Discovery Early Career Award (DE150100969) funded by the Australian Government.

Finally, we give special thanks to our wives, Fleur Slaveska and Olena Malynovs´ka, who have helped so much with their patience and advice over the years.

PREFACE

Russia's full-scale military invasion of Ukraine on 24 February 2022 makes the subject of this book, Oleksandr Shums´kyi (2 December 1890 to 18 September 1946), all the more relevant. Shums´kyi despised the imperialist view of Ukraine as "Little Russia" (*Malorossiia*), a construct advanced throughout the twentieth century by dictators in the Kremlin and promoted by the current president of the Russian Federation, Vladimir Putin. According to this view, Ukraine is not a "real" country, but rather an invention. In fact, according to the "Little Russia" formulation, Ukraine is a subservient appendage of its great neighbor Russia, which is itself the center of the so-called *russkii mir* (Russian world). Armed with this idea, as well as with guns, tanks, bombs, missiles and other murderous instruments of war, Putin has brought the destructiveness of the *russkii mir* to all of Ukraine in our time.

Shums´kyi was one of the staunchest opponents of attempts to mold Ukraine into Malorossiia, and, as a powerful Soviet political leader, he was well placed to oppose it effectively. Like so many of his socialist comrades, Shums´kyi joined the Bolshevik party immediately after the Revolution. Getting involved in the Bolshevik cause during the Civil War, Shums´kyi was inspired by the party's socialist democratic agenda of national self-determination, much discussed in 1917 and adopted as doctrine after 25 October of that year. When the party began to waver from this agenda, Shums´kyi criticized it for "Great Russian chauvinism" and for its wilful ignorance of the differences between Russia and Ukraine. Yet, Shums´kyi thought he could "correct" Bolshevik chauvinism from the inside and help to build a real socialist federation of independent and equal nations that would be true to the ideals of 1917.

This project soon came to naught. Much like Putin today, the people in power and the cultural elite in Moscow in the 1920s maintained that Ukrainian national identity could be subsumed in the unequal power dynamic of "brotherhood" with Russia. Outwardly, the Bolsheviks supported the aims of Ukrainian independence and self-determination; inwardly, they worked against both aspirations. The elite was effectively reinstating Malorossiia, albeit in a new Soviet empire (the USSR of 1924), which could mimic the ideal union of independent republics because only one party, centered in Moscow, ruled in every republic. From the 1930s onward, the elite dropped any pretense of supporting Ukrainian independence and began a massive purge of the thousands of Soviet politicians in Ukraine and other republics who remained committed to the national ideal of 1917. They were arrested, forced to confess under torture to false crimes such as "nationalist counterrevolution," and executed by the thousands.

Shums´kyi was different. He never confessed to the phony charges the Stalinist state leveled at him. He survived in the penal system for over a decade, suffering mistreatment and abuse that left him paralyzed. During this time, the state murdered his wife, yet he continued the struggle for a Soviet socialist Ukraine until Stalin finally had him assassinated in 1946. Shums´kyi's survival for such a long period is unique, and an analysis of it illuminates the general workings of this machinery in new ways and encourages a reevaluation of the mass repressions in the Soviet Union that killed millions.

Though Shums´kyi remains largely unknown in Ukraine outside academic circles, a new generation of Ukrainians has found common cause with his struggle against Russian subjugation. For many, entrance onto the battlefield happened figuratively and actually after Russia's military aggression against Ukraine in 2014. Since Russia's full-scale invasion of 24 February 2022, these Ukrainians have, with much of the democratic world behind them, resisted Putin's attempt to destroy Ukraine as an independent nation. In bringing Shums´kyi's experience to the awareness of the contemporary world, we do not seek to idealize him. We understand him in the context of his time as a tragic figure whose complexities militate against any monochromatic appropriation of a past "hero" for contemporary political purposes. Shums´kyi was a lifelong revolutionary who helped to build Soviet Ukraine by spilling the blood of his enemies and even sometimes his comrades. He understood his world and the value of other human beings only through a revolutionary-socialist lens. But Shums´kyi never lost a sense of dignity or a love for his homeland. Throughout periods of unimaginable torment, he never stopped fighting against Russia's humiliation of Ukraine or Russian attempts to strangle Ukraine's path to independence. His battle, fought alone as a paralytic arrested and exiled to Siberia, can now be known to the world.

Filip Slaveski
Canberra, Australia

Yurii Shapoval,
Tübingen, Germany

November 2023

INTRODUCTION

On 19 September 1946, railway personnel on the train from Saratov to Kyiv discovered the body of a passenger who had died overnight in his carriage. They handed the body over to medical authorities at Kirsanov Railway Station, and an autopsy determined that the passenger's cause of death was a "hemorrhage in the cranial cavity." The authorities concluded that the death was due to natural causes, having little reason to suspect otherwise. Declassified archival sources now confirm that Soviet secret agents murdered the man. They broke into his railway carriage overnight, held him down, and administered the radioactive poison that killed him without leaving any medical trace. The Soviet agents left no criminal trace either, having prepared extensively for their operation. They knew the exact schema of the man's carriage and handover times between railway authorities, allowing them to strike quickly when the train was unguarded. These were the hallmark traits of the Soviet Union's best assassins.[1]

The victim, lifelong Ukrainian Marxist revolutionary Oleksandr Shums′kyi, was lucky to have survived until September 1946. In 1919, with a warrant out for his arrest, Shums′kyi attended a major political conference after the collapse of the Skoropads′kyi military dictatorship in Kyiv. Participating in disguise and under a pseudonym, he revealed his identity once he took the stage to criticize the new regime, the Directory of the Ukrainian People's Republic (the Directorate), for its "bourgeois" policies. His speech was cut short when he was dragged from the stage, beaten, and sentenced to death on the spot. The conference broke down into chaos, allowing Shums´kyi to escape the melee, avoid the subsequent manhunt, and work toward the establishment of Soviet power in Ukraine.[2] Later, Shums´kyi emerged as a key figure in the new Soviet government, serving as Soviet Ukraine's consul to Poland and then as the people's commissar for education from 1924 until 1927, when he was removed on the charge of promoting "Shums´kyism." The charge and his removal were primarily the work of his chief detractors, head of the Ukrainian Communist Party Lazar Kaganovich and general secretary of the Communist Party of the Soviet Union Joseph Stalin. In labeling his commitment to realizing the goals of the Soviet policy of Ukrainization through Ukrainian language and national consciousness "Shums´kyism," they signaled that Shums´kyi had gone too far beyond the narrow and shifting parameters of control they had set.

Shums´kyi's arrest followed in 1933 as part of a broader purge of the Ukrainian political and intellectual elite—the chief adherents of Ukrainization—as Moscow rolled back this policy. Moscow blamed Ukrainization for the mass social unrest in Ukraine that emerged in response to its forced collectivization of the peasantry, which intensified in famine in 1932–33, causing millions of deaths. In addition to violently pacifying the countryside, Moscow responded to the growing unrest by leveling at Shums´kyi and his associates the baseless charge of belonging to the anti-Soviet Ukrainian Military Organization (UMO), which supposedly worked to overthrow Soviet power in Ukraine.[3] Unlike all of his immediate associates, however, Shums´kyi spent his confinement refusing to confess to belonging to UMO, attacking his prosecutors, and demanding public rehabilitation. If not for these demands, his ill health, and his partial paralysis, which led to the commutation of his prison sentence to exile in the Soviet Far East in 1935, Shums´kyi likely would have been shot alongside his colleagues then or during the Great Terror in 1937–38.

After years of failed petitions for rehabilitation, the execution of his wife by authorities in 1937, and the death of his son in combat in the Battle of Moscow in 1942, and with his paralysis only increasing, Shums´kyi tried twice to commit suicide in

July 1946. He survived long enough for Stalin, his "old comrade," to read at least the most inflammatory parts of the suicide letter Shums′kyi had addressed to him.[4] Death by suicide was intolerable to Stalin, who had Shums′kyi killed before he could make another attempt at it.[5]

In addition to his growing hopelessness, there was another motivation for Shums′kyi's suicide attempt. In his 1946 letter to Stalin, whom he had known personally since the 1920s, he protested the Soviet leadership's openly chauvinistic Russian social policies and attitudes toward Ukraine, which had gathered pace in the immediate aftermath of the Second World War. The head of the Ukrainian Communist Party, Nikita Khrushchev, drew the greatest ire of Shums′kyi for his sycophantic speech in October 1945, thanking the Russian people on behalf of Ukraine for their help and leadership in the war. This followed Stalin's own toast of the Russian people when celebrating victory over Nazi Germany in May 1945, in which he drank to their health "because it is the most outstanding nation of all the nations forming the Soviet Union."[6]

Stalin and Khrushchev's celebrations of the ethnic leadership of Russians in the Soviet Union during the war were anathema to the Marxism to which Shums′kyi subscribed and the Soviet project of equality among nationalities to which he remained committed, despite suffering at its hands. Shums′kyi recognized this new wave of Russification based on old racist tropes of Russian leadership; Ukrainian servility was especially pernicious now, given the incredible sacrifices of the Ukrainian population during the war, with millions of Ukrainians killed, maimed, or displaced.[7] He wrote to Stalin:

> Those people of the Little-Russian sort ... always drone on in a servile, flattering, and pernicious way about "our older Russian brother" and about how he is always helping his "younger brother," the Ukrainian people. Nikita Khrushchev, in the lyrical ecstasy of his Little Russianness, not only sang about the "seniority" of the Russian people to the Ukrainian people and about how the Russian people helped the "younger" Ukrainian people, but went so far as to howl on about the gratitude of the Ukrainian to the Russian people. Gratitude for what? For the clear mind, strong character, and indomitable will of the Russian people, it turns out.... Coming from the head of the Ukrainian government ... this is offensive and demeaning for

> the Ukrainian people... Because what? The Ukrainian people don't have clear minds, strong character, or an indomitable will?[8]

As both a lifelong communist and a Ukrainian patriot, Shums´kyi threatened to kill himself if Stalin continued to make incompatible the fundamental institutions of communism and patriotism, which were central to Shums´kyi's existence. Shums´kyi went on to claim that his attempted suicide was a "protest against this new policy of Great Russian nationalist politics toward Ukraine, which insults and humiliates the Ukrainian people."[9]

Stalin and his closest allies in the Soviet leadership read this letter closely and were clearly angered by Shums´kyi's symbolic protest. By the mid-1930s, Stalin, and by extension the state, came to view the suicide of prominent party members—those in line for expulsion and opponents to the regime—as a "political act, an explicit or implicit condemnation of the state [which] accordingly, official rhetoric branded cowardly and contemptible."[10] In addition to the metaphorical sting presented by Shums´kyi's suicide attempt, Stalin and the Soviet leadership had other, more practical reasons to kill him. The authorities delayed Shums´kyi's return to his homeland once he had completed his sentence in exile, particularly because Ukraine remained in the grip of a violent postwar anti-Soviet insurgency that had cost tens of thousands of lives.[11] In the reality that Stalin and his leadership inhabited, the paralyzed Shums´kyi was clearly seeking to return to Kyiv to reconnect with the Ukrainian nationalist organizations that were leading the anti-Soviet insurgency. The secret police even provided "evidence" to this effect, pushing for Shums´kyi's assassination before he got anywhere near Ukraine. That he was innocent of the 1933 charges on which this suspicion was based mattered little to this logic.[12] After all, there were clear antagonisms between Shums´kyi and the right-wing nationalist or émigré groups with which he was supposedly in cahoots; in fact, they despised him as an ardent communist. What did matter to Stalin was that Shums´kyi had declared his opposition to Soviet policy on Ukraine as anathema to the revolutionary principles on which the Soviet state was founded and now threatened to mobilize real opposition toward the state in life or, symbolically, in death, as a martyr.

Though Shums′kyi is largely forgotten in his homeland, he matters more than is indicated by the solitary plaque and street dedicated to him in his hometown of Zhytomyr or the relatively little attention he has received from historians. Shums′kyi's story provides new insights into the purge of the Ukrainian elite and the mechanics of Soviet repression. He survived in the hands of his interrogators by continuing to resist them for over a decade, when most of his compatriots were killed after complying with their demands.[13] His associates were arrested on similar charges and subjected to physical and psychological torture. Nearly all eventually broke under this torture and confessed to the false charges laid against them, implicating Shums′kyi as their ringleader. Those who "broke" accepted that continuing to resist the interrogations was pointless and may have believed their interrogators' assurances that confessing would save their lives. At least, they believed that confessing would save the lives of their loved ones, whom the interrogators also threatened. But the interrogators were lying. Confessing rarely saved the victims' lives—it was often the last step to their execution. As evident in the literature on the interrogation of suspects, either initial resistance or eventual compliance with the state, or indeed anything victims tried to do to avoid being killed, was equally futile.[14]

However, by refusing to confess to the false charges made against him and his compatriots, Shums′kyi posed a problem for the normal functioning of the machinery of repression. He denied his interrogators the key piece of evidence they sought that would demonstrate the necessary "legality," however perverse, of their investigation. When explaining the delay of Shums′kyi's case to their superiors in the late 1930s, his interrogators cited the lack of a confession as the major obstruction to proceeding to his trial (and execution). The problem was, the interrogators complained, that there was no real evidence against Shums′kyi. By "real evidence" they did not mean conclusive evidence of his crimes. If this had been the criterion they used to shoot people, then none of Shums′kyi's colleagues and few of the hundreds of thousands arrested by the state in the waves of mass repression in 1933 and 1937–38 would have been killed. What they meant by the lack of real evidence was that Shums′kyi's refusal to confess denied them the ability to corroborate, and thus make "real," the false statements made against him by his associates.

This was an unusual complaint and by no means a common obstacle posed to Moscow by a provincial arm of the secret police such as the People's Commissariat for Internal Affairs (NKVD) in Krasnoiarsk, where Shums′kyi was serving his exile. Refusal to confess and broader concerns about legality alone were usually insufficient to delay the quick line from arrest to trial and execution, especially during the Great Terror of 1937–38. In many cases, the continued refusal of a suspect to confess their crimes could be taken as further evidence of their intractable criminality, or it would simply be overlooked, especially if they were low-level political or state functionaries, or civilians. When people reneged at trial on confessions given under questioning by police, it rarely helped their defense or saved their lives. This was the case even if their reneging garnered attention from political leaders.[15]

Why was Shums′kyi's case different? Why and how did his refusal to confess keep him alive? Was his case unique, or does an analysis of it provide broader insight into the experience of victims of repression? This book unravels the "Shums′kyi riddle" by tracing his journey through the machinery of mass repression in the Soviet Union from the late 1920s to 1946. A key difference between Shums′kyi's journey and those of his associates was not simply his refusal to confess, but the broader protest he launched against his arrest, including hunger strikes and a letter-writing campaign to political leaders to clear his name and imperil his interrogators. It was this broader, sustained protest, launched mainly from exile in the Russian Far East, that seems to have been effective at critical times to delay the progression from arrest to trial and execution until the waves of mass repression had subsided. Protest kept Shums′kyi alive in 1933, led to the commutation of his hard labor sentence to one of exile in 1935, and kept him from being tried and shot by a military tribunal as incoming head of the NKVD Lavrentii Beria and chief prosecutor of the Soviet Union Andrei Vyshinskii demanded in late 1938.

After the Terror ended, Shums′kyi was released from arrest and sent back into exile. He thus stayed afloat through the two waves of mass repression that drowned nearly all his Ukrainian communist movement associates who were arrested alongside him in 1933 and shot in 1937–38. Nearly all of them falsely confessed to crimes supposedly committed under Shums′kyi's leadership. His wife did not, but nevertheless was arrested in October 1937 and shot in December of the same year.

An analysis of Shums′kyi's unique trajectory through the machinery of mass repression in the Soviet Union provides more general insights into the Soviet Union's operation. This journey arguably began before Shums′kyi's arrest, with his removal from the post of people's commissar for education in 1927. Shums′kyi's protest letters from then until his death in 1946 were read by key Soviet political and police leaders, who discussed the implications of his case, establishing an indirect interplay between a paralyzed "criminal" in the Soviet Far East and the higher echelons of Soviet power. This interplay is recorded in Shums′kyi's declassified documentation, spread between the Russian and Ukrainian security and communist or state party archives, and is now accessible in almost its entirety to researchers.[16] Some files presented here are contained in the Russian Central Archive of the Federal Security Service (TsA FSB) in Moscow, which is closed to most researchers. This collection, which includes files on Shums′kyi's close associates and leading figures in Ukrainization who were also repressed at that time, sheds new light on the broader relationship between political violence and Soviet nationality policy in Ukraine from the 1920s onward. The Soviet regime's distinct pathological attitude toward Ukrainian identity encouraged Soviet leaders to understand complex political and ethnic crises and their solutions in Ukraine in a dangerously reductionist manner. As the 1920s progressed, they came to interpret a wider array of political actions and cultural expressions in Ukraine more narrowly as constituting a threat that was termed "Ukrainian nationalism," even though they had previously permitted, even encouraged, many of these expressions as a matter of official policy. The entire project of Ukrainization—the harmonious union of Ukrainian statehood and Soviet communism that Shums′kyi and thousands of his party compatriots pursued—became, or was revealed as, inharmonious. One could only be built at the expense of the other, and it would not be independent Ukrainian statehood, or at least anything beyond a nominal version of it. The leadership's violent response to those who failed to accept this fact, or anyone they felt might not accept it, fed their pathology with mass purges of Ukrainian political and cultural figures throughout the following decades in a complex, reciprocal relationship for which Shums'kyi's case and those of his close associates offer unique insights.

Beyond that, though, the analysis of this documentary evidence aids in a deeper understanding of the relationship between the NKVD's central and provincial arms and demonstrates how provincial concerns could forestall central demands for blood. Records of the surveillance conducted against Shums'kyi reveal granular details of the daily operations of provincial NKVD agents (Chekists) and the degree to which they carried out, or failed to carry out, orders from above. Some of these themes are well covered in the massive literature on the history of state repression in the Soviet Union during the 1930s and have been the subject of numerous scholarly debates (addressed below).[17] But rarely is a body of documentary evidence available on the fate of a single political leader in relation to his closest associates, a leader whose long journey through the machinery of Soviet oppression opens a small window into lesser-known aspects of its operation, especially the relationship between protest and survival. Some of the well-covered issues of Soviet repression look very different viewed through the frame created by Shums'kyi's case.

* * *

The historical literature on Shums'kyi and Shums'kyism remains small relative to his contribution to the development of the Ukrainian and the broader Soviet communist movement in the 1920s. Most importantly, little connection has been made between Shums'kyi the man and his ideas, meaning that until recently we have had little chance to begin understanding how his fate after his arrest shaped his ideas on Ukrainization and vice versa. This is especially problematic as Shums'kyi continued to develop these ideas while in exile, analyzing from afar the reversal of Ukrainization in the 1930s and the destruction of so many of the policy's achievements—and its adherents—in the purge of 1933 and, later, in the Great Terror. These ideas are now available to researchers in what remains of Shums´kyi's writings in the archives, and they make for compelling reading for those interested in this period.

Until the 1980s, Soviet state publications upheld the Stalinist line of criticism toward Shums´kyism, citing a 1926 letter from Stalin to Shums´kyi in which Stalin criticized him for the "forcible" nature and "fast pace" of Ukrainization. Stalin "feared" that Shums´kyi and his associates, who spoke openly about the need to combat the legacies of Russification in Ukraine, threatened to "undermine the friendship of Russian and Ukrainian peoples" and provided a platform for nationalist insurgency against Soviet power.[18] By the end of the 1980s, with glasnost in full swing, Ukrainian historians began to examine Ukrainization and its adherents more critically. Shums´kyi attracted only minor interest in this broader examination, mostly from Yurii Shapoval, and remained on the margins of broader historiographical interest.[19] In many ways, then, in the intellectual imagination of most scholars in the former Soviet space, Shums´kyi remained either a prisoner to Stalin's 1926 characterization of him or merely a victim of repression.

More ambitious attempts to investigate the relationship between Shums´kyism and Shums´kyi were made in literature abroad. James E. Mace's 1983 work on national communism in Ukraine and Terry Martin's 2001 book on nationalism in the Soviet Union both dedicated sections to the debate within the party over Shums´kyism in the 1920s and Shums´kyi's arrest in 1933.[20] These sections were part of these books' examinations of the effects that the purges of the Ukrainian intellectual and political elite in the 1930s had on shaping Ukraine into the later Soviet period. In the period between these two works, with the Soviet Union collapsing, more Ukrainian historians began looking at Shums´kyi as well, benefiting, like Martin, from access to Soviet archival materials.[21] But in the broader literature on Ukrainization in the 1920s and 1930s, Shums´kyi was often mentioned in passing rather than treated as a topic of investigation. Historians tended to stop discussing his life at the time of his arrest in 1933, even though from the early 1990s Russian memoirs and newspaper publications citing Russian security documents began to appear, giving some details of Shums´kyi's fate thereafter.[22] From these we learned of Shums′kyi's experience in the labor camps in the Soviet Far East, and that his death in 1946 was not by his own hand, as had previously been assumed, but on Stalin's order.

Shapoval's 2017 political biography of Shums′kyi, building on two decades of investigations into Shums′kyi's ideas and fate, was the first major scholarly work dedicated to examining Shums′kyi's entire life and the development of his ideas from the 1920s to his death in 1946.[23] Shapoval's Ukrainian-language biography began to bring Shums′kyi's fate from the margins to the center in the literature's understanding of the broader repression of the Ukrainian political and cultural elite in the 1930s. The present book contains selected parts of this biography and cites numerous archival documents, translated into English for the first time, including those related to Shums′kyi's experience and the evolution of his thinking on Ukrainization during his period of arrest, imprisonment, and exile (1933–46). This book's main purpose is to address key questions raised by Shapoval in the biography that were beyond the scope of that work. These concern the broader implications of Shums′kyi's experience for understanding the state's attack on Ukrainization, its purge of its adherents and the Ukrainian elite generally, and the broader mechanics of repression across the Soviet Union.

We pursue these questions not in a relative lacuna of scholarship, as with Shums′kyi's life and ideas, but, at least in part, in the most overcrowded of research fields in Soviet studies—the Great Terror of the 1930s.[24] On questions of the relationship between resistance and survival, between central and provincial security agencies, and between the purge of social elites and that of the broader citizenry, Shums′kyi's case disrupts established explanations provided in the literature. These disruptions demand examination.

First, from mid-1934 until the assassination of Leningrad Communist Party leader Sergei Kirov in December that year, there was a small window of opportunity for political leaders arrested in the early 1930s to have their sentences commuted or for them to be released. Some did this by reneging on their earlier confessions when standing trial, thus getting the attention of the leadership, or by sending a letter directly to Stalin or other members of the leadership while serving their sentences. Stalin and the leadership reviewed and granted applications for clemency at this time as part of the relaxation of the purge and police powers, and in light of their recognition that they may have gone too far in arresting and killing their erstwhile political allies as enemies in 1932–33.[25] The NKVD now needed to work according to the rules of "socialist legality," which limited its arrest powers and subordinated some of its functions, at least on paper, to the judiciary. Shums′kyi's prison sentence, however, was not commuted during this period, though his case was reviewed. His sentence was commuted only in December 1935, once the purge of political leaders had resumed in response to Kirov's assassination, with those granted clemency often rearrested and some later shot. This resumption of arrests of political figures coincided with the NKVD's actions to arrest tens of thousands of ordinary people living in Ukrainian regions bordering Poland on suspicion of the same charge for which Shums′kyi had been arrested in 1933: working with the assistance of Poland to help Ukraine secede from the Soviet Union.[26] Shums′kyi, the alleged leader of the main organization accused of pursuing this aim (UMO), had his sentence commuted and was "released" into exile when it seemed most unlikely.

The timing of Shums′kyi's release is an exception to the rule and thus seems to make little sense. Analyzing this exception, however, reveals that the police were anxious at least to appear to follow the rules of socialist legality when they resumed mass repression in 1935. Cases that they had clearly fabricated in 1933 and that remained "unresolved"—such as Shums′kyi's, due to his protests—threatened to reveal the extent to which police had disregarded and were still disregarding these rules. In contrast to earlier practice, they could now be punished, or at least embarrassed, for these omissions and the shoddiness of their work. Shums′kyi's continued protest in the new context of exile clearly embarrassed the police before the judiciary and the party, which required his confession in order to move his case forward—indeed, to validate its fabrication. The absence of a confession distinguished Shums′kyi's case from those of others who confessed and later reneged. Without a confession in 1935, he was released into exile, just as the later charges against him would be dropped in 1939, in the wake of the Terror, for the same omission.

The second disruption that demands examination concerns the role of provincial elites in carrying out the Great Terror in 1937–38, a topic of major debate in the literature for decades. Some historians have argued that local elites displayed significant initiative in driving the Terror, pushing Moscow to expand the scope and number of arrests and the severity of the punishment. This process demonstrates the significant interplay between central and local authorities in the Terror, which helps explain its mass scale and points to the limits of Moscow's control over it once it had been launched, in much the same way that it had been limited in other mass campaigns such as collectivization.[27] Other historians have argued that although local initiative was important in executing the Terror (no mass campaign could be conducted without it), the degree of this initiative and broader control over the Terror remained more or less in Stalin's hands at all times.[28]

At the margin of this broader debate on "initiative," some historians have pointed out the inherent bureaucratic resistance to the implementation of campaigns in the Soviet Union. In 1937–38, the development of the procuracy (*prokuratura*, i.e. state prosecutor) and criminal justice in general was stalled. Legal professionals, though also executors and victims of the Terror, at times displayed concern about the Terror's disregard of legal norms. This extended to their own positions of power in relation to the secret police; the role of extrajudicial bodies in processing arrest, trial, and execution; and, more broadly, the NKVD, which was generally pushing to expand the Terror.[29] The political leadership in Moscow voiced the same concerns to the party-state apparatus from late 1938 onward, as it brought a halt to the Terror. The head of the NKVD, Nikolai Yezhov, was replaced by Lavrentii Beria in November 1938, and surrounding this replacement was considerable criticism from the party leadership about the excesses of the NKVD in arbitrary arrest and execution.[30] The leadership issued numerous orders across the country to halt the Terror, partly by restoring procuratorial control over arrest and trial procedures. The NKVD's independent power to arrest and try suspects was reduced, and the makeshift tribunals (troikas) that had decided cases and sent hundreds of thousands to their deaths were disbanded (or at least were supposed to be). Beginning in November 1938, the central leadership berated the NKVD for relying primarily on denunciations and confessions extracted by force as sufficient evidence to shoot people.[31] From now on, it would have to provide more convincing evidence to prosecutors' offices to gain approval before its agents could arrest suspects, and it could no longer expect prosecutors to rubber-stamp their requests.[32] These orders were largely effective; the Terror was halted in most areas but continued in others, albeit on a smaller scale. Some local Soviet elites continued to operate as before, and Chekists, in particular, continued to shoot prisoners into late November 1938 and arrest suspects without procuratorial sanction for months afterward.[33]

Shums′kyi's case is disruptive precisely at this point of resistance from the NKVD to the restoring of procuratorial control over its capacity to arrest and try suspects. In the month following this series of orders, the chief prosecutor in the country and leading legal professional Andrei Vyshinskii approved a request from the emerging head of the NKVD, Lavrentii Beria, for Shums′kyi to be tried in the Military Collegium of the Supreme Court of the Soviet Union. This body was usually reserved for trying (and sentencing to death) political figures, whereas most other people had been tried with little fuss and on little or no evidence by the troikas, which were dissolved (on paper) in November 1938.[34] The Chekists in Krasnoiarsk stalled in fulfilling the order, asking for "real evidence" from the prosecutors and their superiors in the NKVD that they could bring to trial. They likely understood that their request for evidence would not be met because no such evidence existed. All the evidence they had were denunciations gained under interrogation, and Stalin had already criticized the NKVD in November for relying solely on these to shoot people. What they needed was Shums′kyi's own confession to corroborate the confessions of others, to make these fabrications "real." But he would not provide it. Nor would the Krasnoiarsk NKVD seriously attempt to elicit it from a paralyzed, bedridden suspect. Even amid the winding down of the Terror, confessions remained key evidence in Soviet jurisprudence.[35] Without Shums′kyi's confession, Chekists in Krasnoiarsk could argue there was not yet enough evidence to take Shums′kyi before the Collegium. They thus managed to stall the case by inverting the relationship between the

NKVD and the procuracy established by the 1938 decrees, in terms of standards of evidence and zeal for blood.

But why stall it in the first place? The answer to this question reveals a new element for analysis in the relationship between central and provincial elites in ending the Terror and the nuances of political control in a chaotic setting in late 1938. Chekists' intentional stalling of sensitive cases such as Shums´kyi's was evident in other areas beyond Krasnoiarsk, as they were unsure whether the superiors ordering arrest and trial would survive the broader purge of police, procuratorial, and other leaderships in the chaotic period beginning in late 1938 and reaching full steam by the following year. At the pivotal moment in late 1938, Chekists in Krasnoiarsk reckoned that they might suffer under one regime for implementing the orders of the previous one. And they reckoned correctly: even lower ranks of the NKVD were purged, with some Chekists shot for having fabricated cases against innocent people where real evidence was lacking.[36] Whereas during the Terror they kept their jobs exactly by fabricating cases, and thus showing zeal for arrest and execution, now they sought to survive by stalling over Shums´kyi, a "big political figure" who had not yet confessed. Even such powerful figures as Beria and Vyshinskii were unable to sway the Krasnoiarsk Chekists in 1938—nor could they in 1939 or 1940, when the chaos settled.

Some historians demonstrate Stalin's overall control of the process by highlighting the quick end of the Terror once the November decrees were issued.[37] Others cite significant examples of continued arrests by regional NKVD despite the central orders as evidence of the organic nature of the purge and the limits of central control. Chekists also murdered colleagues who, they believed, might work against them in the new regime after the transition from Yezhov to Beria.[38] These questions of control aside, the end of 1938 was a tumultuous time for the NKVD leadership and rank-and-file. What we need to understand is how the provincial offices of the NKVD used stalling as a mechanism of survival when they received unclear instructions from above. Especially with regard to Shums´kyi, we need to understand why the Krasnoiarsk NKVD continued to delay his case for years after this pivotal moment in late 1938, when it became more dangerous not to acquiesce to Moscow's demand for Shums´kyi's head than to do so.

* * *

In addition to parts of the aforementioned biography of Oleksandr Shums´kyi by Yurii Shapoval, this book comprises a further six chapters and a conclusion. Chapter 1, "The Murdered Ukrainian Revolution," traces the rise of Ukrainization in the 1920s and the Soviet leadership's subsequent attack on the policy and its adherents among the Ukrainian intellectual and political elite. Chapter 2, "Shums´kyi's Life and His Rise to People's Commissar," situates Shums´kyi in this environment, providing a brief sketch of his political biography and the collapse of his *Borotbysts* (from Ukrainian *borot´ba*: struggle, endeavor, fight), the most authoritative political party in Ukraine, under Bolshevik pressure, as well as his rise to the position of people's commissar for education in 1924. Chapter 3, "Shums´kyi's Fall as People's Commissar and 'Shums´kyism,'" reconstructs the political scandal that led to his removal as people's commissar for education—his battle with the head of the Ukrainian Communist Party Lazar Kaganovich—and argues that this scandal was the pivot point for the beginning of the Soviet leadership's mass purge in Ukraine.

Chapter 4, "From Political Accusations to Criminal Cases," covers the development from scandal in the late 1920s to mass purge of the Ukrainian political and cultural elite in the early 1930s. It compares the divergent behaviors of Shums´kyi and his associates under arrest and asks why Shums´kyi refused to confess when his associates did so and how this decision contributed to their death or survival. Chapter 5, "Exile, Survival, War, and 'Freedom,'" follows Shums´kyi's subsequent protest campaign against his arrest and exile, and its effect on decision-making among the leading Chekists and political leaders in charge of his fate. An analysis of this interplay within the context of broader changes in the NKVD leadership helps explain why the Krasnoiarsk NKVD delayed Shums´kyi's case. Broadly, it shows how provincial NKVD offices managed to deflect pressure from their superiors in Moscow to implement decisions that could have endangered the local offices.

Chapter 6, "The Tragic Finale," examines the Soviet leadership's decision to kill Shums′kyi in response to his suicide attempts, and the broader fears of his potential assistance to the anti-Soviet insurgency in western Ukraine in the context of rising Cold War tensions. For the Soviet leadership, Shums′kyi, the paralyzed criminal in the Far East confined to a hospital bed for years, became a clear and present danger to Soviet security. When the leadership finally acquiesced to Shums′kyi's demand to return home to Ukraine, after he threatened to attempt suicide again, it did so only as a pretext to kill him, secretly, en route to his final destination. After failing for two decades to silence Shums′kyi's opposition to the regime—for its crimes against him, his nation, and the revolution itself—it finally succeeded in doing so by having its assassins cover his mouth, or "clamp their hands over it" as the assassins recounted, while they poisoned him.[39]

Chapter One

THE MURDERED UKRAINIAN REVOLUTION

One of the most thought-provoking Ukrainian historians of the twentieth century, Ivan L. Rudnytsky, argued that the Ukrainian Soviet Socialist Republic (UkrSSR) could best be understood as the embodiment of a compromise between independent Ukrainian statehood and Russian centralism.[1] This compromise was not a formal agreement between Russian and Ukrainian leaders, but a manifestation of the antagonistic social forces of independence and centralism they represented.

Neither of these forces was strong enough to fully achieve its goals. The Ukrainian liberation movement proved to be too weak to create an independent state. On the other hand, the Bolsheviks, led by Vladimir Lenin, were forced to make concessions to Ukraine and the non-Russian nationalities of the former Russian empire upon taking power in the 1917 October Revolution. Indeed, these concessions became one of the decisive factors in the Bolshevik victory over their Russian rivals in the Civil War that followed the October Revolution. Rudnytsky wrote:

> In Russia, the Bolsheviks won over their internal opponents. Whether one liked it or not, Soviet Russia was the legitimate heir to traditional Russian statehood. In this respect, Ukraine's position was more reminiscent of the "people's democracies" created after World War II. The Soviet regime was thrown at the country from outside; weak local communist forces, where ethnic Ukrainians were only a minority, would never have been able to gain power in Ukraine without external intervention. The Ukrainian Soviet Socialist Republic was a compromise between the fact of restored Russian

> rule and those achievements of the Ukrainian revolution that could no longer be erased.[2]

Another prominent historian in this area, Terry Martin, went further, arguing that the Russian revolutionary government, faced with the rise of national movements from the ashes of the former Russian empire, was the first of the old multinational states of Europe to systematically promote the development of national consciousness among ethnic minorities and create the institutional forms integral to nation-states. The Bolsheviks were Russia's first "decolonizers," though mostly as a means to an end: "The Bolshevik strategy was to assume leadership over what now appeared to be the inevitable process of decolonization and carry it out in a manner that would preserve the territorial integrity of the old Russian empire."[3]

The end of the Civil War, among other things, provided the opportune moment for the Bolshevik leaders of the newly independent states of Ukraine and Russia to expedite the establishment of formal relations between the countries as part of this strategy.[4] In December 1920, the leadership bodies of the Bolshevik Party and state passed resolutions instructing their members to hammer out a treaty between the two countries. The Treaty of Workers' and Peasants' Union was duly signed on 28 December at the Eighth All-Russian Congress of Soviets, the official supreme governing body of the Russian Soviet Federative Socialist Republic (RSFSR), by Russian leader Vladimir Lenin and his people's commissar for foreign affairs Georgii Chicherin, and Ukraine's head of (Soviet) government, the Old Bolshevik Christian (Krŭst′o) Rakovsky.[5]

The treaty's preamble and initial articles declared the independence and sovereignty of both states. The treaty emphasized that, although Ukraine's territory had formerly belonged to the Russian empire, this fact did not imply that any other state, including the RSFSR, now "owned" Ukraine. At the same time, the treaty's agreements on military and economic union did establish Russian ownership over the new UkrSSR by subordinating key spheres of Ukraine's government to Russia, including the commissariats of military and naval affairs, foreign trade, finance, labor, communications, post and telegraph, and the Supreme Council of the National Economy.[6]

The Eighth All-Russian Congress of Soviets ratified the signed document, and on 2 March 1921, so did the Fifth All-Ukrainian Congress of Soviets, which described it as "a new step toward strengthening the united revolutionary Soviet front between workers and peasants of Russia and Ukraine."[7] This Russian-Ukrainian treaty became a template for the RSFSR's treaties with other republics and regions—with Belarus on 16 January 1921, Bukhara on 4 March, Georgia on 21 May, and Armenia on multiple dates. These treaties, along with earlier military-economic unions signed by Russia (with Khorezm on 13 September 1920 and with Azerbaijan on 30 September), formed the contractual spiderweb that reentangled Russia with the periphery of the former Russian empire and further established the Bolsheviks in power.

It soon became clear that Moscow considered even these contractual relations between the republics to be unreliable and potentially dangerous, that the "decolonized" might go too far in pursuing their independence and impinge on the center's power. Indeed, part of the problem for Moscow was the enthusiasm that its "decolonization" policy inspired in national minorities who fought alongside the Bolsheviks in the Civil War for Soviet power, viewing Russia not only as a communist state but also as a vehicle for the realization of their own independence goals. As Vladimir L′vov, a former member of the Provisional Government (which took over from the tsarist regime in February 1917 before being toppled by the Bolsheviks in October), explained in 1922:

> What really is the work of the Soviet government in Russia? Like a magnet, it attracted all the individual nationalities of Russia, uniting them into a single Russian state. What the emperors could not achieve by police action was done naturally in the name of human solidarity and the protection of the oppressed classes. All nationalities felt their belonging to the Russian state, because it protected them from injustice and took their interests under its guard.[8]

Fighting the Civil War against foreign powers and their Russian allies "raised Soviet power to the level of national power because it saved the unity of the Russian state."[9]

But with the Civil War won, "unity" could no longer be had by enticing the national minorities to fight with the Russian center against its enemies with promises of national independence. The Bolshevik leadership sought a new model that would allow it to maintain unity; that is, to ensure that the periphery would serve the interests of the center permanently and more reliably. It would be ahistorical to claim that the Bolshevik leadership in Moscow or the new republics possessed a universal model for what this unity would look like at this time. Some leaders of the party-state, having battled nationalist/anti-Bolshevik forces in the Civil War, understood nationalism and counterrevolution as two sides of the same coin.[10] They proposed eliminating the declarative independence of the UkrSSR and other Soviet republics and suggested instead "autonomizing" them, equating them in status with the autonomous republics that existed within the old Russian empire, provinces established nominally by ethnicity and subordinated to the center. This was seen as perhaps the most effective way of countering Russia's own potential "autonomization"—that is, the RSFSR's loss of status as the center of the old Russian empire.[11]

On the other hand, local leaders in the republics should not be portrayed—as they often were during Mikhail Gorbachev's perestroika—only as supporters of centrifugal, separatist ideologies. Some, especially the Old Bolsheviks—prerevolutionary members of the party who assumed leading positions in party and state structures of the republics—supported the primacy of the Russian center. Other leaders, mostly from leftist parties that joined the Bolsheviks in government in the republics, were often outraged by Moscow's systematic violation of the sovereignty of their national republics and the interference of central bodies in their affairs—which reduced local governing structures to a merely decorative status. Interference in internal affairs went so far that the national republics were concerned and, at the same time, powerless to oppose it. In the end, they willingly supported the formation of the Union of Soviet Socialist Republics (USSR) so that their rights would be clearly enshrined in the new constitution.

Discussions among revolutionaries about the formation of the USSR and the process of its constitutional design were detailed, sometimes heated, explorations of the possible ways to balance power between center and periphery. The revolutionaries were breaking new ground in European history, trying to reconcile historically antagonistic forces of class and nationalism in socialist state-building. The publication of previously inaccessible documents now confirms that the loss of the republics' remaining independence in this process, the dashing of their hopes of what federation and a constitution might bring, was not predetermined. Lenin was indeed committed to the ideal of building a strong multinational state; there is no reason now to question the sincerity of his pronouncements on this matter. The problem was that he was not sure precisely what this state would look like. For all the complexities of the national question in Russia's west, particularly in Ukraine, the national question in its multinational east was even more complex and required more caution and flexibility. Lenin was undoubtedly interested in this broader geopolitical context, as he came to anticipate world revolution erupting less in western Europe and more in East Asia. The question confounding him was what methods would ensure the preservation of a powerful and multinational Russia across both its eastern and western peripheries.

Stalin—whom Lenin charged with overseeing the national question at this time as the people's commissar for nationalities in the Russian government, on the Council of People's Commissars (Sovnarkom)—offered Lenin his advice on this matter in a letter dated 22 September 1922. This letter, despite its extraordinary significance for a true understanding of many events—or perhaps because of this—stayed in the archives until 1989, when it was eventually published in the journal of the Central Committee of the Communist Party of the Soviet Union (CPSU). Stalin wrote:

> Comrade Lenin! We have arrived at the situation where the current state of relations between the center and the periphery—that is, complete chaos and the absence of any order—has become unbearable, creating conflicts, grievances, and irritations; turning the so-called single federal economy into an illusion; and inhibiting and paralyzing any economic activity on the all-Russian scale. We have one of two alternatives [for resolving this problem]: either establish true independence and the noninterference of the center thereafter, with [the republics' having] their own NKVD, their own Foreign Trade, their own Concession Committee [for foreign capital

> investment relations], and their own railways, with common issues being resolved in peer-to-peer negotiations by agreement, and with the resolutions of the [All-Russian] Central Executive Committee [CEC], the RNK [Council of People's Commissars], and the RPO [Council of Labor and Defense] of the RSFSR nonbinding for the independent republics. Or the other alternative: the true unification of the Soviet republics into one economic whole with the formal extension of the power of the RNK, RPO, and the Central Executive Committee of the RSFSR to the RNK, CEC, and the Economic Council over the independent republics; i.e., the replacement of the illusion of independence with the real internal autonomy of the republics [...].[12]

Stalin often proposed two unequal options as a rhetorical device to highlight the necessity of adopting his preferred one. In this case, Stalin clearly preferred the unification of the republics with the center, or the "autonomizing" of them, leaving them completely dominated by the center and enjoying a degree of flexibility only in implementing decisions, not in making them. Stalin laid out the problem of nationality in five points that would eventually become the party's position on the republics. In the third and fourth points, Stalin gives his version of why the early Soviet state had been amenable to nationalism:

> 3. During the four years of the [Russian] Civil War, when we were forced as a consequence of the [Allied] intervention to demonstrate that Moscow was liberal concerning the national question, we managed, against our will, to cultivate among the communists some real, consistent social-independentists, who demand true independence in every respect, and who regard the intervention of the Central Committee of the RCP [Russian Communist Party] to be deception and hypocrisy on the part of Moscow.
> 4. We are experiencing a period of development when form, law, and the constitution cannot be ignored, when the younger generation of communists on the peripheries refuses to understand the game of independence as a game, but instead stubbornly takes words about independence at face value and just as stubbornly demands that we implement word for word the constitution of the independent republics.[13]

For Stalin, who would eventually concentrate power in his own hands, the independence of the Soviet republics was just a game, even before the creation of the USSR. Stalin warned Lenin that the emerging Soviet Union would fall apart if they allowed the "upstarts" in the republics the real independence promised to them in the constitution. Stalin predicted:

> 5. If now we don't try to adapt the form of relations between the center and the peripheries to actual relations, in line with which the peripheries must be subordinated absolutely and in everything to the center—i.e., if now we don't replace formal (fictitious) independence with equally formal (but also real) autonomy—then in a year it will be incomparably more difficult to defend the actual unity of the Soviet republics.
>
> Right now the issue is how not to "offend" the nationals [*natsionaly*]; in a year's time, it will probably be a matter of how not to cause a split in the party on this basis, because the "national" element on the peripheries is not working to the benefit of the unity of the Soviet republics, and formal independence actually favors that activity [of the "national" element].[14]

Stalin's advice was realized before his assumption of power in the party. He and Lenin agreed that the ultimate aim of the nationality policy should be to strengthen central Soviet power, but they disagreed on how to achieve it. Lenin grew impatient with Stalin for making important decisions affecting the republics by himself and clearly in opposition to local leaders. In Lenin's view, Stalin imitated his tsarist predecessors as a "Great Russian chauvinist" in his cavalier attitude toward non-Russians, threatening the entire nationality policy in the republics and thus undermining the policy's ultimate aim. Their dispute erupted in the infamous Georgian Affair of 1922.[15]

But less than three months after Stalin's letter to Lenin, whose input into the nationalities policy and the country's administration was fading along with his health, Ukraine had been quickly "autonomized" and further integrated with the RSFSR, and thus brought under the central control of Moscow. On 10 December 1922, the Seventh All-Ukrainian Congress of Soviets (government councils) opened in Kharkiv (Ukraine's capital at the time). Its delegates approved the declaration on the formation of the UkrSSR and the draft of the UkrSSR Constitution. They appealed to all republics to begin the legislative formation of a single state immediately and proposed to convene an All-Union Congress after the end of the Tenth All-Russian Congress of Soviets, which was to be held in Moscow on 23 December. The All-Union Congress was attended by representatives of all constitutive republics and was held for the first time on 30 December 1922. This congress approved the declaration on the formation of the USSR and the union treaty. The Central Executive Committee of the USSR was elected. Now that the UkrSSR was integrated into the union-state with Russia, it officially fell directly under a one-party dictatorship based in Moscow, which further limited the power of the republic-level government. The leadership of the UkrSSR found it even more difficult to defend the interests of Ukraine. It was bound by party discipline, forced to obey the decisions of the Politburo of the Central Committee of the Russian Communist Party (of Bolsheviks; RCP[b]) in Moscow.

However, the dictatorship itself was not monolithic. A clash of interests between local and central institutions and politicians was inevitable, even if central interests prevailed.[16] A striking example is the Twelfth Congress of the RCP(b), which took place in April 1923, and at which the national question was put on the agenda for the last time in the history of party congresses. An explosive speech by the Old Bolshevik Mykola Skrypnyk, then people's commissar for justice of the UkrSSR and eventually Shums′kyi's replacement as people's commissar for education in 1927, best describes the reason that central interests prevailed, and the detrimental effect this had on those committed to real independence:

> Why, then, did we fight so hard on the national question and, if it was resolved correctly in principle, why did we remain virtually powerless [with its resolution]? The fact was that we were constantly ... trying to find the middle ground. Any indication of great-power [Russian] chauvinism was always countered by its opposite—the chauvinism of non-state nationalities. ... They refused to accept any reference to their own Great Russian chauvinism by filing a counterclaim [against the nationalities]: they said, "First overcome your own nationalism." So, in fact, we did not manage to fight any great-power [Russian] chauvinism. We have to draw a line against this duplicity![17]

Little time would pass after the Twelfth Congress of the RCP(b) before Mykola Skrypnyk, Oleksandr Shums′kyi, and many more political figures of the UkrSSR who dared to fight against Great Russian chauvinism would be repressed by the party. To "draw the line," Shums′kyi used the new policy of *korenizatsiia* (nativization, from the word "root") announced by the Bolshevik leadership after the congress. This policy called for a national revival of local languages and cultures across the former Russian empire and took the specific names of the regions of the USSR where it was implemented (Ukrainization, Belarusianization, Tatarization, etc.). This broad revival would help provide the regime with a means of becoming "rooted" in areas where the Bolsheviks were not identified nationally with the indigenous population. Korenizatsiia would bring ethnic groups into the party and state apparatus to implement decisions and policies from Moscow in the language and customs of their native land. Korenizatsiia, the leadership said, was supposed to liberate the former nationalities of the tsarist empire from the inequalities that had become entrenched by autocracy's exploitation of them—its consequences now inherited by the USSR. Indeed, this is how Shums′kyi and many others understood it: as a policy for the realization of national independence within a Soviet structure. At the same time, much of the Bolshevik leadership, while paying lip service to the liberationist aims of the policy, used it to manage the independence of the republics within increasingly strict boundaries. Others in the party wavered between these two extreme interpretations of the policy's ultimate aim. The tension between these aims and the resultant internal contradictions in the policy's implementation would play out well into the 1930s, until the republics were, as Stalin had always wished, autonomized.

In the early 1920s, not only domestic but also international factors creating threats to national security on the peripheries of the new Soviet Union influenced the Bolsheviks' adoption of korenizatsiia. Concerns about the unity of the republics with the center, allayed temporarily by victory in the Civil War, now resumed with vigor. The coming to power of the fiercely anticommunist government of Stanley Baldwin in Great Britain in 1923 and the beginning of rapprochement between Germany and western

Europe in the Locarno Pact on 1 December 1925 were understood broadly by Bolshevik leaders, especially Stalin, as increasing the prospect of Western military intervention in the Soviet Union.[18] The most clear and present danger was in Ukraine, after Józef Piłsudski retook power in neighboring Poland in a coup d'état in May 1926.[19] Piłsudski had earlier formed an alliance with Symon Petliura's government, the Directorate, in the lead-up to invading Kyiv in 1920 in the Soviet-Polish War. Piłsudski's coup symbolized to Moscow's leaders the possibility of an anti-Bolshevik alliance reforming between Ukrainians and Poles, with Piłsudski again supporting or using as pretext for invasion an uprising against Soviet power in Ukraine.

Korenizatsiia, its supporters argued, was supposed to strengthen Bolshevik control in the republics by giving a "local face" to Soviet power, differentiating it from its tsarist predecessor, which had ruled these areas exploitatively with Russian representatives and in the Russian language. Native people in the republics were trained as communist cadres, and the nascent Bolshevik party-state apparatus was formed by taking into account specific national factors (language, culture, demographics, etc.). Korenizatsiia would enable Soviet power to be exercised "from the inside" by providing for the dissemination of socialist education in native languages, promoting the development of ethnic cultures, organizing a network of schools at all levels, and facilitiating the growth of cultural institutions, newspapers and magazines, and native-language book publishing, among other things. If Soviet power continued to be seen, as L'vov had noted in 1922, as supporting a nationalist revival in culture and language as well as giving "independence," then the nationalist forces battling the Soviets would lose the main grievances with which they recruited for their armies. The party heavily debated the historical and contemporary intersections of class and nationalism, with the policy's supporters ultimately arguing that it would disarticulate nationalism from its bourgeois base and encourage a "healthy" nationalism within a Soviet framework.[20]

Stalin, as commissar for nationalities, officially made these arguments in support of korenizatsiia but, as we have seen, often exhibited the Great Russian chauvinist attitude toward the republics that the policy was supposed to combat. He remained ambivalent about korenizatsiia and always stressed to the party leadership the potential dangers of losing the "game" of independence. The game could be lost in various ways. Korenizatsiia could embolden old class enemies, the anti-Soviet nationalist forces that had survived the Civil War, to remount their challenge to Soviet power. More pressing for Stalin in 1924 was the possibility that the policy might increase expectations among its proponents of a national independence not realizable within the Soviet framework. Stalin's experience in the Georgian Affair, where representatives of national minorities within the party gained support from Lenin to oppose his attempt to reduce the newfound independence of their republics, told him that korenizatsiia could further embolden such members to see Soviet power not as a vehicle for liberation but as a roadblock to true independence. These members might seek or be amenable to other party leaders or foreign powers that promised to help them realize it.

Stalin managed this threat in a variety of ways, most visibly by using public party fora to make examples of ardent supporters of korenizatsiia in the republics who threatened to take independence too far. Stalin pushed through the decision taken by the Politburo of the Central Committee of the RCP(b) on 19 May 1923 to "present the case of [Mirsaid] Sultan-Galiev to show where the logic of secret and anti-party work inevitably leads."[21] The case would be presented at the committee's upcoming "Fourth Meeting on the National Question," to be held with officials from the national republics and regions in Moscow on 9–12 June 1923, though Sultan-Galiev's case had already been decided by the Politburo before the Fourth Meeting was held. Sultan-Galiev would be expelled from the party and arrested for "nationalist deviation," among other things.[22]

Mirsaid Sultan-Galiev, a member of the People's Commissariat for Nationalities in the Sovnarkom (RSFSR) from 1920 to 1923, was one of the first and most consistent critics of Stalin's duplicity in national politics. In his speeches at party meetings, he openly argued with Stalin, effectively his boss as the people's commissar for nationalities, over nation-building issues and great-power (Russian) chauvinism. At the Tenth All-Russian Congress of

Soviets and the Twelfth Congress of the RCP(b), Sultan-Galiev emphasized that, if nationalism was understood as the struggle against great-power chauvinism, "it was not nationalism at all, but simply the struggle against manifestations of great-power chauvinism."[23] Much like Mykola Skrypnyk did at the same congress, Sultan-Galiev identified the duplicity at the heart of the Bolshevik leadership's approach to the national question, though he went further, implying that Stalin was its main proponent.

Sultan-Galiev's speeches greatly irritated Stalin. We now know from declassified archival documents that Stalin fabricated the Sultan-Galiev case immediately after the Twelfth Congress in May 1923, and that the charges made against him as forming a "counterrevolutionary organization" were completely contrived.[24] The Fourth Meeting, which took place the following month, unsurprisingly began with the condemnation and confirmation of the expulsion of Mirsaid Sultan-Galiev from the party. However, Stalin's argument did not rest only on his power to expel party members. Stalin skillfully demonstrated in his speech at the Fourth Meeting how korenizatsiia, though it was the official policy of the party, could be dangerous in stimulating nationalism and thus anti-Bolshevik sentiment in the republics if implemented incorrectly. The materials of this meeting, incidentally, were marked "Top Secret" from the very beginning and were hidden in special repositories for many years. Stalin said:

> It should be remembered that our communist organizations on the peripheries [of the country], in the republics and in the oblasts, can develop and stand on their own two feet and become true internationalist Marxist cadres only if they overcome nationalism... [That is,] only if they are able to resist the nationalist trend that is breaking through to our party on the peripheries, breaking through because the bourgeoisie is coming back to life, the NEP [New Economic Policy] is growing, nationalism is growing, there are remnants of Great Russian chauvinism, which also advance nationalism of the local variety, and there is the influence of foreign states that support nationalism in every way. The struggle against this enemy in the republics and oblasts is the very stage that our communist organizations in the national republics must go through if they want to grow strong as truly Marxist organizations.[25]

Stalin's warning to party members of the republics at this meeting of the potential dangers of korenizatsiia was fundamentally an admonition not to go too far in implementing the policy of the party in the republics. For many in the Ukrainian party-state apparatus, where korenizatsiia took the form of Ukrainization for Ukrainians and other forms for Ukraine's many national minorities, this warning confirmed their own suspicion of korenizatsiia as fomenting, rather than combating, nationalism. Those who, like Shums′kyi and Skrypnyk, were committed to the stated aims of the policy as a "national revival" in Ukraine, figured out how far "too far" was only after they had passed this (ever-shifting) point.

* * *

Ukrainization was not invented by the Bolsheviks, nor was the myriad of problems associated with the policy simply confined to the Bolshevik period of rule. These problems plagued the numerous regimes that lay claim to leadership of Ukraine from 1917 onward. The introduction of the term "Ukrainization" is attributed to Mykhailo Hrushevs′kyi, the great Ukrainian historian and statesman who, in his 1907 collection of articles *Osvobozhdenie Rossii i ukrainskii vopros* (The liberation of Russia and the Ukrainian question) argued against those who believed that "Ukrainization of higher education in Ukraine will adversely affect scientific life."[26] The term began to be used by Ukrainophobes in a much broader sense and with a negative connotation, pointing to the threat of "South-Russian separatism" and the danger of imposing the Ukrainian language on Russians in Ukraine. The notion of imposition, as we shall see later, and as we know from contemporary political life, survived its creators.

In the revolutionary year of 1917, the term "Ukrainization" began to be used outside the field of education. In the article "There Is No Turning Back," published in the spring of 1917, Hrushevs′kyi set the task of "Ukrainizing" new local self-government bodies for the purpose of establishing Ukrainian independence.[27] After the fall of tsarism, under the short-lived Provisional Government in 1917, Ukrainization achieved some success in a short period. The Ukrainian language began to be used as the state language, although it was not given official status, and all state and government acts were written in Ukrainian. This success continued even after the collapse of the Provisional Government. On 7 March 1918, the Ukrainian People's Republic (UPR)—the new Ukrainian government—issued a circular to the provincial and county commissioners on the use of the Ukrainian language. It demanded a translation into Ukrainian of the Provisional Government's resolutions that had not been repealed by the government, and emphasized that "all inscriptions and signs must be made immediately in Ukrainian.... Those guilty of noncompliance will be removed from office and brought to justice."[28] The key efforts were focused on the use of the Ukrainian language in the field of education, from primary to higher levels. In addition, newspapers, magazines, books—especially educational literature—theatrical and musical art, museum publications, and other print media were subject to Ukrainization.

The UPR was overthrown by the military coup of April 1918, which placed General Pavlo Skoropads′kyi in power as hetman, or military dictator, and Ukrainization continued under his regime, the Hetmanate.[29] The *State Gazette* (which published laws and government proclamations) was issued in Ukrainian, and there was a significant increase in Ukrainian-language book publishing and works to codify the Ukrainian language. In 1917–18, a total of 1,831 Ukrainian-language books were published, with a total circulation of 16.2 million copies, which accounted for 70 percent of all book production in Ukraine during that period.[30] The Hetmanate released its own "Main Rules of Ukrainian Grammar" in 1919, which closely followed the "Most Important Rules of Ukrainian Grammar" published under the UPR in 1918.

The brief existence of the UPR and the Hetmanate saw a long-standing tendency emerge that would continue into the UkrSSR. Many people accused the government of "forcing" Ukrainization on the people. Serhii Shelukhin, member of both the UPR and the Hetmanate governments, summarized this trend in a note to the Hetmanate's prime minister, Fedir Lyzohub, in September 1918: "For some time, all sorts of undermining has taken place of the Ukrainian language, the clearest sign of Ukrainian state independence and the country's separation from Russia. It should be noted that the campaign against the Ukrainian language was growing at the same time as the campaign against Ukrainian statehood was growing."[31] According to Shelukhin, the participants in this campaign included the Bolsheviks, Russian centralists, chauvinists, and Russifiers—those who sought to "destroy Ukrainian statehood and recreate their disintegrated 'single indivisible' Russia with the enslavement of Ukraine." Shelukhin demanded from Lyzohub action to resist this drive against Ukrainization, arguing, "It was undoubtedly necessary to issue a law establishing that in the Ukrainian state, the state language was Ukrainian and only Ukrainian."[32] Nevertheless, the Senate, of which Shelukhin was a member, by a majority vote, gave Russian, not Ukrainian, the status of the state language.

The Directorate, which replaced the Hetmanate of Skoropads′kyi, had little time to continue the policy of Ukrainization before the Bolsheviks overthrew it. Despite the change in regimes and resistance against Ukrainization, the status of the Ukrainian language from 1917 to 1921 "changed dramatically, and in many respects decisively, in comparison with previous decades. After a break of almost two hundred years, the Ukrainian language was firmly established as the language of legislation, administration, army, and assemblies." This tendency did not change when the Bolsheviks overthrew the Directorate in 1920, and the Bolsheviks would play the most decisive role in "determining the zigzags of Soviet language policy in Ukraine in the future."[33]

The Bolsheviks zigzagged sharply in relation to Ukrainization throughout the 1920s and 1930s, though the party's official support for Ukrainian language use remained steadfast from the revolution. On 9 March 1919, the Provisional Workers' and Peasants' Government, the Soviet government in Ukraine during the Civil War, adopted the resolution "On Compulsory School Study of Local Language, as well as the History and Geography of Ukraine." On 21 February 1920, the All-Ukrainian Central Executive Committee of the All-Ukrainian Congress of Soviets adopted the resolution "On the Use of the Ukrainian Language on an Equal Footing with Russian in All Institutions." On 21 September 1920, the Soviet Ukrainian government, Sovnarkom (UkrSSR), passed a resolution on the compulsory study of the Ukrainian language in schools and Soviet institutions.[34]

Not all party and state figures in Ukraine were optimistic about these initial Ukrainization efforts and about the need to promote a national language. Indeed, as Shelukhin noted as early as 1918, some Bolsheviks resented these efforts and their "own" political figures, such as Shums′kyi, who were responsible for implementing them. During the Fifth Conference of the Communist Party (of Bolsheviks) of Ukraine (CP[b]U), in November 1920, the head of the Communist International (Comintern), Grigorii Zinov′ev, stressed, "It doesn't matter what language the workers speak, all we have to say is how many hides, one or five, we will skin off the kulaks [supposed rich peasants] for the benefit of the poor, the peasant, or the worker."[35] The October plenum of the Central Committee of the CP(b)U in 1922 officially proclaimed bilingualism and the free development of Ukrainian culture, but all this was "balanced" by statements that the "Ukrainian counterrevolution" was taking cultural affairs into its own hands; that is, Soviet support for the Ukrainian language threatened to lend support to the nationalist forces of counterrevolution.[36] Thus, from the very beginning of the talks on supporting Ukrainization, an ambivalent attitude to Ukrainization was present in the upper and lower party structures. Resistance to it was inevitable, especially given the acceleration of Ukrainization efforts with the Bolsheviks firmly in power in Ukraine, as demonstrated below.

On 27 July 1923, Sovnarkom (UkrSSR) issued a decree "On Measures to Ukrainize Schools and Cultural-Educational Institutions," which introduced the use of Ukrainian language into all types of schools. A few days later, on 1 August, it issued a related decree, this time "On Measures to Ensure the Equality of Languages and to Promote the Development of the Ukrainian Language." These decrees anticipated that the education system would be "Ukrainized" in two years, while also promoting the Ukrainian language in government: civil servants who were already working had to study the Ukrainian language for a year or risk being fired, and those entering the civil service were obliged to master the Ukrainian language in six months.[37]

Many members of the party-state apparatus resisted not only these provisions, but also the rise of new native cadres brought into the party-state apparatus under Ukrainization. This element of the policy, aimed at "rooting" the party in the republics, threatened to destabilize the Soviet system. This was primarily because the embedding of local power—training, educating, and promoting native personnel in the party-state apparatus—was carried out under the slogan of overcoming great-power (Russian) chauvinism and inevitably led to the formation of local ethno-elites. Over time, Moscow came to block native cadres out of important administrative positions and prestigious social niches for fear that these elites would become too powerful and challenge the center. The relationship between these elites and the center would inevitably change, less through open confrontation than through a formal central recognition of the status of Ukrainian officials, to whom the center afforded a certain amount of autonomy and respect.

This tension among the party leadership was part of a broader friction wrought by Ukrainization and, indeed, by korenizatsiia between the center and the republics across the Soviet Union. On the one hand, the process of party-bureaucratic centralization continued to concentrate power in Moscow, while on the other, the number of separate national-territorial entities grew, and for a while, so did their formal status and that of their representatives. By 1931, twenty-five national districts and over a thousand national village soviets (councils) had been established in Ukraine in places of residence of Jews, Germans, and Poles, among others.[38] Ukraine became the first region of the USSR with an extensive system of ethnic soviets.[39] In these ethnic districts, people were allowed to use their own language in courts and civil work. Thus, korenizatsiia in Ukraine was not limited to Ukrainization, though, given the predominance of ethnic Ukrainians, it became dominant in the country.

Because, in practice, korenizatsiia meant de-Russification for the non-Russian ethnic groups of the USSR, especially in terms of promoting local language use, it was inevitable that many people would associate Russian with centralism and local languages with tendencies toward "independence" in the republics. Indeed, de-Russification is probably why korenizatsiia was so widely accepted by representatives of the Ukrainian intelligentsia across the political spectrum, even as it inspired suspicion among the centralists, who came to understand the wholesale promotion of local language as a threat to the party-state structure. Those committed to korenizatsiia included party members who sought to disentangle these negative associations; that is, those who were first pro-communist but also in favor of local language use and national traditions within this structure.

Indeed, for many party members who were trying to answer the self-contradictory national question in Ukraine of how to build a state that was simultaneously independent and socialist, promoting local language use was not the problem but the solution. Shums′kyi best explained the "contradiction" felt by Ukrainian socialists:

> Ever since I became a socialist, when addressing the question of Ukrainian statehood, I proceeded from the position of the Marxist doctrine of socialism that one of the main tasks of a socialist society is to eliminate the chaos of production and competition inherent in the capitalist system, and to organize production and distribution according to a strictly determined plan. From this point of view, I could not help reacting negatively to the demand for the independence of Ukraine, since this demand was incompatible with and contradicted the tasks of the struggle for socialism.[40]

Shums′kyi's solution to this contradiction—to establish Ukrainian statehood within a socialist setting—lay in the development of the Ukrainian language. By language, he meant

> the entire language culture from the school curriculum to the Academy of Sciences, from everyday conversation to the speech of an orator and state acts, from a drama or technical group at an enterprise to a state theater and a technical institute, scholarly books and fiction, the press, etc. I assigned language the central place in solving the Ukrainian national question under the conditions of Soviet power. This was based, of course, on the fact that I loved the Ukrainian language—it was my mother tongue.[41]

Shums′kyi skillfully distinguished between the national question's two major elements—the question of Ukrainian statehood and the question of language and culture—to offer the second as the solution to realizing the first. Shums′kyi promoted Ukrainian language through the policy of Ukrainization, which he advanced as the people's commissar for education from 1924 to 1927. He was responsible for implementing this policy in at least three areas: educational institutions, from schools to universities; the party-state apparatus created by the Bolsheviks in Ukraine, including its structures, civil work, and operational language; and cultural products, including books, newspapers, and magazines in Ukrainian and other native languages.

Shums'kyi's areas of responsibility and the main policy settings of Ukrainization were defined and regulated by special resolutions of party and government organs, which limited Shums'kyi's capacity for independent Ukrainizing initiatives or improvisations. Though Shums'kyi operated within a strict legal framework in implementing Ukrainization, he enjoyed greater freedom in shaping Ukraine's broader cultural environment. As people's commissar for education, he automatically occupied the position of editor in chief of the journal *Chervonyi shliakh* (Red path), a monthly journal founded in 1923 and published in Kharkiv until 1936. The journal was established to help unite the Ukrainian intelligentsia around the Bolshevik government and to oppose the Ukrainian émigré intelligentsia. *Chervonyi shliakh* was quite successful in this respect and became widely seen as a counterweight to the powerful monthly journal *Nova Ukraïna* (New Ukraine), the émigré periodical published under the editorship of Mykyta Shapoval in Prague.

Shums'kyi stacked *Chervonyi shliakh*'s editorial board with some of Ukraine's youngest revolutionary literary figures: the executive secretary, for example, was the futurist poet Mykhailo Ialovyi who wrote under the pseudonym Iuliian Shpol, and Mykola Khvyl'ovyi was a board member.[42] Shums'kyi was also keen to allow people from diverse political backgrounds, including the old Ukrainian intelligentsia, access to the editorial boards and broader institutions of Ukrainian literary and social culture, even those he distrusted and disliked. Some he respected deeply but nonetheless clashed with politically. He continued to associate with them because he understood their importance in promoting and legitimating Ukrainization in various fields domestically and abroad, especially in art, literature, and the creation of an authoritative Ukrainian dictionary—within strict boundaries.

Shums´kyi's troubled relationships with Mykhailo Hrushevs´kyi and Vasyl´ Ellan-Blakytnyi are the main cases in point and are discussed later.

Under Shums´kyi's broad-minded editorship, as Mykhailo Ialovyi later recalled, "the liveliest atmosphere of literary and artistic creativity arose around the journal *Chervonyi shliakh* and [extended broadly] to the party writers' circle, and all circles, one might say, not only literary, but also cultural intelligentsia in general."[43] This atmosphere, nurtured by Shums´kyi, reached beyond the editorial board into the broad avenues of Ukrainian culture, in which Ukrainization could flourish. Shums´kyi also nurtured this atmosphere by funding literary bodies to promote revolutionary literature, such as the Free Academy of Proletarian Literature (VAPLITE), founded in November 1925 under Ialovyi's presidency.[44] VAPLITE included many talented writers, most notably Khvyl´ovyi.

Panas Fedenko, the Socialist-Revolutionary who served in the UPR government and was critical of Soviet communism, offered a positive evaluation of this period in his work *Ukraïns´kyi rukh u XX stolitti* (The Ukrainian movement in the twentieth century):

> The policy of Ukrainization ... produced some useful outcomes for Ukrainian culture. The Ukrainian language prevailed in the public schools of Ukraine. After the return of M. Hrushevs´kyi to Ukraine from emigration in 1924, the Ukrainian Academy of Sciences developed a wide range of activities. Over the course of several years of diligent cultural work, new cadres of the Ukrainian intelligentsia were created.[45]

In February 1925, Dmytro Levyts´kyi, leader of the influential Ukrainian National Democratic Union, a political party that opposed Polish rule over western Ukraine (where it was based), wrote that "in Soviet Ukraine, the Ukrainian national idea was growing, strengthening, and developing, and along with the growth of this idea, the foreign framework of fictitious Ukrainian statehood was being filled with the native meaning of true statehood."[46] Evaluating this period, Professor George G. Grabowicz argued:

> Many sources show that, in the eyes of the public, institutions such as the Ukrainian Academy of Sciences gained extremely high authority. This attitude to the humanities could have in principle become a paradigm for national revival overall. This discourse, although overloaded with authoritarian, voluntaristic rhetoric, could have been, at least in its external form, a discourse, albeit not of an open, but of a non-totalitarian society. Despite all the difficulties of the day, we see it as a real civil society—even though in the Soviet state it had no chance of survival; it is a society based on a truly patriotic, Ukraine-centric consensus, where formal ideology is subject to a broader awareness of national goals.[47]

The impact of Ukrainization should not be overestimated. At the same time, its achievements should not be ignored. These include the widespread prevalence of Ukrainian literacy and education at all levels and the formation of specialized institutions for the study of the humanities and natural and technical sciences.

Much has been written about the development of the arts, especially literature, theater, music, and cinema.[48] Among other efforts to revive the Ukrainian language and implement it in the broadest strata and branches of society, work on the creation of terminological dictionaries, whose codification of the Ukrainian language endures today, should be singled out as a key success in this period. In addition, the Commission for Compiling the History of the Ukrainian Language, the Commission for the Etymological Dictionary of the Ukrainian Language, the Commission for Normative Grammar of the Ukrainian Language, and the Dialectical Commission of the All-Ukrainian Academy of Sciences (VUAN) were launched. In 1927, formal orthography (*pravopys*) was adopted, called the "Kharkiv orthography," which was officially approved by the VUAN on 31 March 1929.[49]

The Tenth Congress of the CP(b)U in November 1927 outlined the numerous successes of Ukrainization. From the materials attached to the transcript of the congress, specifically "National Politics and Ukrainization—Raising the National Question by the Party and Achievements in This Area," we glean that the circulation of all Ukrainian newspapers increased from ninety thousand copies in 1924 to five hundred thousand in 1927. Ukrainians made up 33 percent of the CP(b)U's membership in 1924, 38 percent in 1925, and 49 percent in 1926.[50] It is worth recalling that the Ukrainian-language Bolshevik press did not exist until 1918; in 1920–21, there were about seven to ten Ukrainian-language newspapers throughout Ukraine, most of which had half of their pages printed in Russian. In 1929, fifty-four Ukrainian newspapers were published in the UkrSSR, including twenty newspapers in Russian and eleven in the languages of ethnic minorities. Ukrainian-language newspapers accounted for 65 percent of the total circulation.[51]

Shums′kyi's fostering of a relatively liberal environment (as much as this term can be applied to a Soviet state) in which Ukrainization could be successful raised the ire of his critics, who claimed he was getting "carried away" or "going too far" with Ukrainization. None of his accusers ever explained exactly how he was getting carried away, although it is clear what they meant. Shums′kyi painted these accusers, mostly from the Russian-speaking party-state apparatus of the UkrSSR, as the main enemy of Ukrainization. Shums′kyi was "carried away" in publicly declaring that this apparatus, which was supposed to both help implement Ukrainization and be Ukrainized itself, was the major obstacle to the policy's realization.

To better understand the source of this resistance to Shums′kyi and Ukrainization, it pays to look at Ukraine's demography in the 1920s. According to the census of 17 December 1926, over 29 million people lived in Ukraine, including 23 million Ukrainians, 2.7 million Russians, and over 1.5 million Jews. More than 22 million people reported Ukrainian as their mother tongue, and about 4.5 million reported Russian. In the cities, almost 2 million people reported Ukrainian as their mother tongue, and over 20 million in the villages.[52] The question was, who was supposed to be Ukrainized? First, there were the government officials and the party apparatus, which mainly consisted of non-Ukrainians. It was clear that the strongest resistance to Ukrainization came from the ranks of the structure that had in fact been called upon to implement the policy, the CP(b)U. The decree of 1 August 1923, "On Measures to Ensure the Equality of Languages and to Promote the Development of the Ukrainian Language," was, in actuality, sabotaged.

According to the 1923 data, only 797 out of 11,826 officials of the party-state apparatus of the UkrSSR stated (only stated!) that they knew the Ukrainian language. In 1924, a survey was conducted among 599 executives of central Soviet institutions. Three hundred and two people, or 52 percent, knew Ukrainian, and the proportion was even lower (46 percent) among the party's leadership.[53] The problem was further complicated by the fact that even those who knew the Ukrainian language preferred to speak Russian. This state of affairs was addressed by the March 1923 plenum of the Central Committee of the CP(b)U and the party conference of May 1924. Both required all party members to learn Ukrainian—but nothing happened.

The requirements established in 1923 and 1924 were not implemented properly. The central Ukrainian archives contain almost no information about Ukrainization until April 1925. As befits officials—in this case, Soviet officials—many in the leadership found ways to avoid the unpleasant duty of Ukrainization.[54] As in the days of the Ukrainian Central Rada (Council) and Hetmanate, Ukrainization did not receive support from everyone in the leadership, and some did not accept declarations of policy even when they came from the party congresses. According to Terry Martin, this resistance should not have come as a surprise, as korenizatsiia had not been popular among ordinary party members, and in Ukraine, given the bitter experience of the Civil War, it was even less so. In addition, if the highest positions in most of the leading state structures, the Ukrainian commissariats, were held by staunch supporters of Ukrainization (indeed, this applies to all commissars for education between 1921 and 1939: Volodymyr Zatons′kyi, Shums′kyi, Skrypnyk, and Hryhorii Hryn′ko), this was not the case within party structures.[55]

In fact, many representatives of the party leadership shared the opinion of the first secretary of the Central Committee of the CP(b)U, Emmanuil Kviring. He belonged to the Katerynoslav group of communists, who were fundamentally opposed to Ukrainization. Even after the party's resolutions of 1923 were adopted, Kviring expressed concern that communist Ukrainization would turn into "Petliurist" (counterrevolutionary) Ukrainization.[56] Another CP(b)U party leader, Dmitrii Lebed′, a staunch opponent of

Ukrainization, defended the "theory of the struggle of two cultures" in March 1920, a theory that anticipated the inevitability of the struggle between the predominantly urban Russian culture and the predominantly rural Ukrainian culture. Moreover, Lebed′ gave priority, of course, to the victory of urban culture, as it was a symbol of large-scale industry, in contrast with the small-scale peasant agricultural economy and rural culture. He wrote:

> If there are cases in which it is better to use the Ukrainian language, then one should be able to do it. However, in cases where the [Ukrainian] language is used as a means of nationalization [building national awareness] ... [or] of Ukrainization out of [nationalist] sentiment rather than out of [Marxist-communist] consciousness, then it should be opposed by the actual Marxist truth that for communist-internationalists, the national question does not in principle exist; it is merely one of the means of changing [speeding] the pace of socialist construction.[57]

The aim of the party, according to Lebed′, was to subdue the development of agricultural industry by inserting large-scale production into agriculture. And the "culture of the city" had to do this because it had "more socialist, proletarian elements."[58]

Crucial for combating these sentiments in Kharkiv in early April 1925 was a thirty-one-year-old Jewish party leader from Kyiv, Lazar Kaganovich.[59] Having extensive experience in party administrative work, and with Stalin's assistance, he was appointed to the Central Committee of the CP(b)U. The primary purpose of his appointment was to ensure support for Stalin within the CP(b)U, neutralize the anti-Stalinist opposition in the UkrSSR, and promote the creation of a pro-Stalinist party-state monolith. The party leader of Ukraine, Kviring, began to flirt with Stalin's political rivals in Moscow. Some of them, particularly Iurii Larin, launched attacks on Ukrainization, equating it with "Petliurism."[60] Kaganovich cleverly used this situation to his advantage; he criticized the opposition for not understanding Ukrainization and started to promote the policy, within the limits set by Stalin, as a wedge against his opponents.

On 5 April 1925, the plenum elected Kaganovich general secretary of the Central Committee of the CP(b)U, and he met with

Shums´kyi. The next day, Shums´kyi gave the report "On Ukrainization" at the plenum of the Central Committee, and Kaganovich, in his new role, listened. For Shums´kyi, the concept of Ukrainization meant "the study of the Ukrainian language and culture, but not the transformation of anyone into the Ukrainian nationality." He openly stated that the biggest failure of Ukrainization was in the party, where it was largely ineffective among the membership.[61] According to Shums´kyi, in no case could the Ukrainian national-cultural movement be bestowed on public and cultural figures who were "hostile" to communism. It was a fairly orthodox report that was supported by the majority of the participants.

Even then, party and state figures accused Shums´kyi of being the front man for "radical Ukrainization." While supporting Ukrainization as a wedge against their opponents, Stalin and Kaganovich had to reckon with Ukrainization's supporters, who, in their implementation of the policy, were exceeding the limits Stalin set to contain it. The lively atmosphere that Shums´kyi fostered for the policy to flourish was ripe for "nationals" (*natsionaly*), as Stalin called them, to really believe that true independence was possible, to go too far in pursuing it, and, in doing so, to threaten Stalin's own centralization of control in the party-state structure. Unable to officially stop Ukrainization at this time—the party remained committed to korenizatsiia as a whole to keep the union together—centralists would remove the policy implementers who shared the so-called nationals' ideals and failed to understand the national question as a "game," including Shums´kyi and his successor as people's commissar for education.

Kaganovich and Stalin removed Shums´kyi with bureaucratic aplomb. As part of the lively literary and cultural atmosphere fostered by Shums´kyi, VAPLITE's members met often at his apartment, or at Khvyl´ovyi's or Ialovyi's, to discuss current affairs in Ukraine and read their poems and pamphlets. At Shums´kyi's apartment, Khvyl´ovyi read his satirical novella *Ivan Ivanovych* (1929) and then his polemical article "Ukraine or Little Russia [Malorossiia]?" (1926) which advocated that Ukraine shift from a historically Russian to a pro-western-European "psychological" orientation in its moral values. This article became a lightning rod for attacks by more conservative elements within the party apparatus against this "lively atmosphere," where everyone was getting "carried away" with Ukrainization. The article would later be declared counterrevolutionary and would be banned by state censorship in 1928, but Shums′kyi supported Khvyl′ovyi against serious party criticism in a series of literary debates from April 1925 until this time, and then beyond. He debated Khvyl′ovyi's article with Kaganovich, who was sharply critical of Khvyl′ovyi and his views. Mykhailo Ialovyi recalled that Shums′kyi returned "in a very agitated state" after a conversation with Kaganovich about Khvyl′ovyi's article, telling him "he was going to fight" Kaganovich over Khvyl′ovyi.[62]

Shums′kyi's broader war with Kaganovich over Ukrainization is the topic of the next chapter. In this specific fight, as with the war, Shums′kyi was defeated. VAPLITE was forced, as its members said at the time, to self-liquidate on 12 January 1928. Even earlier, Kaganovich conveyed to Stalin the most important points of Khvyl′ovyi's article, translated into Russian. In April 1926, Stalin established Khvyl′ovyi and Shums′kyi as two sides of the same anti-Russian coin. In a letter to the members of the Politburo of the Central Committee of the CP(b)U (discussed later), he criticized Khvyl′ovyi's anti-Russian passages and Shums′kyi's calls to "forcibly" Ukrainize the proletariat in Ukraine.

But Shums′kyi never actually made such statements. Stalin simply claimed that he did, echoing the old criticisms of "forced Ukrainization" leveled at ardent supporters of Ukrainian language use, criticisms that predated the Bolsheviks' assumption of power in Ukraine. This episode reiterated Shums′kyi's sense that Stalin had sent Kaganovich to Ukraine not to carry out Ukrainization but to build political support for him in the Ukrainian party organization by using the policy as a wedge against both its staunch opponents and its more enthusiastic proponents. In deliberately distorting Shums′kyi's statements, Stalin opened the way for Kaganovich to attack him politically with various accusations, such as "national bias," which grew into larger accusations of counterrevolutionary intentions.

The escalation of Shums′kyi's transgressive rapsheet from his removal as people's commissar in 1927 to his arrest in 1933, as for so many of his party colleagues, was a result of the relationship between the GPU (the State Political Directorate, the secret police) and party leadership in opposition to Ukrainization. This relationship was already well established in 1926, when the GPU of the USSR organized surveillance of the policy's supporters. In early September 1926, a GPU circular entitled "On Ukrainian separatism" was issued to its local leaders. It was marked "Top Secret. Not to be reprinted. ... Under the responsibility of the head of the GPU." The circular called for the gathering of comprehensive information about supporters of Ukrainization, primarily those Ukrainian intellectuals who had returned, or still wanted to return, to Ukraine from Europe to support the cause.[63] Indeed, the circular identified the most dangerous centers of "Ukrainianness," that is, supposed nationalist and counterrevolutionary groups, as those who would pursue their own interests under the guise of supporting Ukrainization. These included the Ukrainian Autocephalous Orthodox Church (UAOC), "a powerful stronghold of nationalism and a wonderful propaganda tool," and the VUAN, which "gathered a compact mass of former notable figures of the Ukrainian People's Republic."[64] The circular analyzed in detail the situation in the countryside, the beginning of industrialization, and trends in Ukrainian emigration. This analysis concluded that "the work of the Ukrainian public should be given the most serious attention" and emphasized the growing activity of "social and political strata hostile to us."[65]

The circular thus makes clear that long before the open attack on Ukrainization, the secret police and central party leadership to whom its members reported were already preparing their own counter-Ukrainization scheme. The first step of this scheme was to gather compromising information on all proponents of Ukrainization (though it was a legal policy) whom the police considered "dangerous" to the communist regime, including members of the academic class the regime was building.[66] The second step, as Kaganovich's report to the Ninth Congress of the CP(b)U clarifies, was for the political leadership to use the police to purge the threats it identified. Responding to the European socialist thinker Karl Kautsky's accusation that the Bolsheviks had mastered the art of political policing better than the teachings of Karl Marx, Kaganovich wrote:

> We do not dispute that we have really learned the art of political policing, as [Kautsky] put it, that the GPU works very well with us, and if Kautsky came to us, we would give him the full opportunity to see this for himself. In this regard, we do not argue, because Kautsky does not know that the GPU organization not only does not oppose, but in fact follows entirely from Marx's teachings, because none other than Marx was the first to put forward the idea of the dictatorship of the proletariat as the idea of a rigid dictatorship that suppresses any resistance of the exploiting classes and their lackeys.[67]

Shums´kyi was removed as people's commissar for education in September 1927 for upholding a "national bias" and professing a "national-communist ideology." These collaborations between party and GPU members and their creative extrapolations of Shums´kyi's criminality provided the political outline for Chekists to later fabricate a criminal case against Shums´kyi. Shums´kyi and Khvyl´ovyi were thus easily turned into so-called Ukrainian nationalists and fascists, and Shums´kyism and Khvyl´ovyism became dangerous political labels. Andrii Khvylia (real name Olinter), deputy people's commissar for education in 1933, wrote at the height of the purge of the Ukrainian intelligentsia:

> No wonder the Ukrainian fascists—Shums´kyi, Maksymovych, Solodub, and others—under the guise of party membership cards fought so zealously against Khvyl´ovyi's classification as a nationalist troubadour. It is because they saw him as a [useful] sniper who, in the communist camp, could shoot the communist army in the back with the poisoned bullets of Ukrainian nationalism.[68]

The centralists saw Shums´kyi's support of Khvyl´ovyi less as a problem in its own right and more as a scandal providing an opportunity to discredit him. Their main problem with Shums´kyi was twofold. First, Shums´kyi could never be a staunch ally to the emerging dictators in Kharkiv and Moscow because he always proceeded from the premise that every leader should be open to criticism. This absolutely contradicted the imperatives that guided Kaganovich and Stalin as authoritarian leaders. No wonder Kaganovich perceived Shums´kyi's criticism of his position on Ukrainization as an attempt to undermine his credibility. With Stalin affording Kaganovich special trust and protection in

Ukraine to do his bidding, it is also no wonder that Stalin perceived Shums′kyi's attack on Kaganovich as an attack on himself.

Second, Shums′kyi refused to understand Ukrainian independence and specifically Ukrainization and the path to Ukrainian statehood as a game. For him, it was a do-or-die mission. The policy was thus not a platform for him to strengthen his position within the party as it was for Stalin and Kaganovich. Shums′kyi's different interpretation, especially compared to Kaganovich's, was not due to Shums′kyi being a radical or even an anti-Stalinist at the time. He was not a fundamentally different type of party member than his detractors, and he was as much a bureaucrat as Kaganovich was. The documents of the People's Commissariat for Education confirm that he followed the party and state resolutions in matters of Ukrainization very much to the letter, as did his successors. Like Kaganovich, Shums′kyi was a politician with many years of experience, high political intuition, and a deep understanding of the context in which he had to work. Shums′kyi's different understanding of Ukrainization stemmed from the fact that he felt himself to be a Ukrainian *and* communist politician; this was his primary identity. The fundamental difference between him and Kaganovich was that, despite being born and raised in Ukraine, Kaganovich and many like-minded communists thought of Ukraine as no more than a geographical area.

As long as many in the party-state structure understood themselves as Shums′kyi did, as specifically "Ukrainian" communists committed to the policy of Ukrainization, it would continue its revival of Ukraine's national culture even after Shums′kyi's removal. As would continue Stalin and Kaganovich's growing sense that the policy was fomenting and unleashing dangerous, anti-Russian, and thus counterrevolutionary forces (and party members). Even when Mykola Skrypnyk replaced Shums′kyi as people's commissar for education in 1927, duly criticizing his predecessor for all his faults, it was not long before Skrypnyk, too, was subjected to exactly the same criticisms and eventually removed from the post and arrested like Shums′kyi (actually, Skrypnyk shot himself before his arrest). Skrypnyk suffered this fate even though he was potentially a much better ally to Stalin and Kaganovich, being an Old Bolshevik, not a member of another party, unlike Shums′kyi, who joined the Bolsheviks after the revolution. Many Bolsheviks never really trusted these new members, especially outside Russia. The problem Stalin and Kaganovich had with Skrypnyk was that he, like Shums′kyi, was Ukrainian in the sense that he still understood statehood as a mission and Ukrainization as a means to achieve it. He, too, firmly believed in the possibility of synthesizing communist ideas imbued with internationalism with Ukraine's national revival.[69]

For all of the supposed differences between Skrypnyk and Shums′kyi, Skrypnyk made no fundamental revisions to Ukrainization's conceptual basis or its practical implementation during his tenure as people's commissar for education. Skrypnyk's following statement could just as easily have been made by Shums′kyi: "For most members of our party, Ukraine, as a national unit, did not exist. It was Little Russia [Malorossiia], an inseparable part of a single indivisible Russia, something inconspicuous with respect to its relations with Russia as well as regarding its territory, and even language."[70] This was a common, not radical, position at the time. Indeed, no less than the head of the CP(b)U, Panas Liubchenko, who roundly condemned Shums′kyi and then Skrypnyk, agreed: "Our CP(b)U for quite a long time had taken a rather wrong point of view on the Ukrainian national question, although it completely agreed with Lenin and fully subscribed to his foundations of the national question."[71] Skrypnyk's opponents made his position radical by narrowing the acceptable parameters of Ukrainization in the late 1920s and early 1930s. Even when Skrypnyk sought to amend the policy to fit within these parameters and avoid the same charges of "national bias" and forced Ukrainization that had been laid against his predecessor, his opponents continually narrowed them. Eventually, it was impossible for Skrypnyk to operate without being accused of these crimes, indeed, with Shums′kyism, which was quickly becoming a byword for all of them.

For instance, Skrypnyk attempted to differentiate his implementation of Ukrainization from Shums′kyi's in important areas. He blunted Ukrainization's "anti-Russian" direction by distinguishing between the policy and de-Russification (Shums′kyi's opponents claimed he had conflated these). The latter process, in Skrypnyk's opinion, now more limited in scope and by no means forcible, applied only to those Ukrainians by birth who spoke three quarters in Russian and one quarter in Ukrainian. He called those people "half-Russians." Skrypnyk's critics could not forgive even his clumsy attempts to dilute the implementation of de-Russification by fractions. One of them, for example, saw no distinction between Skrypnyk's "moderate" and Shums′kyi's "extreme" version of the policy. Indeed, by 1933, any mention of de-Russification was problematic:

> Comrade Skrypnyk suggested the need for de-Russification, which was a very gross distortion of Comrade Stalin's directive. Comrade Skrypnyk branded the Russified proletarians of Ukraine as the "half-Russians" and this characterization had a bad nationalist smell. This was no better than the argument about the "Little Russians" that was used by the provocateur Shums′kyi.[72]

Having established the "nationalist diversion" of both Skrypnyk and Shums′kyi in their roles as people's commissar by 1933, the party leadership found it easy to move to the next logical step in its denunciation process—linking them with foreign counterrevolution; that is, "work for the interventionists," in the mass purge that saw tens of thousands arrested.[73]

For Terry Martin, Shums′kyi's case clearly shows that by the late 1920s, most Bolshevik leaders in Moscow and even Kharkiv understood Ukrainization not as neutralizing nationalism but as exacerbating it. Shums′kyi's removal and the party's campaign against Shums′kyism were the party's first major and official steps toward counteracting Ukrainization.[74] Shums′kyi was not without his defenders in this drawn-out repression. The leaders of the Communist Party of Western Ukraine (CPWU), with bases in enemy Poland, defended him. However, this moved Shums′kyi's case into the international arena and made it easier for his detractors to define Shums′kyism now as an attempt to separate Ukraine from the USSR, especially given the growing tensions with Piłsudski's Poland. From the 1920s, and for a long time after—in fact, until Gorbachev's perestroika—these assessments were dominant in Soviet historiography and political propaganda.

The party's campaign against Shums′kyism and its progressive countering of Ukrainization into the late 1920s and early

1930s did little at first to stem the national revival in Ukrainian culture that the policy had helped foster under Shums´kyi and Skrypnyk. According to Rudnytsky, the 1920s were the happiest years in the history of the UkrSSR:

> Under the new economic policy [NEP], industrial production more or less returned to the pre-revolutionary level, and the not-yet-collectivized peasantry lived relatively prosperously. It was also a time when Soviet Ukraine had real autonomy in cultural affairs. Its achievements in the fields of education, scholarship, literature, and art are truly impressive. Cities quickly lost their Russified appearance. By 1930, Ukraine was approaching the state of a fully developed, culturally mature nation.[75]

Even considering the slightly inflated optimism of this assessment, a serious expert would be hard pressed to disagree with it.

Skrypnyk continued to foster the development of this "culturally mature nation" from 1927 to 1933, and his name was used at the time to mark this period ("Skrypnykivshchyna"). This maturity, particularly in urban culture, was evident in the unprecedented outbreak of creative activity in Ukrainian literature. More Ukrainian-language books and journals reached a much wider and more educated audience than ever before. This Ukrainian renaissance would later be renamed the "executed renaissance," because many participants of the cultural revival were arrested and shot from 1933 onward, after Stalin decided to end Ukrainization, or at least end it as a serious policy.

This decision to end Ukrainization was a long time in coming. Its origins were multifaceted and warrant their own works.[76] Suffice it to say here that by the 1930s, Stalin's long-time concerns about the policy undermining the balance of power between the communist regime and the Ukrainian national movement had come to a head. As one historian points out, Ukrainization led to "the transition of some communists to national positions, the formation of the Ukrainian proletariat, the increase in the share of the urban population, and the growth of educational, cultural, and scholarly activities by the old and young. [Now the] Ukrainian elite posed a serious threat to Moscow's control over the UkrSSR."[77] This threat intensified in the midst of the greatest transformation in Ukraine's, and the USSR's, history: the forced collectivization of the peasantry and its resultant catastrophes. Compelling onto collective farms tens of millions of Ukrainian peasants, who had operated as subsistence farmers or private traders in the 1920s under the NEP, elicited massive resistance across the country, including from some parts of the party-state structure. The murderous Soviet response to Ukrainian resistance in the countryside and in the cities helped to forge the famine of 1932–33, the Holodomor, which killed millions of Ukrainians.[78]

This massive shift away from the NEP to forced collectivization and Stalin's consolidation of his own personal dictatorship over the party-state structure after defeating his rivals by the end of the 1920s also removed the old impetus for Ukrainization—keeping the support of the republics for the union among both the population and the elites. The former was being decimated by forced labor and famine, and the latter by mass purges by the center to reform it into a more compliant base. Stalin was reducing Ukraine—and, indeed, other republics—to the subservient, peripheral position he had always anticipated. He was autonomizing them. In doing so, he strengthened his power over both periphery and center as domestic catastrophes raged and international tensions rose.[79]

Party propaganda offered nationalism (fostered by the misimplementation of Ukrainization and korenizatsiia more generally), rather than Stalin's policies, as a key cause of Ukraine's and much of the union's catastrophes, including famine. Nationalism was the key threat to the Soviet Union and could only be countered by ending korenizatsiia and purging its "nationalist" proponents. This change in the party line on korenizatsiia took place between the Fifteenth (1930) and Seventeenth (1934) Congresses of the All-Union Communist Party (of Bolsheviks; ACP[b]).[80] During this period, purges of local communists and nonparty intelligentsia were carried out in all non-Russian republics, and a significant number of cadres educated during the process of korenizatsiia were removed from their posts, with many arrested. The action targeted various kinds of "national prejudices" and manifestations of "bourgeois nationalism," under which it was easy to bring down even members of the Communist Party, if they professed their dedication to national traditions and patriotism.

Terror against the intelligentsia began to unfold in 1930. The first major show trial—a public court case against political "enemies"—commenced in March against the Union for the Liberation of Ukraine (SVU). This fabricated case was symptomatic of the secret police's method of operation. It established a fictitious organization, the SVU, in Ukraine in 1927—the year Shums′kyi was charged with "national bias"—claiming that this counterrevolutionary organization united anti-Soviet intellectuals, activists of the UAOC, and kulaks against Soviet power. Fictitious anti-Soviet organizations provided a useful tool for police to use in establishing the criminality of numerous innocent figures. The police claimed that their targets were members of these institutions and thus part of broad criminal conspiracies that fomented counterrevolution. The first report about the discovery of the SVU was published in the press in November 1929, and in February 1930, the newspaper *Visti VUTsVK* (News of the All-Ukrainian Central Executive Committee) began to publish materials from the indictment, referring to the fictitious organization by name. According to the official version, the SVU was led by the vice president of the VUAN, the "anticommunist" Serhii Iefremov. It was associated with the real-life anti-Soviet emigrant organization of the same name, which had existed between 1914 and 1918. The fictitious SVU supposedly aimed to overthrow Soviet rule in Ukraine through an armed uprising with the help of foreign powers, as well as to segregate the UkrSSR from the USSR and restore the capitalist system there. Through the press, the leadership claimed that the SVU had separate sections—academic, school, and pedagogical, among others, including medical, which was supposed to have poisoned communist patients. The SVU was alleged to have branches across the USSR, with a suborganization, the Union of Ukrainian Youth, dedicated to young counterrevolutionaries.

Forty-five people were tried at the show trial, which took place at the Kharkiv Opera House, prompting contemporaries to call the process the "Theater within the theater" or "Opera SVU, Music GPU" (that is, the music to the opera of the show trial was provided by the police). Among the defendants were two academics from VUAN, fifteen professors, two students, one high school principal, ten teachers, one theologian and one priest of the UAOC, three writers, five editors, two lawyers, and one librarian. Fifteen defendants worked in the VUAN system, thirty-one were former members of various Ukrainian political parties, one was the prime minister, two were ministers of the UPR government, and six were members of the Central Rada. Another seven hundred people were arrested shortly after in connection with the case, and, in all, according to some estimates, more than thirty thousand people were arrested, killed, or deported as a result of the SVU trial.[81]

The SVU as presented in 1929–30 did not exist. The police had to create it. The GPU of the UkrSSR did so by recruiting several young people, beginning in 1928, as double agents (some of whom would later be found in exile), inviting them to initiate contact with nationalists and report relevant information. In December 1929, the preparation of the SVU entered a decisive phase. The GPU received a number of documents that became available to the Central Committee of the CP(b)U, the Central Committee of the ACP(b), and the Joint State Political Directorate (OGPU) of the USSR. Stalin personally directed the preparation of the process, as evidenced, in particular, by an encrypted message he sent to the leaders of the CP(b)U on 2 January 1930. In developing the SVU case, the GPU provided the basis for the subsequent purge, which was launched full-scale in 1932–33, when Stalin decided to violently curtail Ukrainization.

For Stalin, ending Ukrainization and ending the chaos in the Ukrainian countryside were interconnected problems. On 14 December 1932, Stalin, together with his key ally and head of the all-union Soviet government (Sovnarkom), Viacheslav Molotov, signed a joint state-party resolution on the removal of grain produced on collective farms. This resolution also called for the "proper conduct of Ukrainization" in Ukraine and abroad, in the regions where Ukrainians lived. This signaled the death of Ukrainization as a policy. The next day, Stalin and Molotov signed a similar telegram together, and, on 24 January, the Central Committee of the ACP(b) instructed Pavel Postyshev, a Russian Old Bolshevik, to move to Ukraine as the second secretary of the Central Committee of the CP(b)U both to solve the famine and to eliminate the country's "nationalist danger."[82] At the joint November plenum of the Central Committee and the Central Control Commission of the CP(b)U, Postyshev stressed that "without eliminating the errors in the implementation of the party's national policy, without defeating the nationalist elements that have settled in various sections of social construction in Ukraine, it will surely be impossible to eliminate the backwardness of its agriculture."[83] This plenum not only became the apotheosis of the political campaign against the Skrypnykivshchyna, but also stated unequivocally in the resolution that "at the moment, the main danger is local Ukrainian nationalism combined with imperialist interventionists."[84] This "moment" stretched for years and meant a steady destruction of Ukraine's intellectual forces, including the communist intelligentsia—those who yesterday had crushed the nationalists were today declared an enemy of the system they had faithfully served.

Stalin supported the defeat of Skrypnykivshchyna, mentioning it in a report at the Seventeenth Congress of the ACP(b) about Ukraine and the "fall" of Mykola Skrypnyk:

> They argue which trend is the main danger, the trend toward Great Russian nationalism, or the trend toward local nationalism? Under the current conditions this is a formal and therefore empty debate. ... The main danger is the trend against which fighting has stopped, and which, thus, has been allowed to grow into a danger to the state. (*Long applause.*) In the [sic!] Ukraine, until very recently, the trend toward Ukrainian nationalism was not the main danger, but when fighting against it stopped and it was allowed to grow to the point where it closed ranks with the interventionists, this trend became the main danger.[85]

Now the "explosive" material that the GPU (NKVD) had been accumulating for years started to bear fruit, used only against those they considered a potential or real enemy. This included yesterday's adherents of the system. More than one hundred cases against fictitious anti-Soviet organizations—the Ukrainian National Center (1932), the Ukrainian Military Organization (1933, 1938), the Union of Ukrainian Nationalists (1934), the Counterrevolutionary Former Borotbysts, an imagined association of Shums′kyi's former party colleagues (1935, 1937), the Ukrainian Counterrevolutionary Nationalist Organization (1936), and others—featured not only representatives of the nonparty Ukrainian intelligentsia or non-Bolshevik political parties, but also figures from the party and state leadership of the UkrSSR. As the macabre joke at the time went, those arrested and exiled as a result of these cases began to intensively "Ukrainize" the peripheries of the Soviet Union from the prison camps where they were sent (Solovki, Siberia, and Central Asia). Otherwise, they were sentenced to death.

In January 1938, a new leader of the CP(b)U, Nikita Khrushchev, replaced Stanisław Kosior in Ukraine.[86] With his arrival, the policy of korenizatsiia came to an official end. In particular, a resolution of the Politburo of the Central Committee of the CP(b)U of 10 April 1938, "On the Reorganization of National Schools in Ukraine," described the establishment of educational institutions that used the languages of national minorities as "the planting of special national schools" that were hotbeds of "bourgeois-nationalist, anti-Soviet influence on children," and their functioning as "inexpedient and harmful." These schools and other educational institutions were liquidated, and students were transferred to schools with Ukrainian and Russian languages of instruction.[87]

Khrushchev blamed this "sabotage" in the field of public education on former people's commissar for education Volodymyr Zatons´kyi—who replaced Mykola Skrypnyk in 1933 and was arrested in November 1937—and the staff of the People's Commissariat for Education of the USSR. In his report to the Twelfth Congress of the CP(b)U, Khrushchev stated: "Zatons´kyi, the enemy of the people, confessed in his testimonies ... that the recertification of teachers by the government was carried out in such a way as to discredit honest teachers and kick them out of school in order to leave Petliura's, Trotsky's, Bukharin's, and bourgeois-nationalist spy gangs." Recalling his predecessor as head of the CP(b)U, Panas Liubchenko (who committed suicide in August 1937), Khrushchev claimed that "Liubchenko and other bastards did everything to knock the Russian language out of Ukrainian schools."[88]

On 20 April 1938, the Soviet People's Commissariat of the USSR and the Central Committee of the CP(b)U adopted a joint resolution, "On the Compulsory Study of the Russian Language in Non-Russian Schools in Ukraine."[89] This resolution was an outgrowth of a broader decision of all-union Sovnarkom and the Central Committee of the ACP(b), "On the Compulsory Study of the Russian Language in the Schools of National Republics and Regions." On 8 May 1938, the Politburo of the CP(b)U adopted a resolution "On Compiling a New Ukrainian Spelling," and in October 1938, it discussed the question of reorganizing national schools. It noted that "[m]any schools are not provided with teachers. Much worse than Russian schools, the Ukrainian schools are not provided with textbooks and do not have methodological guidance, and therefore work poorly."[90]

In April 1940, a special government decree regulated the teaching of Russian in the national schools of the UkrSSR.[91] Notably, at the Fifteenth Congress of the CP(b)U, held that same year, neither Nikita Khrushchev's report nor the speeches of the delegates mentioned korenizatsiia or Ukrainization. By this time, Stalin had won the "game" of independence he had described to Lenin in 1922. Everyone now understood what it meant to be Ukrainian and represent Ukraine in party and state structures. This new generation of apparatchiks (communist officials) would be symbols of Stalin's power "rooted" in the peripheries. Their loyalty to him was established during the Great Terror of 1937–38, when Stalin elevated them to positions of power at the expense of almost the entire old guard, whom he killed or imprisoned. However, Oleksandr Shums′kyi, unlike his former friends and enemies, did not die. How was this possible? Before answering this question, we need to follow Shums′kyi through these turbulent times on his way to the highest government office in Ukraine.

Chapter Two

SHUMS´KYI'S LIFE AND HIS RISE TO PEOPLE'S COMMISSAR

Oleksandr Iakovych Shums´kyi hailed from Ukraine's Zhytomyr region. He was born in the village of Turchynka on 2 December (OS 21 November) 1890 as one of eight children. Shums´kyi's father, Iakiv Danylovych (born in 1851), was of Polish descent but born in Zhytomyr, and his mother, Ieva (born in 1862), was German. Like many other Soviet citizens who did not originate from clear worker or peasant backgrounds, Shums´kyi lied about his family's class origins when filling out Soviet census documents and questionnaires. He wrote that he was born "into a family of hired laborers [*naimyty*]."[1] In fact, his father was a forester on the estate of a wealthy landowner, Mykola Iakovych Muraviov, and Shums´kyi's grandfather, Danylo Iakovych, as well as his great-great grandfather, was a priest. The parish register of 1899 listed Iakiv as a "hereditary honorary citizen and resident of Borovaia Rudna."[2] Hereditary honorary citizens were seen as forming an intermediate class somewhere between the merchant class and the bourgeoisie. The son and even the grandson of a hereditary honorary citizen had the right to be included in the nobility.

Shums´kyi grew up in Turchynka and, in 1906, graduated from a two-grade village school in the village of Saly, Zhytomyr Oblast. This meager education was sufficient for Shums´kyi to pass external exams to attend and graduate from high school, and then study at university. Before that, he worked at the large (for

Zhytomyr) sawmill enterprise named Gottesman and Brochman. Shums´kyi wrote about this in his autobiography:

> During breaks, when the factory was not working, we went to earn money on the estate. At that time, we had a group of workers at the factory, which included me. This group had connections with the Ukrainian Social Democrats [union], to which we also belonged. Therefore, from that time, from 1908, I joined the labor movement. Then from the factory I went to work as a surveyor's assistant.[3]

Shums´kyi was referring to the Ukrainian Social Democratic Union, a political party that emerged in late 1904 because of the split of the Revolutionary Ukrainian Party (RUP) and, on 12 January 1905, became a part of the Russian Social Democratic Labor Party (RSDLP), with autonomous rights.[4] Thus, at the age of nineteen, Shums´kyi joined the socialist movement. In the Korosten-Chernihiv Oblast, he took part in a strike for the first time at the factory where he worked.

After studying to become a technician, Shums´kyi would work as an assistant to a land surveyor named Biel´s´kyi at the Land Management Commission of the Volyn Oblast for one year. In January 1910, Shums´kyi wrote an official application for the position.[5] Of course, the relevant background check was carried out. On 27 March 1910, the head of the Volyn Provincial Gendarmerie informed the Volyn governor that "there was no information that could compromise the political credibility in the affairs of the Department entrusted to me of Oleksandr Iakovych Shums´kyi, who lived in Zhytomyr, at 38 Kroshenska Street."[6] It is difficult to say why and how, but Shums´kyi at that time did not attract the attention of the gendarmes. He took up this position but soon attempted to leave it.[7]

As early as September 1911, he submitted a request for sick leave, and in October 1911, he was found to be incapable of work in the field. On 6 October 1911, Shums´kyi wrote a report to his former boss, the Volyn provincial land surveyor, stating that he had been granted a month's leave. A month passed before Shums´kyi asked for another month's leave and attached a medical certificate signed by Moscow doctor Nikolai Kron. The address Shums´kyi listed is noteworthy: "Moscow. 55th Post and Telegraph Office.

Attention: O. Ia. Shums´kyi."[8] Therefore, Shums´kyi was already in Russia, in Moscow, and he did not want to return to Zhytomyr. He wanted to combine the incompatible: receive the salary of an assistant land surveyor (six hundred rubles a year) without working in this position. His Zhytomyr bosses quickly realized that, and, on 30 November 1911, the governor of Volyn dismissed Oleksandr Shums´kyi from his position "for a negligent attitude to his duties." Shums´kyi wrote a letter of resignation in December 1911 in any case, and he later asked Biel´s´kyi for work documents and a reference letter on his performance as assistant surveyor before taking leave. He received all this in February 1912, with a positive character reference from Biel´s´kyi.[9]

Why did Shums´kyi move to Moscow? He later admitted that it was to escape from his father and "to see the world and people." Iakiv Danylovych had wanted his son to work on the estate and "not be associated with any mischief." Apparently, the latter had been reported to his father by an official at the estate of Muraviov, who, according to Shums´kyi, had "sniffed out" his connection with the revolutionaries.[10] In any case, an acquaintance of Shums´kyi's who had previously moved to Moscow helped him find accommodation and work there.

The only work Shums´kyi could immediately take up was in the same field—land surveying—so he sought to become an assistant land surveyor in the Land Management Department of Moscow gubernia (province). Not having enough money to study, he attended evening courses at the first democratic university in Russia, the A. L. Shaniavskii Moscow City People's University. It was named after Al´fons Shaniavskii (1837–1905), a general in the Russian army, a colonizer of the Far East, and later a gold miner, who had left money to create a university where anyone could study, regardless of gender, religion, political beliefs, or level of previous education.

Students did not need to present a school certificate or any other documents to enroll and could choose which lectures to attend. Shums´kyi described his experience there as follows:

> I entered Shaniavskii University for an evening popular science course, but nothing came of it, because I was only semiliterate. ...

> But I wanted to study, and I started to prepare for the "certificate of maturity" externally. For a long time, I was confused by this training, earning a living, but I was a persistent guy, and in 1915 I still passed the exam in Moscow, although it undermined my health.[11]

There is no detailed evidence of Shums′kyi's stay in Moscow, but it is known that Shums′kyi was increasingly drawn into the whirlpool of the revolutionary movement. As French politician and contemporary of Shums′kyi Georges Clemenceau is rumored to have said, he who was not a socialist in his youth would be a complete villain in his old age.[12] And long before Clemenceau is said to have uttered these words, Ivan Franko, the great national literary figure and founder of the socialist movement in western Ukraine, describing the atmosphere of the 1870s and early 1880s, wrote:

> Socialist ideas inflamed people to fanaticism; at the same time, those ideas were far from the criticism that was gained later. Marx's first volume [of *Capital*] was the gospel, and what it did not contain was supplemented by imagination and feeling. Everyone dreamed of a great social revolution; Engels and other western European socialists predicted its onset in ten years, and when those years passed, they postponed it for another ten years, and so on.[13]

Shums′kyi was fascinated by socialism. Until 1913, he had contact with representatives of the Ukrainian Social Democrats in Moscow, and from 1914, he was a member of the Socialist-Revolutionary circle. Shums′kyi explained this shift in his exposure to revolutionary ideas as follows: "It is impossible to say that I have radically changed my worldview, because at that time I was a revolutionary-minded but unconscious ordinary worker, and I followed individual people whom I knew and trusted more than I understood differences in programs and worldviews."[14] Later, in his 1923 article "Old and New Ukraine," Shums′kyi provided an assessment of the activity of the Ukrainian Socialist-Revolutionaries before 1917:

> First, they did not have their own consolidated party organism before the revolution. These were separate circles with little connection. And second, with regard to their program, it was a terrible mix, starting with Russian populism, which grew on the basis of

community, with the addition of anarchism and syndicalism, and ending with Marxism; and with regard to social composition, especially during the revolution, it was a conglomerate of proletarianized labor and real landowners. In short, it was just a community of Ukrainians.[15]

At the beginning of the First World War, the political situation in Ukraine changed radically. The Tsarist government banned all official Ukrainian organizations, then all Ukrainian-language publications, then imposed martial law on the right bank of Ukraine. Military courts began to operate. Ukrainian political life shifted to the underground.

Like most other revolutionaries, Shums´kyi sought to avoid conscription. For this purpose, he enrolled in a veterinary institute, which he would have supposed would provide him with a student exemption. It did not; he was conscripted into the engineering corps of the Russian army, anyway. At the end of 1916, he was arrested for possession of illegal literature and eventually sent to the Southwestern Front, directly to the front line. Interestingly, his friend Serhii Litoshenko, who used Shums´kyi's identity documents in Moscow, was also arrested for Shums´kyi's crime. He was arrested as Shums´kyi's double, so to speak, and was imprisoned until the February Revolution.

During the February Revolution of 1917 in Russia, Shums´kyi was elected a delegate to the corps, army, and later front congresses of soldiers' committees, before being sent as a specialist from the army to the Kyiv Provincial Land Administration. Based in Kyiv, Shums´kyi would become one of the "most active participants" in revolutionary affairs.[16] His sympathies lay with the Ukrainian Party of Socialist-Revolutionaries (UPSR), which represented the interests of the Ukrainian peasantry primarily and enjoyed its strong support. According to some eyewitnesses, it sometimes happened that an entire village of peasants enrolled in the party as a group. In September 1917, there were seventy-five thousand party members.[17]

The first signs of an organized Socialist-Revolutionary movement date to the early twentieth century, but as an all-Ukrainian party it took shape at the Constituent Congress in Kyiv in April 1917.[18] It was then that Shums´kyi joined the UPSR. For some time, he worked in the editorial office of the party newspaper, *Narodna volia* (The people's will).[19]

Mykola Kovalevs′kyi, noting that Shums′kyi was a surveyor and economist by education, said of him at this time:

> He knew the land issue quite well, and he worked in the editorial office in this area, covering issues related to land reform. In discussions on this subject, Shums′kyi held rather radical views and always expressed the opinion that not only should large land ownership be abolished, but also peasant land ownership should be thoroughly audited. He defended the idea of socialization of land—that is, the abolition of peasant property and the socialization of land in the hands of rural communities.[20]

Kovalevs′kyi's memoirs reveal another important detail for understanding Shums′kyi at that time:

> In national-Ukrainian affairs, Shums′kyi was less radical than in land affairs and often expressed the opinion that the future political and state system of Ukraine would depend on future developments in Russia. During an editorial discussion on this topic, I called him a defeatist and a person who did not believe in the people's own strength. Shums′kyi was very ambitious, and he was terribly offended by this remark.[21]

Both Kovalevs′kyi's assessment and Shums′kyi's response were well grounded. It was Shums′kyi's revolutionary experience from 1917, including his dealings with the Bolsheviks or "Russian developments," that would radicalize his position on Ukrainian independence. His growing radicalism placed him on the left wing of the party.

The UPSR was unequivocally a party of the peasantry and its membership was young—mostly between seventeen and thirty years old, and rarely older than thirty. Shums′kyi later wrote: "In the Ukrainian Party of Socialist-Revolutionaries, I stand on the left wing of the internationalists; because of this, I was considered to be a Bolshevik provocateur in the party."[22] Yet, he was not a provocateur. His desire to combine national and socialist slogans seemed deep and sincere, and, at this stage, this desire, along with his opposition to the Central Rada, united him and his associates with the Bolsheviks. Although they formed only a small group within the UPSR in the summer of 1917, by the end of that year, the internationalists had grown into a complete faction.

In late November 1917, at the Third Congress, Shums´kyi was co-opted into the Central Committee of the UPSR as a representative of the left wing. From there, he was sent as a delegate to the Parliament of Ukraine, the Ukrainian Central Rada. Thus, Shums´kyi was among those who formed the left-wing opposition in the Rada. He saw the Rada's leadership as immobilized, unable to control the situation in the country, and ineffective: it talked a lot and did little, and it could adopt the right laws but could not implement them. It was solely bourgeois and also nationalist. Shums´kyi and the left faction in the UPSR were also dissatisfied with the Rada's agrarian policy. The UPSR demanded the abolition of private ownership of land and the establishment of "state workers' control over industry," which the Bolsheviks proclaimed when they came to power in late 1917.

Shums´kyi and his colleagues believed in their own messianic role: they, not the Central Rada or the Bolsheviks, represented the interests of Ukraine. To oppose the Central Rada, they entered into an alliance with the Bolsheviks. Shums´kyi soon learned that the Bolsheviks knew how to cheat and cheat well. In 1917, he and other members of the left wing of the UPSR demanded the resignation of the government, the creation of a left-wing government, and immediate reconciliation with the Bolsheviks. Shums´kyi was involved in the attempted coup to realize these demands. Isaak Mazepa, head of the Directorate from August 1919 until May 1920, recalled this incident sometime later:

> As is known, in January 1918, during the struggle between the Central Rada and the Bolsheviks in Kyiv, a group of left-wing SRs [Socialist-Revolutionaries] emerged from a party of Ukrainian SRs that was headed by members of the Central Rada M. Poloz, O. Shums´kyi, M. Liubchenko, V. Ellans´kyi, and others. With the help of the Bolsheviks, this group wanted to overthrow the Central Rada and proclaim Soviet rule in Ukraine. This plan did not materialize ... the conspirators were arrested.[23]

On 16 January 1918, the day of a Bolshevik-inspired armed uprising at the Arsenal plant in Kyiv, Shums′kyi and other left-wing Socialist-Revolutionaries were indeed arrested as Bolshevik supporters.

The Rada commission established to investigate the coup found that the Bolsheviks, in the event of their success, had promised positions in the future government to some of the rebels. Borys Martos, who reported on the work of the commission, did not want to disclose the names of those to whom the Bolsheviks had promised things, although he did say that the plan had been to divide Ukraine so that the Katerynoslav (Dnipro) region, Taganrog district, and some other mining districts of Ukraine would "join the Moscow region."[24] It is still unclear what was promised and to whom. Shums′kyi's logic in this situation is not entirely evident. He was convinced that the Ukrainian Central Rada was preparing for war with Bolshevik Russia. At the same time, it was known that on 17 December 1917, Vladimir Lenin and Leon Trotsky had issued an ultimatum to the Rada with impossible demands, in effect making a declaration of war.

This type of ultimatum would become classic Soviet "diplomacy." Lenin and Trotsky's ultimatum had been issued in the name of the Soviet government, Sovnarkom, and it accused the Rada of "pursuing an ambiguous bourgeois policy" in the Civil War by disarming pro-Bolshevik military units and letting Cossack units pass through Ukrainian territory to the Don, from which they waged hostilities against the Bolsheviks. The ultimatum demanded that the Rada not only stop these actions, which were merely allegations, but also take part in the struggle "against the counterrevolutionary Kadet-Kaledin uprising." If these demands were not met within forty-eight hours, Sovnarkom would declare the Central Rada to be "in a state of open war against the Soviet authorities in Russia and Ukraine."[25] Lenin and Trotsky knew full well that the Rada could not cease behavior over which it had little control and openly support the Bolsheviks—indeed, they counted on it. Sovnarkom had approved military intervention in Ukraine a few days before the ultimatum was sent.[26]

Along with other detainees from the failed coup, Shums′kyi was imprisoned in the Kyiv Pedagogical Museum—but only for a few weeks. The detainees were liberated, by default, by an attack on Kyiv by Bolshevik troops under the command of Mikhail Murav´ev.[27] When this assault on Kyiv began, the parliamentarians and guards fled the museum, leaving it unguarded, and Shums´kyi and his comrades simply left. Shums´kyi's detractors accused him of thus taking part in a conspiracy against the Ukrainian Central Rada. Here it would be possible to brand him a pro-Bolshevik figure, as they did, but the situation was not so simple. As early as April 1918, he labeled the revolution in Ukraine a "Bolshevik onslaught."[28] Vasyl´ Ellan-Blakytnyi described the Bolshevik policy of that time most clearly in a publication in February 1918, arguing that the policy was aimed at inciting ethnic hatred and that "the whole path of the second revolution was only a struggle, but, to a greater extent, it was repressions, arrests, cowardice, and arbitrary murders without measure, without end."[29] Even as they allied with the Bolsheviks, the Borotbysts categorically condemned the Bolsheviks' proclamation of a separate Donetsk-Kryvyi Rih Soviet Republic as an attempt to prevent the spread of Ukrainian power to Donbas and Kryvbas.[30]

Shums´kyi and his colleagues sought to achieve their revolutionary aims in alliance with the Bolsheviks. They strove to reconcile national and socialist interests harmoniously and were in solidarity with the Bolsheviks' belief that revolutionary transformations could not be carried out within the existing so-called bourgeois-capitalist system. This belief distinguished the left wing of the UPSR, which later formed a separate Borotbyst party with Shums´kyi among its leaders, from those in the Central Rada. The Borotbysts began to set up radas (councils) as central bodies to govern political affairs and defend the working class. Within their alliance with the Bolsheviks, they had the right to organize governing bodies on a national basis, so long as they did not conflict with the interests of workers. These bodies were created on the basis of nation, not class, and constituted parliamentary self-government in this alliance. They worked in accordance with the Constitution, which distinguished between the roles and functions of "national" and "supreme" (class) authorities.

In analyzing this model from the perspective of what happened to the Borotbysts later—in the 1920s and 1930s, when the Bolsheviks purged them—it is tempting to talk about the naivete of the former and the insidiousness of the latter, who never wanted to share power with anyone. This is an ahistorical argument. If we consider the situation in early 1918, its fluidity, and the fact that the Bolsheviks were not popular in Ukraine, the ideas of the Borotbysts could be seen as a reasonable (albeit imperfect) attempt to create a model of Ukrainian statehood completely different from the one that emerged later under the Bolsheviks. The Bolsheviks may have needed the Borotbysts in Ukraine, given their lack of reach in the country, especially in rural areas, but it must also be said that the Borotbysts may have felt they needed the Bolsheviks. Though the Borotbysts were the most authoritative party in Ukraine, they, too, lacked widespread representation across the country and had failed to offer a platform that would unite pro-Ukrainian political forces, not to mention their lack of military strength.

After the return of the Ukrainian Central Rada to Kyiv and the arrival of the German army in February 1918, Shums′kyi moved back to Zhytomyr. On 16 March, he was elected chairman of the Volyn Land Committee, and on 14 April, he became a member of the Volyn Regional Committee of the UPSR.[31] He later recalled: "With the arrival of the Germans, I fled to Volyn and worked in the Land Committee, where, despite the protection of the Germans, we carried out the destruction of landowners and the seizure of estates."[32] Incidentally, Shums′kyi lived in the same building in which the Volyn Land Administration was located. He already had a family by this time. His wife, Liudmyla, was a teacher, though there is no other information about her, other than that she was the daughter of a priest. Shums′kyi and his wife had three children: a daughter, Kateryna, and two sons, Petro (born in 1914) and Oles′ (born in 1918).

At the end of April 1918, the Germans, who had been invited by the Ukrainian Central Rada to eject the Bolsheviks from Ukraine, dispersed the Rada. A former tsarist general and now a hetman (historically, an elected military chief among the Zaporizhzhian Cossacks), Pavlo Skoropads′kyi came to power. The leftist Socialist-Revolutionaries decided to continue the struggle underground. Shums′kyi rallied against the Hetmanate, living by the laws of the underground. According to some researchers, it was during the period of the anti-Hetmanate underground that Shums´kyi began to rethink his previous ideas and finally changed his political platform. A turning point in the political mood of the Ukrainian peasantry played a decisive role in his transformation. Having been largely indifferent to earlier divisions between Hetmanate and anti-Hetmanate camps, the peasantry turned decisively to the leftists in the summer of 1918.[33] In the Zhytomyr region, Shums´kyi organized an anti-Hetmanate movement, and here the Borotbysts formed joint revolutionary committees with the Bolsheviks. At the time, Shums´kyi was hiding in his parents' house in the village of Turchynka. He was almost arrested, though he managed to escape. Fate saved him again from arrest and likely execution.

After the Fourth Congress of the UPSR, which gathered illegally in the suburbs of Kyiv on 13–16 May 1918, the party ceased to exist as a single organization. The leftist Socialist-Revolutionaries proposed a resolution that would become the first position document of the left wing (later the Borotbyst party), calling for the "steadfast ... consolidation of all revolutionary socialist forces in order to achieve the final victory of socialism through class struggle."[34] The leadership of the left wing of the party included Levko Kovaliv, Hnat Mykhailychenko, Oleksandr Shums´kyi, Vasyl´ Ellan-Blakytnyi, Anton Prykhod´ko, Andrii Zalyvchyi, and Panas Liubchenko, among others.[35] This leadership passed a resolution on 3 June 1918 to conduct illegal struggle against the Hetmanate. Shums´kyi would take more and more of an active part in this struggle. The left wing, now the Borotbyst party, had evolved ideologically toward communism and tactically toward the Bolsheviks. Another resolution of the Borotbysts' Central Committee, on 4 November 1918, spoke of the need for a "class-based armed uprising" against the Hetmanate, the transfer of power to the workers and the poorest peasants, "world revolution," the "dictatorship of the proletariat," and rapprochement with "revolutionary socialist parties"—including the Communist Party (of Bolsheviks) of Ukraine (CP[b]U), created under Lenin's control in Moscow in July 1918.[36] Several agreements between the Borotbysts and Bolsheviks were concluded during the uprising against the Germans and the regime of Pavlo Skoropads´kyi. Thus, Vasyl´ Ellan-Blakytnyi was included in the Bolsheviks' Poltava Military Revolutionary Committee, and Shums´kyi in the Kyiv Committee.

After the overthrow of Skoropads´kyi's regime, power shifted to the Directorate of the Ukrainian People's Republic (UPR), against which Shums´kyi also fought. He was in danger again. This was how he later recalled this period:

> After the fall of the hetman, the Directorate convened a congress of the Workers' Soviets [Councils] in Kyiv to gain political approval and support. ... [As I was] in an illegal situation, I went to this congress and got the floor under someone else's surname, and revealed who I was only at the podium, when it was impossible to deprive me of my word without a political scandal. However, I could not speak for a long time—I was pulled from the podium, beaten, and sentenced to death ... for exposing the policy of the Directorate. However, the goal was achieved—the congress was split and disrupted. And I survived by a happy coincidence.[37]

This "happy coincidence" was that, among the Cossack guards, Shums´kyi had an acquaintance who organized his escape in the melee that followed the agitation. The sequence of arrest, sentence, and escape would happen to Shums´kyi again soon after, in Nizhyn, his destination after leaving Kyiv.[38] We see the incredible temperament and talent that helped Shums´kyi survive time and again.

Upon his return to the Kyiv region, Shums´kyi worked with the Bolsheviks to establish the Kyiv Provincial Revolutionary Committee. In December 1918, he became chairman of the Bolshevik Revolutionary Committee, which organized an uprising against the Directorate in the area of Rzhyshchiv, proclaiming a (short-lived) socialist "Rzhyshchiv Republic." According to Shums´kyi's somewhat exaggerated claim, the Revolutionary Committee's forces scored decisive victories against the Directorate and Civil War enemies by striking "Petliura's army near Kyiv, during Antonov's attack, [which] defeated Petliura's main headquarters in Vasylkiv and caused his army to be dispersed."[39]

Shums´kyi's successful collaboration encouraged him to push for a formal unification between the Bolsheviks and the Borotbysts. At a meeting of the Kyiv faction of Borotbysts on

15 February 1919, he explained his rationale for unification, noting that, although the UPSR had twice organized successful uprisings in Ukraine, both had been short lived. The Directorate took advantage of the first uprising, and the Communists came to power the second time. To achieve longer-lasting success, the USPR needed to stop fighting against the Communists in the struggle for power over Ukraine. Indeed, Shums´kyi proposed that, to prevent a counterrevolution, "we needed the most sincere and decisive support of the Communists."[40] However, the leaders of the Borotbysts did not support Shums´kyi's proposal—they simply did not trust the Bolsheviks. And the leaders of the CP(b)U were likewise in no hurry to merge with the Borotbysts, as this could be seen as recognition of the legitimacy of the Borotbysts' ideology and policy.

Despite these concerns, there was political rapprochement. At the Third All-Ukrainian Congress of Soviets in March 1919, the All-Ukrainian Central Executive Committee was formed on a bipartisan basis, with ninety Communists and ten Borotbysts, including Shums´kyi.[41] Shums´kyi was also a member of the editorial board of the newspaper *Kommunist*, a body of the Central Committee of the CP(b)U.[42] At the beginning of April 1919, Mykhailo Poloz, a representative of the Borotbyst faction on the Central Executive Committee, joined its Presidium and the board of the newspaper *Visti VUTsVK*.[43] In an 8 April telegram, the Central Committee of the Russian Communist Party (of Bolsheviks; RCP[b]) insisted on the inclusion of Ukrainian Socialist-Revolutionaries in the government. By a resolution of the Politburo of 12 June, Shums´kyi was introduced into the Halychynan (Galician) bureau of the CP(b)U. From July through August, he headed the People's Commissariat for Education under Christian Rakovsky's government.

Shums´kyi's first experience working in the People's Commissariat for Education revealed the limits of Bolshevik generosity and should have served as a lesson for his future career. Shums´kyi introduced a draft project in August 1919 to promote the development of the culture of the Ukrainian people, subject to approval by the All-Ukrainian Central Executive Committee. The proposals contained in the project were limited to the introduction of teaching in the Ukrainian language in areas where the Ukrainian population predominated. Where representatives of other ethnicities predominated, the plan was to introduce school teaching in the language of the predominant ethnicity. The language of instruction was to be determined through the bodies of the People's Commissariat for Education. Particular attention was paid to the need to train appropriate staff capable of implementing these policies and to obtain appropriate literature and teaching aids. But the Collegium of the People's Commissariat for Education rejected the draft decree in a vote of five to three (Bolsheviks to Borotbysts).[44] The point is not that the Bolsheviks underestimated the national question. Rather, they immediately understood and rejected the assumption that underlay Shums′kyi's proposal: that the Bolsheviks could not and should not rule Ukraine without the involvement of the local, ethnic Ukrainian elite.

At the same time, in 1919 and the beginning of 1920, Shums′kyi and his associates made a decisive attempt to use their relationship with the Bolsheviks to realize their own state-building project in Ukraine. This was the period in which the Borotbysts most irritated the Bolsheviks. The Borotbysts were convinced that, without them, the Bolsheviks were doomed to failure, as they would be unable to rule Ukraine—especially its rural regions. Nevertheless, the Borotbysts' state-building attempts were thwarted by their inability to form their own power structures or create their own militias, which led to a growing crisis among Borotbyst leaders. Some—particularly Viacheslav Lashevych, Serhii Pylypenko, and Andrii Khvylia—and a number of ordinary party members were frustrated at these limitations and individually joined the CP(b)U.[45] Shums′kyi sought to stop this outflow. In the summer of 1919, he returned to his proposals for unification with the Bolsheviks, and insisted at the meetings of the Central Committee of the UPSR in June and July that they be adopted. On 6 August, the non-Borotbyst wing of the UPSR (communists) merged with the Ukrainian Social Democratic Workers Party (USDRP; leftist independents). The Borotbysts then changed the name of their party to the Ukrainian Communist Party of Borotbysts UCP(b). Shums′kyi was one of its founding leaders, along with Hnat Mykhailychenko, Levko Kovaliv, Mykhailo Poloz, Panas Liubchenko, Mykhailo Panchenko, and others.[46]

At this stage, Shums'kyi and other Borotbyst leaders realized that, although they needed formal unification with the Bolsheviks to achieve their own political ends in Ukraine, they also needed to be wary of becoming too dependent on them. This was the balance that Shums'kyi tried to strike when reporting on the unification of the parties at the meeting of the All-Ukrainian Central Executive Committee on 6 August 1919.[47] He first emphasized that the Borotbysts sought the concentration of communist forces in Ukraine, while the Bolsheviks professed a different line: they sought to drive other political forces into a political "corner." To retain some independence from the Bolsheviks, the Central Committee of the UCP(b), on 28 August, sent a request to the highest governing body of the Communist Party in the world, the Executive Committee of the Comintern, to include the Borotbyst party among all recognized international communist parties.

It was not difficult to predict how the Executive Committee of the Comintern, which was under the decisive influence of the Bolsheviks, would respond to this letter. It rejected the request and the fundamental notion behind it, that the Borotbysts would be equal to the Bolsheviks at the international level. Nevertheless, the Borotbysts and their national-communist ideology continued to grow as a serious force, claiming political hegemony in Ukraine and thus threatening their Bolshevik partners. In October 1919, the Bolshevik Andrei Bubnov prepared the pamphlet "On the Party of the Borotbysts," which was to be discussed at a meeting of the Central Committee of the CP(b)U. His pamphlet blamed the Borotbysts for "inconsistencies." First, in the author's opinion, these were manifested in the focus on "internal Ukrainian forces," which in fact meant "defending independence under the guise of verbal recognition of the federation."[48] Second, Bubnov stated that the Borotbysts were constantly opposed to the Bolsheviks' land and food policies—no doubt in reference to their failure to approve of the violence and requisitions that marked the policy of "war communism." Finally, Bubnov criticized the Borotbysts for their efforts to unite with other political forces and for "the desire of the newly formed so-called Ukrainian Communist Party to distance itself from the CPU [Communist Party of Ukraine], portraying it as a predominantly 'Muscovite' party, and presenting itself as the only representative of the Ukrainian proletariat of the 'village and city.'"[49]

Bubnov proposed to correct the mistakes of the Bolsheviks regarding the Borotbysts: "It was necessary not only to withdraw support for the organizationally independent existence of the Borotbysts, but also to strive by all means for the greatest possible organizational disappearance of this party as an independent whole."[50] According to Bubnov, this could be achieved by pushing the Borotbysts to unite with the CP(b)U. In the process, "those who hesitate" should be excluded from the communist ranks, and the "best, truly communist part" of the Borotbysts should join the CP(b)U.

In November 1919, the Borotbysts declared that there could remain "either a 'single indivisible Russia of workers and peasants, as the Red Army political committees shout at every crossroads ... or our production, a separate Ukrainian Socialist Soviet Republic subject to a common Federal Soviet center."[51] Not *one* republic that included others, but an association of *separate, independent* republics: this was the political ideal of the Borotbysts. This was the ideal of Oleksandr Shums′kyi.

Overtly, Lenin sought to reconcile opposing Bolshevik and Borotbyst voices, bringing the two groups to recognize the need for unification in order to ensure the survival of the revolution in Ukraine. However, as we will see, Lenin covertly shared Bubnov's position, and he pursued unification to eliminate the Borotbyst "threat." His masterful subterfuge was successful against the Borotbysts, including Shums′kyi. In November 1919, Lenin wrote a draft thesis of the Central Committee of the RCP(b) on politics in Ukraine, which remained unpublished until 1999. Its first point said: "Great care should be given to nationalist traditions, the strictest observance of the equality of the Ukrainian language and culture, the obligation to learn the Ukrainian language for all officials, and so on."[52] At the Eighth All-Russian Party Conference, held on 2–4 December 1919, Lenin addressed the question of the Borotbysts. This was not accidental, as the local Bolshevik leaders in Ukraine (Dmytro Manuïl′s′kyi, Stanisław Kosior, Volodymyr Zatons′kyi, Christian Rakovsky, and Andrei Bubnov) were against a political compromise with the Borotbysts.[53] Lenin argued that they needed a bloc with the peasantry of Ukraine, and that in order to obtain this bloc, it was necessary for the Bolsheviks to rethink their approach toward the Borotbysts, as their previous approach had not worked.[54]

Some Borotbysts suffered under the illusion that they had played an influential role in Lenin's position. The Borotbysts' press enthusiastically quoted his letter to the workers and peasants of Ukraine on the occasion of the victory over General Anton Denikin in the Civil War. It said that the Great Russian communists should be compliant in disagreements with the Ukrainian Bolshevik communists and Borotbysts if the disagreements concerned Ukrainian independence, its alliance with Russia, or the national question in general. Shums´kyi and his supporters among the Borotbysts even imagined that Moscow's leaders, though not all, sometimes looked somewhat "more liberal" and "more progressive" than the cadres they sent to Ukraine to conquer it. In January 1920, speaking at the Kyiv City Conference of Borotbysts, Shums´kyi dared to state that there were no objective grounds for the existence of the CP(b)U in Ukraine. He cited as a key reason a split in the ranks of this party: the lower classes demanded a separate centralized policy in Ukraine, and the upper classes relied solely on the Red Army.[55]

These illusions soon began to dissipate. In the early 1920s, the Borotbysts appealed to the Executive Committee of the Comintern for a second time, demanding that they be recognized as the main communist force in Ukraine. Again they were refused. On 6 February 1920, Lenin wrote a secret resolution on the need to exterminate them as a political force:

> The Borotbysts are hereby recognized as a party that violates the fundamental principles of communism with its [the Borotbyst party's] propaganda campaign aimed at dividing the military into separate forces and its support for banditry, which just comes in handy for the Whites and international imperialism.
>
> Their struggle against the call for a close—the closest possible—alliance with the RSFSR is also contrary to the interests of the proletariat.
>
> All policy must be conducted systematically and unswervingly toward the liquidation of the Borotbysts in the near future. To this end, not a single transgression of the Borotbysts is to go without

> immediate and severe punishment. In particular, evidence is to be collected on the nonproletarian and highly unreliable nature of the majority of their party members.
>
> The liquidation timeline is to be established within the near term. The time is to be set by the Politburo and communicated to the Ukrainian Revolutionary Committee.[56]

Lenin's resolution was immediately approved by the Central Committee of the RCP(b), and, on its basis, a directive was developed for all its party organizations and urgently conveyed from Moscow to Kharkiv. On 11 February 1920, the Central Committee of the CP(b)U approved the "Theses on Our Attitude to the Borotbysts," developed on the basis of Lenin's resolution and sent to all provincial committees of the CP(b)U. Among other things, the party organizations were instructed to "mount the most serious, attentive, and energetic campaign against the party of Borotbysts."[57] On 12 February, the Central Committee of the CP(b)U sent abstracts and a telegram to the provincial committees, demanding that the campaign against the Borotbysts be launched immediately. Finally, on 24 February, the Central Committee of the CP(b)U decided to publish the theses and end the bloc with the Borotbysts.[58]

Shums´kyi, like other representatives of the left of the Central Committee of the UCP(b), faced a dilemma: oppose the Bolsheviks or compromise with them—that is, in effect, bow to them. If the latter was chosen, the Borotbysts would instantly lose the status of a separate Ukrainian party and join the CP(b)U, the Ukrainian regional structure of the Russian Communist Party. According to Mykhailo Poloz, senior Borotbysts fell into two opposing camps on this question. The first, led by Poloz, "insisted that before joining [the CP(b)U], [they] should adopt a resolution that would reflect the Borotbyst positions on the national question and thus reveal our political face."[59] The second camp, led by Shums´kyi, argued that they should join the CP(b)U without any resolutions, so as to not complicate the issue or tie their hands for further political maneuvering. Poloz claimed that Shums´kyi "managed to carry out his line by some formal maneuver."[60]

Whatever the differences, there was a glimmer of hope that the Borotbysts could be kept alive as a political force. Mykhailo

Ialovyi later revealed that, by joining the CP(b)U, he and his fellow party members hoped that they could work "within the Bolshevik party to correct it, in particular, on the national question."[61] They would work for change within the system. This hope also proved to be illusory, as the Bolsheviks soon eliminated them as a separate party. Contemporary researchers explain the Borotbysts' miscalculation by pointing out that their leaders were mostly young people who lacked political experience. They were unable to effectively coordinate their political action to defend their demands for the establishment of Ukrainian military and economic centers of power independent of Russia.[62] Undoubtedly, the resolution of the Executive Committee of the Comintern had a negative effect on the strategic decisions of the Borotbysts. It deprived them of the prospect of becoming an independent political force among the communist structures of the world. In addition, we must remember that fundamental decisions—such as Lenin's 6 February 1920 resolution to eliminate the Borotbysts—remained unknown to Shums´kyi and his colleagues.

In any case, at the end of February 1920, negotiations began on the "self-liquidation" of the Borotbysts. Without unnecessary euphemisms, some claimed that the Bolshevik leaders, including Vladimir Lenin, Leon Trotsky, and Joseph Stalin, guaranteed the Borotbyst leaders high party and state positions, the possibility of implementing the policy of Ukrainization, and the privileges of membership in the CP(b)U in exchange for supporting the self-liquidation of the party. The Borotbysts probably had their own personal reasons in mind—an unwillingness to lose their acquired status and influence—for which they paid by repeatedly putting their lives at risk.

On 14 March 1920, the All-Ukrainian Conference of the UCP(b) began its work. At this conference, attendees expressed varying opinions about joining the CP(b)U. This was the point at which Shums´kyi and his associates channeled Ialovyi's thinking to invent a new strategy: "We will merge, disperse, and flood the Bolsheviks!" That is, key Borotbysts would take up major positions in the Ukrainian Bolshevik government and from there work to achieve Borotbyst aims. This note, written in Russian by Vasyl´ Ellan-Blakytnyi, was circulated among the delegates of the

Borotbysts' last forum. On 25 March 1920, at the personal insistence of Vladimir Lenin, Shums´kyi was included in the "temporary bureau" of the Central Committee of the CP(b)U, which had been established "to direct party work."[63] This bureau was headed by Stanisław Kosior and included, in addition to Shums´kyi, Christian Rakovsky and two other Bolshevik figures. At the meeting, Shums´kyi reported on the second item on the agenda, "Liquidation of the Party of Borotbysts."

Contemporary researchers rightly point out that, at the time of their self-liquidation, the Borotbysts were more numerous than the Bolsheviks. The UCP(b) had roughly fifteen thousand members, while the CP(b)U had 11,087 members and 2,439 candidates for party membership.[64] From 1918 through 1920, the Borotbysts had strong support in the central and western provinces of Ukraine, while the CP(b)U was supported mainly by residents of large cities in eastern and southern Ukraine. This urban support was a significant advantage in party politics in the early 1920s, although, as Stanislav Kul´chyts´kyi rightly notes, it is important to remember that the general influence of the representatives of both parties on the population of Ukraine was relatively small.[65]

The Bolsheviks gained a more substantial political advantage in Ukraine in the spring of 1920, not due to the growing influence of the CP(b)U over the population, but due to the Red Army's military offensive from Russia and the influx of RCP(b) cadres into the Ukrainian provinces. That is why the "self-liquidation" of the Borotbysts, which in truth was simply their liquidation, was a true victory for Vladimir Lenin and his protégé in Ukraine, the Trotskyite Christian Rakovsky. Lenin boasted of his successful political maneuver against the Borotbysts at the Ninth Congress of the RCP(b):

> We reregistered this party and, instead of the uprising of the Borotbysts, which was inevitable, thanks to the correct line of the Central Committee and the perfect execution by Comrade Rakovsky, we had all the best that were among the Borotbysts join our party under our control, with our recognition, and the rest disappeared from the political scene. This victory is worth several good battles.[66]

What was really behind Lenin's words that "all the best that were among the Borotbysts join[ed] our party"? First, these figures would play a significant role in the party-Soviet leadership of the UkrSSR before the purges of 1933. Among them were Oleksandr Shums´kyi, Hryhorii Hryn´ko, Vasyl´ Ellan-Blakytnyi, Panas Liubchenko, Andrii Khvylia, Iurii Ozers´kyi, Petro Solodub, Todos Taran, and Iurii Voitsekhivs´kyi.[67] Mykola Doroshko has rightly pointed out that involving people from other parties in the party-state apparatus, the Politburo, and the Organizing Bureau of the Central Committee of the CP(b)U enabled the Bolsheviks to increase their representation in the All-Ukrainian Central Executive Committee, the People's Commissariat of the UkrSSR, and other institutions of authority. The Bolsheviks now exerted greater control over the publication of newspapers and the direction and amount of monetary subsidies to different bodies.[68] Having skillfully consolidated their power at the expense of the Borotbysts, the Bolsheviks soon began to undermine them. Of the fifteen thousand Borotbysts, more than four thousand joined the Communist Party. At that point, people from other political parties accounted for at least 30 percent of the total number of party members in the CP(b)U.[69] By the fall of 1920, during the re-registration of the CP(b)U, almost all of the Borotbysts had been expelled from its ranks, and, after the party purge in August 1921, only 118 of them remained. Mykola Skrypnyk first mentioned this figure in his speech at the Twelfth Congress of the RCP(b). He stated that "some of them moved to Russia, some of them left, and most of them were expelled from the party on the grounds that they had preserved the remnants of nationalist sentiments."[70]

Obviously, the Borotbysts did not "flood" anyone. And the situation got worse. At the end of 1922, only forty-five former members of the UPSR (Borotbysts) and thirty-four former members of the UCP(b) remained in the CP(b)U. After that, former Borotbysts were admitted into the party with caution. Sixteen former Borotbysts were admitted in 1921–23, thirty-three in 1924–27, forty-seven in 1928–30, and six in 1931–32. At the end of 1936, only 180 former Borotbysts and UCP(b) members remained throughout the ACP(b).[71] Thus, soon after 1920, the leaders of the Borotbysts remained in the CP(b)U without the support of the majority of their fellow party members, whom they had so consistently led to the Bolsheviks to build communism with a Ukrainian face. In fact, Shums′kyi and his closest associates had sacrificed their party. They personally took on the entire burden of realizing the ideals nurtured by the Borotbysts. They now had to answer for their intentions, their political position, and their past actions and words in an increasingly hostile party without their base of support.

Shums′kyi's relationship with Lenin and key Bolshevik figures, however, enabled him to rise in the party. On 1 April 1920, he was confirmed as the head of the Department of Rural Work by the Central Committee of the CP(b)U. During the Civil War, Shums′kyi served as a member of the Revolutionary Military Council of the Twelfth Army and headed the Kyiv Provincial Revolutionary Committee.[72] Shums′kyi's primary job was to mobilize human and economic resources for Red Army forces traveling across the Poltava and Odesa regions. The ongoing social and economic upheavals and military confrontation continued into 1920. Amid these tragic events, Oleksandr Shums′kyi had remarried, taking Ievdokiia Oleksiïvna Honcharenko as his wife. We have no more information on his first wife and children. Honcharenko was born in the city of Myropole in the former Kursk province. Until 1917, she studied at a gymnasium (secondary school) in Kharkiv, where she became involved in revolutionary activities. From 1918 to 1920, she was a member of the Borotbysts and was the secretary of the organizational-foreign department of the Central Committee, as well as an underground organizer of party logistics, mainly safe houses. At the time of their meeting, Honcharenko was twenty-two years old, and Shums′kyi was thirty. In 1921, their son, Iaroslav, was born.

Shums′kyi took up diplomatic work in the aftermath of the Civil War, first as a member of the Soviet delegation to the negotiations relulting in the Treaty of Riga with Poland in October 1920, and then, from April 1921, as the head of the Plenipotentiary Representation (Embassy) of the UkrSSR in Poland. Another notable Borotbyst worked in the Warsaw mission of the UkrSSR: Shums′kyi's personal secretary and close friend Karl Maksymovych (real name Savrych).[73] As we will see, he would later play an important role in the fate of his former boss and friend. The trade mission of the UkrSSR was headed by Isai Khurhin, who had been active in and sympathetic to the Borotbysts since the days of the Ukrainian Central Rada.[74] Shums´kyi's colleague in the UPSR Ievhen Filipovych also worked with him on this mission.

Shums´kyi was not impressed by Bolshevik diplomacy, as all decisions were made in Moscow. He applied to be recalled from Warsaw, hoping to return to Ukraine. On 29 July 1922, the CP(b)U Politburo discussed the question of the Warsaw mission and decided that "Comrade Shums´kyi's request to be recalled from the Warsaw mission should be granted in principle, leaving him temporarily in the line of duty."[75] In autumn of that year, Shums´kyi was recalled to Kharkiv. Although he was officially recalled, he could not leave Warsaw immediately and remained in diplomatic service for some time as acting head of the UkrSSR Representation. Finally, Shums´kyi was replaced by the Russian diplomat Grigorii Besedovskii, who would become a nonreturnee, seeking political asylum in France in 1929.[76]

After the proclamation of the founding of the USSR in December 1922, the collapse of the "independent" foreign policy structures of the UkrSSR began. The People's Commissariat for Foreign Affairs was closed, with the formal consent of Kharkiv. An authorized representative of the secret police in Ukraine was appointed in its place. At its meeting on 6 February 1923, the Politburo of the Central Committee ACP(b) specifically considered the liquidation of the UkrSSR Representation in Warsaw. Shums´kyi was invited to this meeting and was instructed to take part in the closure of the mission's activities for one month.

The question was, what would happen to Shums´kyi? He seems to have had some suggestions, but they were not recorded, as a transcript of the Politburo meeting was not made. However, the meeting resolved to "stay with the previous decision to send Comrade Shums´kyi to work in Vserobitzemlis as an authorized representative of the Central Committee of Vserobitzemlis."[77] Vserobitzemlis (Vserabotzemles) was the All-Union Trade Union of Land and Forestry Workers, which had branches in Ukraine. Undoubtedly, Shums´kyi's appointment to the post of Ukraine's commissioner of this secondary structure was a demotion, though only a temporary one before his rapid rise in the party. The Seventh

All-Ukrainian Conference of the CP(b)U, held in April 1923, elected Shums′kyi as a candidate for membership in the Central Committee. The June plenum of the Central Committee admitted him to the Organizing Bureau, where he remained until February 1927. The Eighth Conference, in May 1924, admitted him to the Central Committee and its Secretariat.[78] At that time, Shums′kyi was working as the head of the Propaganda Department of the Central Committee of the CP(b)U. In 1923, he became the editor in chief of the monthly magazine *Chervonyi shliakh*. Serhii Pylypenko, Pavlo Tychyna, Mykola Khvyl′ovyi, and Mykhailo Ialovyi served with Shums′kyi on the editorial board.[79]

On 29 September 1924, the Politburo made the decision "to nominate Comrade Shums′kyi as a people's commissar [for education], leaving him a member of the Organizing Bureau."[80] The former Socialist-Revolutionary and Borotbyst became the leader of a powerful communist structure. It is clear Shums′kyi wanted this position as a means to legally contribute to what the Borotbysts had aspired to and fought for—the development of the UkrSSR with a distinct Ukrainian cultural and political face. The pressing question is why the Bolsheviks appointed a former Borotbyst to such a prominent position in the nomenklatura when there were "safer" Bolshevik options. We have no way to confirm whether the Bolsheviks offered Shums′kyi this position in return for his support for the unification and then sacrifice of the Borotbyst party. What we can confirm is that at the time, Shums′kyi was an attractive candidate for this position for numerous reasons.

First, the Twelfth Congress of the RCP(b) announced that the pace of Ukrainization was disappointing in the second half of 1924, reflecting the view expressed by many Ukrainian leaders in party conferences and plenums of the Central Committee of the CP(b)U. The pace needed to be quickened, mainly because the policy enabled the Bolsheviks to infuse themselves into the Ukrainian political and cultural context more rapidly. This was a matter of their survival in Ukraine. In this situation, Shums′kyi, an unfailing supporter of rapid Ukrainization and someone who had demonstrated loyalty to the Bolsheviks, clearly showed great promise to accelerate the policy within Bolshevik limits.

Second, at least in 1924, the Bolshevik leadership was confident that Shums´kyi would rely on the procommunist intelligentsia (rather than, for example, the prosocialist part) to carry out Ukrainization. The leadership knew of his negative attitude toward the leaders of the Central Rada and the UPR, including especially Mykhailo Hrushevs´kyi, Volodymyr Vynnychenko, Serhii Iefremov, and Symon Petliura. They also knew about his critical attitude toward members of the Ukrainian intelligentsia who remained in Ukraine and used Ukrainization as a vehicle to achieve their own anti-Soviet ends—especially those who fought for the revival of the UPR.

Third, Shums´kyi's appointment was clearly a Bolshevik concession to the Ukrainian segment of the CP(b)U and Ukrainians in general. These concessions were common practice at the time as a way for the Bolsheviks to buttress loyalty and manage instability on the outskirts of the newly created Soviet Union and above all in Ukraine. Stalin was pressed to make concessions on the national question in exchange for support from the republic's party organizations.

Even before 1927, however, Stalin figured that he and the Bolshevik leadership had miscalculated in appointing Shums´kyi, who turned out to be far too friendly with anti-Soviet intellectuals and who went beyond the "limits" in implementing Ukrainization. It mattered little to Stalin that it was not Shums´kyi but instead the limits that had changed, as did Bolshevik definitions of anticommunist intellectuals. In any case, as he strengthened his personal dictatorship, Stalin became less interested in making concessions to the peripheries or, indeed, to anyone. Shums´kyi was no longer useful by this time; he was now dangerous. His removal, as the first step in the destruction of his career and life, is the subject of the following chapter.

Chapter Three

SHUMS´KYI'S FALL AS PEOPLE'S COMMISSAR AND SHUMS´KYISM

In 1924, Shums´kyi took up the role of people's commissar of education, replacing Volodymyr Zatons´kyi, who had taken over this position from Hryhorii Hryn´ko. Hryn´ko had been in the role only from 1920 to 1922, before he was removed on the grounds of "excessive" Ukrainization. In July 1920, even his subordinates, members of the communist faction of the Collegium of the People's Commissariat, complained:

> The essence of our differences was that the Borotbysts wanted to justify the forcible Ukrainization of schools, promote Ukrainian national culture above all, and bring to the fore not class but the national content of education. The logical conclusion was that the system of education was naturally to be transferred to the national intelligentsia, not the proletariat.[1]

Undoubtedly, this should have been a warning for Shums´kyi, who might have learned from the experience of his fellow Borotbyst. However, upon assuming the post of people's commissar, Shums´kyi did not alter the priorities of Ukrainization in deference to its detractors. His commitment to these priorities when the party departed from them, or at least dropped the pretense of pursuing them, would be his undoing. This chapter traces Shums´kyi's fall and the fate of Ukrainization in this period.

In his new position as people's commissar, Shums´kyi enjoyed the support of Hryhorii Hryn´ko, Vasyl´ Ellan-Blakytnyi, and

Mykhailo Ialovyi—or the former "nationals" (*natsionaly*), as the Bolsheviks called the Borotbysts—as well as, behind the scenes, people from other political parties. In return, Shums′kyi would later call the Bolsheviks "the leading Russian minority." His deputies were Petro Solodub, Ian Riappo, and former Borotbyst Anton Prykhod′ko.[2] The economist Mykhailo Volobuiev also worked with him and, like Shums′kyi, would later have his name attached to a "dangerous" political movement created by the Bolsheviks, the "Volobuievshchyna."[3]

These former Borotbysts and activists in the People's Commissariat were alarmed by the appointment of Lazar Kaganovich to the post of the head of the CP(b)U in Kharkiv in 1926. Shums′kyi seemed to sense that this figure would soon play a fatal role in his destiny. As Shums′kyi's former colleague Iurii Voitsekhivs′kyi later testified under interrogation in 1933, Shums′kyi gathered his colleagues Ellan-Blakytnyi, Ialovyi, Hryn′ko, Khvyl′ovyi, and Arkadii Liubchenko at his apartment for numerous meetings to discuss this appointment.[4] At these closed meetings, the former Borotbysts freely expressed their dissatisfaction that Stalin's protégé had been sent to Ukraine from Moscow, and that the role of CP(b)U head had not been given to a leader who knew the local conditions—that is, a Ukrainian.

It was probably then that these former Borotbysts developed their hypothetical plans to position Ukrainians as heads of the Central Committee of the CP(b)U and the Council of People's Commissars of the UkrSSR. According to Voitsekhivs′kyi, Vlas Chubar was offered for the former, and Shums′kyi for the latter post. Not all Borotbysts were on the same page, however. Andrii Khvylia, deputy head of the Agitation and Propaganda Department of the CP(b)U Central Committee, and Panas Liubchenko, secretary of the Kyiv Provincial Committee of the CP(b)U, refused to take part in creating a "counterweight" to Kaganovich and ultimately sided with the Bolsheviks.[5] Later, Khvylia and Liubchenko would be among the most active opponents of Shums′kyism, though this would not save either of them from being labeled Borotbysts or from being executed in the 1930s. (Liubchenko shot himself before he could be arrested.)

These cracks in the CP(b)U in 1925 widened with the scandal surrounding Mykola Khvyl′ovyi, one of Shums′kyi's closest allies. By 1928, when the scandal was over, Khvyl′ovyism would form the third element of the Bolshevik's trifecta of national bias in Ukraine, along with Shums′kyism and Volobuievshchyna. As noted in chapter 1, Khvyl′ovyi's publications decried the corrosive influence of Russian culture on Ukraine's national development, which sparked a much broader political crisis in which Shums′kyi and his commissariat were immediately embroiled. This was the crisis that provided the pretext for his removal as people's commissar in 1927.[6]

In the spring of 1926, Khvyl′ovyi published the pamphlet that sealed Shums′kyi's fate, a pamphlet with the scandalous title "Moscow Slums":

> The Ukrainian economy is not the Russian economy, and cannot be it, because Ukrainian culture, growing out of its economy, affects the economy, insofar as our economy takes on specific forms and character. In short, the Union will remain a Union, and Ukraine is an independent unit. ... Little Russia has already acquired the "tradition." ... Is Russia an independent state? It is independent! Well, we are "independent," too.... We will go to Europe to study, but with the hidden thought that in a few years we will shine with extraordinary light. Do you hear, Moscophiles from the Moscow slums, what we want?[7]

Shums′kyi grossly miscalculated how this pamphlet would be received in Moscow. Moscow leaders—like those in Kyiv, including Kaganovich—considered it a betrayal by Ukrainization and not, as Shums′kyi saw it, an indication that Ukrainization was overcoming the "secondary" and provincial nature of Ukrainians, which should have been a great benefit to Moscow and a decisive influence on the further formation of the Ukrainian nation. Shums′kyi offered this argument to his enraged party colleagues in justifying his defense of Khvyl′ovyi, and he continued his moral and financial support for Khvyl′ovyi's VAPLITE, which Khvyl′ovyi's detractors would call the hotbed of national bias in Ukraine.

Shums′kyi's disagreements with Kaganovich started innocuously enough, before this row, over funding, but quickly developed into a personal feud. Shums′kyi, for instance, constantly monitored levels of government support for cultural development in Russia compared to those in Ukraine. On 15 June 1925, at a meeting of the Politburo of the Central Committee of the CP(b)U, during a discussion of the Ukrainian budget, Shums′kyi reported that expenditures on cultural needs in the UkrSSR were declining, while in the RSFSR they were increasing. Mykola Skrypnyk supported Shums′kyi, although later he would ruthlessly criticize him. Kaganovich agreed that funding for the People's Commissariat for Education should be increased, but rejected Shums′kyi's claim that Russia's cultural development was better funded.[8]

Lazar Kaganovich's stubborn refusal to acknowledge facts, his dismissive attitude toward the opinions of others, and his boundless servility toward Stalin irritated Shums′kyi immensely. Shums′kyi began to speak openly about Kaganovich's poor behavior and statements, which enraged Kaganovich and exacerbated their emerging personal feud. A clear clash occurred when Shums′kyi insisted on the appointment of former Borotbyst F. Samutin to a position in the Vinnytsia district committee, a demand that was opposed by some members of the Central Committee of the CP(b)U, as well as by Kaganovich.[9] For Shums′kyi, this was a typical example of the attitude toward the "former," that is, people from other political parties who were now in the ranks of the Bolshevik party.

In the summer of 1925, Kaganovich informed Stalin that he had some disagreements with Shums′kyi. The continued sabotage of the implementation of Ukrainization by Kaganovich and the nomenklatura in general prompted the emotional Shums′kyi to cross the Rubicon.[10] On 12 October 1925, during a visit to Moscow for the Second Congress of the CPWU, Shums′kyi addressed Stalin on the problems in Ukraine. The two had been well acquainted since the Civil War, and Stalin usually responded to Shums′kyi's telephone calls.[11] Mykhailo Tesliuk, a former member of the Central Committee of the CPWU, was present at the meeting.[12] Decades later, on 5 March 1965, during an interrogation in the Committee for State Security (KGB) Department at the Council of Ministers of the Ukrainian SSR in the Lviv region, Tesliuk recalled the strategy Shums′kyi chose in his talk with Stalin. Shums′kyi began by saying that many notables of science and culture who had previously cooperated with the Ukrainian Central Rada or the Directorate had returned to Ukraine. Due to their authority, these individuals influenced the cultural processes in Ukraine and "used them for the nationalist purposes."[13]

However, he went on, it was not these individuals but the Central Committee of the CP(b)U that had to control and direct processes in the national and cultural life in Ukraine. Here Shums´kyi moved to the main problem. He said that Moscow was interfering because it was sending to Ukraine "officials who did not understand Ukrainian national issues." Tesliuk thought that "probably, Shums´kyi meant L. M. Kaganovich, who was then the first secretary of the Central Committee of the CP(b)U." Shums´kyi then stated that the "Ukrainian communists had already matured and could elect the leaders of the party and the government by themselves."[14] After hearing all this, Stalin replied to Shums´kyi that he was right but that it was too early to let them do so.

On 4 December 1925, Vasyl´ Ellan-Blakytnyi died. Shums´kyi lost his closest friend and adviser, one who would likely have encouraged Shums´kyi to take a strategic course of action against Kaganovich. Despite his controversial statements in Moscow, Shums´kyi attended the Presidium of the Ninth Congress of the CP(b)U in December 1925, and, at the end of the congress, was elected to the Central Committee. In his speech at that congress, Kaganovich spoke a great deal about Ukrainization, but this time it was not Shums´kyi but other delegates who began to criticize Kaganovich's leadership methods. For example, the rector of the Artem Communist University, Isaak Dashkovs´kyi, said that a special environment had been created in the party in which everyone who disagreed with Kaganovich and Stalin "were not Leninists, they were deviators."[15] Emboldened by this criticism of Kaganovich, Shums´kyi decided to continue his battle against him. On 20 April 1926, Shums´kyi was once again admitted to Stalin's office, and once again he reminded Stalin of his vision for Ukraine and insisted on personnel changes.[16] That conversation was not officially recorded; however, it later emerged that this meeting was secretly recorded using a phonograph. The record of this meeting would eventually be used against Shums´kyi. Evidence of this can be found in the weekly report of the Secret Department of the GPU of the UkrSSR for 23–29 January 1927. From this source, we also learn that Hryhorii Petrovs´kyi read this conversation at a party conference—probably the First All-Ukrainian Conference of the CP(b)U, on 17–21 October 1926 in Kharkiv—to "expose" Oleksandr Shums´kyi.[17]

The result of this second conversation (not the first one, as researchers previously believed) was Stalin's letter of 26 April 1926, addressed to members of the Politburo of the Central Committee of the CP(b)U, headed by Kaganovich. Kaganovich had previously provided Stalin with typewritten copies of excerpts from the works of Ukrainian writers translated into Russian. Stalin carefully read what Mykola Khvyl´ovyi wrote in the pamphlet "Apologists of Writing" and made numerous annotations with a red pencil.[18] Stalin's letter of 26 April was thus a reaction to both the meeting with Shums´kyi and Khvyl´ovyi's works. Although Stalin agreed with some of Shums´kyi's views on the need to control Ukrainization and even guardedly criticized Kaganovich for over-administration, Stalin unequivocally stated that the movement for Ukrainian culture and society was turning into an anti-Russian undertaking and declared that "this danger was becoming more serious in Ukraine."[19]

To support this view, Stalin gave an example of Khvyl´ovyi's demand for "immediate de-Russification of the proletariat" in Ukraine and his call for "Ukrainian poetry [to] flee from Russian literature and its style as soon as possible." In these and other opinions, Stalin saw the manifestation of the struggle "against the Russians in general, [and] against Russian culture and its highest achievement—Leninism." In the letter, Stalin criticized Shums´kyi, as the people's commissar for education, for insufficient opposition to these tendencies. Resorting to his inherent demagoguery, Stalin rejected Shums´kyi's proposed personnel changes—in particular, to nominate Hryhorii Hryn´ko as head of the Council of People's Commissars and to replace Kaganovich with Vlas Chubar:

> How would the party in general and party cadres in particular view this case? Would they not understand it as that we were pursuing a course to reduce the share of the Council of People's Commissars? Because it was impossible to hide from the party that Hryn´ko's party and revolutionary experience was far less than Chubar's party and revolutionary experience... Wouldn't it be better, both in the

> interests of the cause and in Hryn´ko's interests, to abandon these plans for the time being? I am in favor of strengthening the composition of the Secretariat and the Politburo of the Central Committee of the CP(b)U, as well as the Soviet leadership, with Ukrainian elements.[20]

This letter contained an afterword that was not published in Stalin's collected works, but in which he wrote that former Borotbysts should not be harassed for their past but should be involved in party work, and that "Shums´kyi should be participating in the leading party work."[21]

Though Stalin directed these instructions to the leadership of the CP(b)U, in practice his letter gave the mortally offended Lazar Kaganovich carte blanche to expose what would later be called Shums´kyism and Khvyl´ovyism. Kaganovich launched a powerful and public campaign against Shums´kyi, accusing him of establishing a national bias. The outcome of the Shums´kyi-Kaganovich confrontation depended largely on the Politburo of the Central Committee of the CP(b)U. Even before Stalin's letter was received, Shums´kyi could no longer maintain his composure. At a meeting of the Politburo of the Central Committee of the CP(b)U on 19 March 1926, he heard Kaganovich say that no one planned to Ukrainize Russian workers in Ukraine. Shums´kyi understood this inadvertently categorical statement to be a Freudian slip and proof that Kaganovich was not going to carry out Ukrainization. He protested. Kaganovich maneuvered; because his speech was not transcribed, he found a way out in one word. On 2 April, the Politburo of the Central Committee of the CP(b)U specifically discussed this issue and adopted the following resolution: "Comrade Kaganovich, during a discussion of the issue of Ukrainization at the Politburo on 19 March 1926, stated in his speech: We should not FORCIBLY Ukrainize Russian workers. The Politburo was in full solidarity with this statement (adopted unanimously)."[22]

Thus, it turned out that Lazar Kaganovich meant forcible Ukrainization. Witnessing the Politburo's complicity in Kaganovich's sleazy play on words, Shums´kyi exploded. Not for the first time, he threatened the Central Committee with his resignation. He accused the Politburo of adopting the wrong national policy and stated that Kaganovich was not the leader that Ukraine needed. A few days later, the CP(b)U Central Committee sent a letter to Stalin from Kaganovich and Chubar accusing Shums′kyi of careerism and of aiming to seize leadership positions in the party.[23] Kaganovich, the consummate apparatchik and a master of behind-the-scenes intrigues, did not stop there. He conspired to convene a new meeting to further attack Shums′kyi.

On 12 May 1926, at this meeting of the Politburo of the Central Committee of the CP(b)U, Volodymyr Zatons′kyi presented a report titled "Preliminary results of Ukrainization." The second issue at the meeting was the "exchange of views" in connection with Shums′kyi's statement. Zatons′kyi cited statistics on Ukrainization and switched the conversation to "how much we had mastered Ukrainian language outside the party and outside industry." He noted a certain positive change in the mood of the noncommunist intelligentsia in connection with the deployment of Ukrainization, but warned that these representatives were keen to take part in Ukrainization only to "snatch the initiative from the Communist Party and seize it."[24] Aggravating the conversation, Zatons′kyi pointed to Mykola Khvyl′ovyi as one example of individual party members who had begun to reflect bourgeois ideology in their works. He said that Khvyl′ovyi urged them to focus first on European values and culture, rather than on Russian literature and culture, and to seek their own path and not confuse a political alliance with Russia with literature. "We will have to deal with Khvyl′ovyi's ideology," Zatons′kyi concluded. He did not mention Shums′kyi at all and insisted at the end of the report that "in the current situation, when the majority in our party still did not speak Ukrainian fluently and undertook Ukrainization with little desire ... the Central Committee of the CP(b)U had done if not everything, then enough to be worthy of its role in advancing [Ukrainization]."[25]

Kaganovich spoke after Zatons′kyi. In his opinion, three tasks were the most urgent: strengthening Ukrainian statehood as an integral part of the USSR, furthering cultural development, and maintaining the party's leading role in Ukrainization. Kaganovich cited figures designed to confirm that, despite all the difficulties, his leadership did not harm Ukrainization. He continued Zatons′kyi's theme of dangers to Ukrainization from the influence of hostile ideology.[26] As an example, he, too, cited Khvyl´ovyi. Kaganovich raised the issue of the pace of Ukrainization and reiterated that no one would forcibly Ukrainize the Russian workers: "It was clear that the people who were oppressed for hundreds of years, the people whose language was banned by the tsar, now they had a very big impulse. However, as a political party, we could not act on the basis of feelings, impulses, and good intentions—we had to take the possibilities into account." In his first speech, Kaganovich avoided mentioning Shums´kyi and, at the end, called for a struggle against "the ideological distortion of opposing Ukrainian culture to Russian culture, opposing Ukraine to Moscow" and against "manifestations of any tendencies toward chauvinism within the party."[27]

What Kaganovich did not say, his subordinates did. Almost all representatives of the party's top leadership blamed Shums´kyi for his indulgence of Khvyl´ovyi. Mykola Demchenko stated:

> Literary discussion was also a political act because participants in politics such as Comrade Shums´kyi shared the views that were discussed. I spoke to him repeatedly on this topic and did not hear from him that he dissociated himself from Khvyl´ovyi. ... No one dared speak out against Khvyl´ovyi, not one of the people who were credited with being so-called Ukrainian civil society, neither Shums´kyi nor Hryn´ko. They considered Khvyl´ovyi to be an official from the Central Committee apparatus.[28]

Mykola Skrypnyk said that he would be glad if Shums´kyi voiced his refusal to show solidarity with Khvyl´ovyi. Vlas Chubar mentioned Shums´kyi's name only once and resolutely rejected Shums´kyi's proposal to appoint him head of the CP(b)U, as Stalin had advised in his letter of 26 April 1926.[29] Fedir Korniushyn claimed that "Shums´kyi was trying to create a crisis within the Ukrainian [communist] organization."[30] This selection of statements is enough to convey the purpose of the meeting.

In response, Shums´kyi stressed that many of the speeches indicated that "gossips were sufficiently involved in the issue discussed here. I wanted to say from the very beginning that I did not argue with or answer to those here who operated on marketplace rumors."[31] In his speech, he drew a detailed picture of his differences with the leadership of the CP(b)U and analyzed his position and the arguments of his critics. He made clear that he was not against criticism of Mykola Khvyl′ovyi, but cautioned against invoking only fragments of his works. It was at this meeting that Shums′kyi uttered the words that would in some ways lead to his assassination in 1946. The leaders who heard him would recall these words for the rest of Shums′kyi's life and even after his death:

> The party is dominated by a Russian communist who treats the Ukrainian communist with suspicion and hostility, if not worse. He reigns based on the pathetic selfish type of a Little Russian [*maloross*], who, in all historical epochs, has been equally unprincipled, hypocritical, slavishly insincere, and treacherously flattering. Now he calls himself a communist and shouts a lot about "internationalism," boasts of his indifference to everything Ukrainian, and is always ready to spit on it (sometimes in Ukrainian) if it gives him the opportunity to serve and get a warm place. That's the thing. The fact is, our party must become Ukrainian in language and culture.[32]

At the end of his speech, Shums′kyi explained his conversation with Stalin:

> Finally, about Comrade Kaganovich, as general secretary, and about the statement I made to Comrade Stalin. I asked Comrade Stalin to transfer me from Ukraine in connection with the current situation. I explained to him the state of national affairs and said that, in my opinion, Comrade Kaganovich, as general secretary, was not the political leader of our organization that we needed and that Comrade Chubar would be better suited to this role. I was asked who the head of the Council of People's Commissars could be. I said that we have a lot of people who could be appointed to this post and named three people: Comrades Skrypnyk, Hryn′ko, and Zatons′kyi. I repeated that I was guided in this by the interests of the party and our development as I understood them—that is, above all by motives of a political nature—and I would always protest the introduction of elements of squabbling here. Comrade Stalin rejected my proposal to leave Ukraine and said that he would speak to the Central Committee of the CP(b)U about the issues I had raised, which he did after that. I replied that I would stay to work in Ukraine with Comrade Kaganovich, although I doubted that anything good would come of it because the situation for work was difficult.[33]

Criticism of Shums´kyi among the meeting participants crescendoed as they discussed his statement. Vlas Chubar (whom Shums´kyi had suggested as a replacement for Kaganovich as leader of the CP[b]U), proposed writing a letter to Stalin to assure him that the Politburo had confidence in the current leadership. Chubar and Zatons´kyi were instructed to write the letter, and Shums´kyi abstained from voting.[34] All members of the Politburo of the Central Committee of the CP(b)U except Shums´kyi eventually participated in writing the proposed letter, with Kaganovich personally making many changes.[35]

At the plenum of the Central Committee of the CP(b)U on 2–6 June 1926, a new round of brutal criticism of Shums´kyi began. Defying popular sentiment in the party leadership, Shums´kyi again defended Khvyl´ovyi. The June plenum would be the last battlefield in the conflict between Lazar Kaganovich and the former Borotbysts. But the story was to continue for Shums´kyi. Before the closing session of the plenum on 6 June, in Kaganovich's office, members of the Politburo spent seven hours trying to convince Shums´kyi to issue a public statement, a letter, admitting his errors in defending Khvyl´ovyi. It was a difficult situation and an extraordinary test of Shums´kyi's nerves. Shums´kyi hesitated but did not write the letter, as Chubar announced to the plenum at the beginning of the closing session.[36] At the meeting, Shums´kyi categorically denied the accusations of "malicious distortion" of the situation, hinting that Stalin had distorted something in his letter when he retold the content of their conversation. Shums´kyi said, "I would not put my signature under a series of questions formulated by Stalin and presented as my statements." He insisted that he could not stay in Ukraine and announced that in the coming days he would apply to the Central Committee of the ACP(b) in Moscow with a request to be transferred.[37]

However, at the end of the meeting, after a heated discussion, he changed his position and declared that he recognized his proposal to remove Kaganovich as erroneous. Hryhorii Hryn´ko also "repented." The plenum approved the work of the Politburo and recorded Shums´kyi and Hryn´ko's retraction of their proposal to nominate above all local staff. Kaganovich's authority was confirmed, and neither Shums´kyi, nor Hryn´ko, nor anyone else could encroach on it.[38]

In July 1926, Kaganovich became a candidate member of the Politburo of the Central Committee of the ACP(b), and supported Stalin even more rigorously in his struggle against Leon Trotsky, Grigorii Zinov´ev, and Lev Kamenev. Kaganovich's rise was useful to Stalin, partly because he could draw on Kaganovich's support in the event that Shums´kyists attempted to form an alliance with the anti-Stalinist opposition. Kaganovich worked immediately to stop this (hypothetical) threat from emerging. He began with Hryhorii Hryn´ko, whom he had transferred to the post of deputy chairman of the USSR State Planning Committee in November 1926. On 16 November, Kaganovich received a report from the secretary of the party committee of the People's Commissariat for Education of the UkrSSR, O. Kyrychenko. It said that Shums´kyi was not attending the People's Commissariat for Education board meetings and was not paying party dues. On 20 November, the Politburo of the central Committee of the CP(b)U dismissed Mykhailo Ialovyi and Mykola Khvyl´ovyi from their positions on the editorial board of *Chervonyi shliakh* for "political errors." Volodymyr Zatons´kyi was appointed editor in chief instead of Shums´kyi. At the same time, at the instruction of the Central Committee of the CP(b)U, the party committee of the People's Commissariat for Education heard Shums´kyi's report on his work.[39]

Shums´kyi did not actually report on his work as people's commissar but instead talked about Ukrainian literary debates and their participants. This "report," which was later published in the magazine *Bolshevik of Ukraine*, was an attempt at compromise. It criticized Khvyl´ovyi, whom Shums´kyi had so stubbornly and uncompromisingly defended before.[40] On 4 December 1926, Shums´kyi sent an abridged version of his speech to Lazar Kaganovich, and on 7 December, he received a reply. The leader of the CP(b)U was dissatisfied with the nature of the criticism of Khvyl´ovyi and the assessments of Mykhailo Hrushevs´kyi's personality contained in the text. Shums´kyi reworked the text and sent it to Kaganovich again on 11 December. Kaganovich showed the text to Hryhorii Petrovs´kyi, expressed dissatisfaction again with the political content, made many changes to the text, and, most importantly, demanded that Shums´kyi make a public speech condemning his own personal mistakes. At the same time, Kaganovich returned the text, knowing how the ambitious and emotional Shums´kyi would perceive it.

On 15 December 1926, Shums´kyi sent a new version, but again "Iron Lazar" was not content. On 18 December, enraged, Shums´kyi wrote to Kaganovich:

> I must say, Lazar Moiseevich, that, in general, your amendments made a depressing impression on me of being treated as a stranger and alien to the Central Committee. Although I did everything at the June plenum to put an end to the frictions that took place before this plenum, and I do not fundamentally disagree with the Central Committee ... I think I did everything, even said that I defended the wrong positions when in fact I did not. It was done to eliminate any possibility of anyone speculating about my apparent opposition to the Central Committee.[41]

We need to pay particular attention to Shums´kyi's "confession" to Kaganovich. He admitted that he had played along with Kaganovich and his allies, claiming that he had defended erroneous positions for the sake of the party. And what did he get in return for his confession? Nothing. It was a false confession with zero effect. Shums´kyi would learn this lesson well; when he was eventually in the clutches of the Chekists, despite their sometimes violent interrogation of him over many years, Shums´kyi would never give them the false confession they coveted (see chapter 5).

But Shums´kyi understood that his position—indeed, his residence—in Ukraine was no longer tenable, at least for the time being. In December 1926, at the same time that he sent the letter to Kaganovich, Shums´kyi sent a letter to the Politburo of the Central Committee of the CP(b)U requesting that he be dismissed as people's commissar for education. On 7 January 1927, this letter was considered at a meeting of the Politburo. However, his request was not granted. Shums´kyi was instead "offered" the opportunity to continue his work, and later to present his report on the work of the People's Commissariat for Education.[42]

Kaganovich would not release Shums´kyi so easily; he had to finish off his opponent. On 2 February 1927, the Politburo heard a report on Shums´kyi's performance as people's commissar. It was then that Kaganovich noted the incredible collapse in the work of the People's Commissariat for Education and asked the specific commission within the Politburo hearing the report to issue a resolution on this point. That commission, which consisted of Volodymyr Zatons´kyi, Mykola Skrypnyk, Andrii Radchenko, Mykola Demchenko, Shums´kyi, and his deputy Ian Riappo, engaged in heated debate.[43] For the resolution, the commission members were told what to write and given eleven bullet points to include in it. Ten points were negative assessments of the commissariat's work, while one was positive: the need to note "achievements in the field of cultural development, as well as in the work of People's Commissariat for Education."[44] That was all.

The ten shortcomings in the work of the People's Commissariat for Education included, among others, Shums´kyi's poor leadership of "the process of the cultural growth of Ukraine"; Ukrainization's "separation from society"; insufficient attention to workers' education; weak management of school and research work; insufficient attention to teaching, art, literature, and cinema; and insufficient communication of local People's Commissariat bodies with party organizations. The most severe shortcoming with the most serious consequences was twofold: the "incorrectness of the People's Commissariat for Education's line on the main issues of national policy and deviation from the party line," and its lack of authority (according to the criticism, it was necessary to "raise the authority" of the People's Commissariat for Education and strengthen the leadership of the party in it).[45] In addition, at the meeting, Kaganovich demanded that Shums´kyi admit the mistakes mentioned in Stalin's letter, because in June 1926, Shums´kyi had hinted that he would not sign the Stalinist version of their conversation. This time Shums´kyi was firm and rejected the demands for confession, angering Kaganovich further.

This farcical meeting of the Politburo of the Central Committee of the CP(b)U on 2 February 1927 ended with Shums´kyi's finally being dismissed from his post. His future was now in the hands of the Central Committee of the ACP(b).[46] On 16 February, he was again received by Stalin—for the last time—though it is not known what they spoke about. Shums´kyi would soon be in Leningrad.[47]

The Secret Department of the GPU of the UkrSSR took numerous statements and carefully collected information on the response of various social strata to the removal of the former Borotbyst. "Shums´kyi's departure was a strong blow to us, to nonpartisan Ukrainians," said one former member of the UPSR.[48] Another report stated: "There was a belief within the Russian part of the People's Commissariat that the pace of Ukrainization would weaken with Shums´kyi's departure." The Chekists also recorded that "among some part of the Ukrainian intelligentsia, there were rumors that Khvyl´ovyi or Panas Liubchenko would be appointed the people's commissar for education in place of Shums´kyi."[49] However, neither would head the People's Commissariat for Education. As already mentioned, Mykola Skrypnyk became the next people's commissar. Like Shums´kyi, he would be removed from his post. Rather than face a show trial, he committed suicide before his arrest in 1933. Beginning in 1927, Shums´kyi would live in a form of political purgatory. He was gradually pushed downward into the hell of arrest and eventual death by his detractors, including Skrypnyk, who would help transform Shums´kyism from a "national bias" into a counterrevolutionary crime.

Chapter Four

FROM POLITICAL ACCUSATIONS TO CRIMINAL CASES

At the beginning of 1927, Shums´kyi's travails with Kaganovich and the party's charges of national bias against him gained international attention. Shums´kyi was publicly defended by Karl Savrych (Maksymovych), a leading figure of the CPWU, the head of its Foreign Section, and a candidate for the Central Committee of the CP(b)U. Maksymovych had worked with Shums´kyi in the UkrSSR delegation in Warsaw, but it was not simply that they had a strong friendship. Maksymovych and other CPWU leaders were outraged at the criticism of Shums´kyi at the February–March plenum of the Central Committee of the CP(b)U in 1927, when Kaganovich and his supporters spoke about Shums´kyi's alleged national bias. Shums´kyi described his treatment as follows:

> Comrade Kaganovich said something incomprehensible about my bias and mistakes. And what was the bias, and what were the mistakes? It remained shrouded in obscurity and a secret for the party. It had to be said that the party could overcome this bias and gain some experience in correcting these mistakes. However, the fact was that the talk about my bias and mistakes was just empty talk, and the reasons for my departure were not to be found here. The reason for my leaving was a failure to work with Secretary General Comrade Kaganovich. With his arrival in Ukraine, despite my full desire, I could not manage to establish relations with him as the most responsible (at least formally) political leader and establish political cooperation, although for my part I did my best in this direction.[1]

Maksymovych shared Shums′kyi's view of Ukrainization, and both took an active part in the work of the CPWU. Founded in 1919 as the Communist Party of Eastern Halychyna (Galicia), the party changed its name in 1923, becoming the Communist Party of Western Ukraine. A separate Communist Party was created not only for Ukrainians but also for Belarusians in Poland, the Communist Party of Western Belarus. In December 1924, the Communist International (Comintern) passed a resolution calling for the transfer of all territories in Poland, Czechoslovakia, and Romania with Ukrainian-majority populations to Ukraine.

From 1921 to 1938, the CPWU was a "corporate" member of the Communist Party of Poland (CPP) as an autonomous organization with its own Central Committee.[2] The party mostly operated underground but sought to create mass legal organizations—"outbuildings"—by attracting other leftists and like-minded political forces. In 1926, it managed to form the Ukrainian Peasants' and Workers' Socialist Alliance (Selrob), which became the most influential of the Ukrainian parties in Volhynia and also operated in Halychyna. However, the spread of CPWU's influence—the growth of its outbuildings—was clearly hindered by the party's barely veiled manipulation from Moscow and Kharkiv, as well as by its members' Bolshevik sectarianism, their refusal to work with other leftist parties, to which they often referred as fascist, socially treacherous, and so on.

As a member of the Executive Committee of the Comintern since its Second Congress, in 1920, Shums′kyi attended party meetings of the CPWU and maintained constant contact with it. Beyond influencing leading Ukrainian political figures in national politics, including Volodymyr Zatons′kyi and Mykola Skrypnyk, Shums′kyi influenced Soviet foreign policy decisions and was not afraid to criticize the communist parties of Czechoslovakia and Poland for their disregard of Ukrainian problems.

Maksymovych, for his part, was a former soldier of a formation of the Ukrainian Sich Riflemen in the Austro-Hungarian army, a former prisoner of Russia, a former Borotbyst, and one of the most influential figures in the CPWU. He was as categorical as possible in his defense of Shums′kyi at the February–March 1927 plenum of the Central Committee of the CP(b)U.

He stated that he did not see a fundamental difference on the national question between Shums′kyi and the political line of the Central Committee of the CP(b)U, and he therefore disagreed with the decision to remove Shums′kyi as people's commissar for education.[3] Maksymovych's position was supported by other CPWU leaders, including Iosyp Vasyl′kiv (real name Krilyk) and Turians′kyi (real name Kuz′ma).[4] CPWU activists even protested at a Comintern meeting against the recall of Shums′kyi from Ukraine. This was a real mutiny, as the CPWU was financed by the Bolshevik party treasury.

But it was not only the CPWU causing difficulties for Moscow. Its leaders came to Shums′kyi's defense during the height of international military turmoil, in 1927, when it was least opportune to do so. Shums′kyi's detractors justified their attack on him in part on the grounds that his national bias made the Soviet Union more vulnerable to hostile international forces, especially from Poland. Józef Piłsudski's coup d'état in Poland in May 1926 was interpreted by communist leaders as the first step toward the inevitable aggression of international imperialism against the USSR. Piłsudski's widely publicized domestic policy initiatives to improve relations with the Ukrainian and Belarusian populations in Poland further alarmed the Soviet leadership, which saw this as an attempt to secure Piłsudski's "rear in the event of a conflict with the USSR" and argued that he was "definitely conducting a policy aimed at such a conflict."[5]

Kaganovich immediately took measures against the schismatics (or "breakers," as they were called). On his initiative, on 9–12 April 1927, a special "underground" plenum of the Central Committee of the CPWU was held in Polish-controlled Gdańsk, where the party had a secret apartment. Mykola Skrypnyk arrived from Kharkiv and reported on the national policy of the CP(b)U. He read a letter from its Central Committee accusing Shums′kyi and condemning Maksymovych and Turians′kyi for the positions they had voiced openly at a meeting of the Secretariat of the Executive Committee of the Comintern on 28 March. Here, they had protested against a speech by Vincas Mickevičius-Kapsukas (one of the founders and leaders of the Lithuanian Communist Party), who claimed that Shums′kyi's activities were in line with "Piłsudski's plans to create a bourgeois Ukraine." There was a heated discussion at the plenum, with most members of the Central Committee of the CPWU disagreeing with the accusation that Shums'kyi diverged from the party line. They argued that there was no difference between his position and the party's, and therefore no reason to talk about any bias.[6] This angered Skrypnyk, who, in his closing remarks at the plenum, insisted that Shums'kyi opposed the party line as a "National Bolshevik" and old Borotbyst. Skrypnyk issued an ultimatum: either the CPWU supported the CP(b)U, or it supported Shums'kyi and Maksymovych.

The CPWU did not take Skrypnyk's bait. On 10 April 1927, the plenum passed a resolution that did not criticize either Maksymovych or Shums'kyi. The resolution was adopted with twelve votes, with only Natan Sukhyi (real name Shapiro), Pinkhus Bremer (real name Mintz), and two representatives of the CPP voting against it.[7] But Skrypnyk was a tough nut to crack. On 12 April, he organized the continuation of the plenum and tried again to squeeze out more votes against Shums'kyi and Maksymovych from the members of the Central Committee of the CPWU, but again failed. After that, Skrypnyk stated that Nikolai Bukharin, the central Bolshevik leader who had become the head of the Comintern at the end of 1926, had authorized him to "put an end to National Bolshevism."[8] Thus, the resolution proposed by the Central Committee of the CPWU was regarded as "a break with the Communist International, the ACP(b)and the CP(b)U." However, the members of the Central Committee of the CPWU did not capitulate, though they were likely blackmailed. Only two people voted for Skrypnyk's resolution—it is easy to guess that they were Sukhyi and Bremer—and thirteen abstained.[9]

Skrypnyk was somewhat satisfied with this result, spinning it into a tangible victory he could take back to Kharkiv (that is, to Lazar Kaganovich). Both would use the 1927 plenum in Gdańsk as the starting point for accusations against the majority of the CPWU leadership of all sorts of betrayals, ploys, and subversive activities against Soviet power. These accusations led to a split in Selrob in October 1927 between left and right factions. In November 1927, Kaganovich said that he did not know whose side the CPWU would take in the event of war against the Soviet Union.[10]

At the beginning of 1928, the CPWU also split into two factions. One faction was recognized by the Comintern, and the other was the opposing CPWU majority, whom the Bolsheviks derided as Vasyl′kivites or the Vasyl′kiv-Turians′kyi group, named after the supposed leaders of the CPWU breakers (schismatics) Vasyl′kiv and Turians′kyi. The split significantly reduced the influence of the CPWU.[11] Kaganovich succeeded in expelling the "treasonous" Vasyl′kiv-Turians′kyi faction from the Comintern on 18 February 1928. The official CPWU faction continued to harass the Vasyl′kivites in every possible way and ascribed to them the label of the social-fascist parties. Shums′kyists from the CPWU were even accused of falling under the ideological influence of the Ukrainian nationalist thinker Dmytro Dontsov.[12] Meanwhile, as historian Oleksandr Zaitsev aptly reminds us, while the western-Ukrainian communists were fighting among themselves, the real enemies of Soviet power, radical Ukrainian nationalist groups in Halychyna and in exile, were consolidating their strength, culminating in the formation of the Organization of Ukrainian Nationalists (OUN).[13]

In Kharkiv, the scandal over the CPWU break continued to rage. On 9 May 1927, the leadership of the CP(b)U recalled Maksymovych from the post of the CPWU representative in the Comintern and then deprived him of the status of candidate for membership in the Central Committee of the CP(b)U.[14] In March 1928, the plenum of the Central Committee of the CP(b)U stated that Shums′kyi not only "openly opposed the line of the CP(b)U, but also conducted general factional work on the shoulders of the CPWU," and, further, that he "was preparing for a future rift." The plenum culminated in a resolution that was formulated as a verdict for the so-called breakers: "The plenum of the Central Committee of the Communist Party (b) noted with indignation the fact of the betrayal of Vasyl′kiv-Turians′kyi's group, which broke up the CPWU in favor of the fascist dictatorship of Piłsudski. The plenum condemned traitors and renegades of communism before the working class around the world."[15]

The orgy of accusations and remorse continued. On 25 January 1929, the Comintern's Political Secretariat instructed the Comintern's Executive Committee to clarify the role of Shums′kyi and Maksymovych in the activities of the Vasyl′kivites. A special commission of the Comintern was set up, which stated that Shums´kyi and Maksymovych had not dissociated themselves from the group but, rather, defended it. On this basis, Maksymovych was removed from the Comintern and expelled from the party. He had to publicly atone for political "sins" in letters to the newspapers *Pravda* and *Kommunist*. In response, the Central Committee of the CP(b)U raised the issue of his return to the party. However, this would not save him from repression later. Unable to withstand the pressure, almost all the Shums´kyists from the CPWU capitulated and admitted their mistakes by 1930.

But the actions supposedly initiated by the breakers did not end there. At the end of 1933, the leaders of the CPWU, Myron Kosar (real name Zaiachkivs´kyi) and Hryhorii Baraba (real name Ivanenko), were summoned to the USSR and arrested as members of the mythical UMO, on whose orders they had allegedly infiltrated the CPWU leadership. Both died in the camps. Shums´kyi was declared to be the head of the so-called Ukrainian Military Organization (UMO, which will be discussed later), and other CPWU activists, including Vasyl´kiv, Maksymovych, and Turians´kyi, were accused of participating in the UMO, then convicted and executed on false charges.[16] The last nail in the coffin of the communist movement in the Second Polish-Lithuanian Commonwealth came on 16 August 1938. The Executive Committee of the Comintern accused the CPP and its constituents—the CPWU and the Communist Party of Western Belarus—of having been infiltrated by Piłsudski's spies and provocateurs under the guise of oppositionists, and of promoting these agents to leading positions in the communist parties. The party organizations were dissolved.[17]

* * *

In September 1927, the party posted Shums´kyi to Leningrad, where he would stay until the early 1930s. He was made rector of the Leningrad Institute of National Economy and then, in August 1929, rector of the M. I. Kalinin Leningrad Polytechnic Institute (now Peter the Great Saint Petersburg State Polytechnic University). Founded in the late nineteenth century, the Polytechnic had eight thousand students in the late 1920s. It was a large university with longstanding traditions, and its name had changed many times. Judging by the available sources, Shums´kyi did not feel comfortable in the rector's chair, but because he had been assigned to this position by the party, he had little option but to stay there. In any case, this proved to be a short-term posting. According to an order dated 31 December 1929, he was to take leave from 1 January through 1 March 1930 due to illness (rheumatoid arthritis). He resigned in February 1930 and did not return to the institute.

Even in Leningrad, Shums´kyi was in constant contact with like-minded people, particularly those who came from Ukraine on business, for example, former Borotbysts Iurii Ozers´kyi and Panas Liubchenko. During an interrogation in February 1934, Ozers´kyi recalled a meeting with Shums´kyi in 1928, and the academic Matvii Iavors´kyi did much the same when he was interrogated.[18] Petro Solodub acknowledged that he had met in Leningrad with Shums´kyi, Maksymovych, Oles´ Dosvitnii, and Omelian Volokh.[19] Another of Oleksandr Shums´kyi's visitors was the writer and former Borotbyst Mykhailo Ialovyi. Shums´kyi explained to him that the reason for his exile was that the pro-Russian forces temporarily ruling in Ukraine were taking their revenge upon him. Ialovyi spoke to Shums´kyi about the situation in the UkrSSR with pessimism, listing "the complete defeat of cultural personnel ... the formalism of Ukrainization, publishing and research in neglect, the grave situation in the countryside, and the same in industry."[20] Shums´kyi remained optimistic. While agreeing that "the revanche of Russophilism (*rusotiapstvo*) in Ukraine is inevitable," Shums´kyi nevertheless insisted that "in a year or two ... [they] will see for themselves how they have bungled it by becoming disconnected from the Ukrainian element represented by the peasantry and intelligentsia, and then we will have to get back to work." Ialovyi said during interrogations that Shums´kyi "thought that he would have to stay outside Ukraine for two or three years, and then he would be given the opportunity to return to high-level political work."[21] This was excessive optimism; it would never happen.

Shums´kyi's expulsion from Ukraine became the subject of attention outside the UkrSSR. On 30 August 1928, a columnist in the Lviv newspaper *Dilo* (Action), Galaktion Chipka (the pseudonym of the poet Roman Kupchyns´kyi), wrote ironically:

> Hryn′ko was sent to Moscow to defend Ukraine's interests ... and Shums′kyi and Maksymovych continued the policy of Ukrainian hetmans. ... They went to deep Russia to Ukrainize everything in their path. And on the Solovki Islands, the Ukrainian intelligentsia was finishing what [Petro] Kalnyshevs′kyi, the Sich Army's Kish ataman, failed to do. This was nothing other than ... Ukrainian imperialism. ... There were the cunning Little Russians [*malorossy*]! They were pursuing an imperialist policy quietly, without violence and shouting ... and so someday, they would squeeze Moscow so that it would become Ukrainized and would be forced to agree to a single, indivisible whole.[22]

Declassified security documents reveal that the Chekists surveilled Shums′kyi during his time in Leningrad. For example, on December 1927, the Secret Department of the GPU of the UkrSSR sent a request to its agents in the Leningrad Military District to determine whether Oleksandr Shums′kyi and Petro Solodub had left Leningrad in the second half of November, and, if so, to identify their destination.[23] In January 1928, the head of the Secret Department of the GPU of the UkrSSR, Valerii Horozhanin, received the response that, "according to the personal observations of our resident," Shums′kyi had not traveled during this period.[24]

In Ukraine, the Chekists were carefully gathering information on how members of the Ukrainian public were reacting to the removal of Shums′kyi, and communicating the information to the Ukrainian party leadership via the weekly reports of the Secret Department of the GPU of the UkrSSR. In a report dated 19–25 February 1928, for instance, an agent stated that "the national opposition was headed by Shums′kyi, who led its political activities, while Khvyl′ovyi led the Ukrainian opposition in literature." The report of 26 February–3 March contained rumors that Shums′kyi and Maksymovych had fled abroad, that Shums′kyi was allegedly already in Lviv, and that he had been elected secretary of the Central Committee of the CPWU. Soon, however, the Chekists became aware that none of this was true.[25]

A GPU report dated 6–11 May 1928 contained the following record of conversations among former Socialist-Revolutionaries in Kyiv:

> The Ukrainian opposition has grown out of Ukrainian autonomy's struggle with Great Russian chauvinism. The hard-core Great Russian chauvinist in Ukraine is Kaganovich. A campaign was conducted and continues to be conducted against him. Shums´kyi, Maksymovych, and Khvyl´ovyi have been especially bold in fighting against Great Russian chauvinism. Kaganovich tried to remove Shums´kyi from the path and honorably "sent" him into exile outside Ukraine.[26]

Gathering evidence and various opinions about Shums´kyi in Ukraine, the Chekists could well interpret all this as evidence that Shums´kyism could become a kind of counterrevolutionary symbol and catalyze an eventual opposition.

At the end of 1929, this emerging understanding of Shums´kyi's potential threat encouraged the party to cajole Shums´kyi into swearing to it a new oath of allegiance. On 19 December, Shums´kyi wrote a statement to the Executive Committee of the Comintern, the Central Committee of the ACP(b), and the Central Committee of the CP(b)U. Though written in the genre of ritual repentance for past political "sins," this statement was measured and even self-justifying in its tone, unlike the groveling letters written by many other repressed political figures. Shums´kyi explained why, three years before, he had insisted on accelerating the pace of Ukrainization and nominating Ukrainian cadres to leading party positions. The statement ended:

> I accept that my proposals could have led to a general weakening of the party's political power, including a weakening of its leading role in the Ukrainian sociocultural process; that is, they could have led to results directly opposite to those I wanted to achieve with my proposals. I did not take this side of the issue into account at the time, and this was my main mistake. In defending my incorrect position before the Central Committee of the CP(b)U, I made a number of derivative mistakes that followed from the logic of the struggle. The most important of these were the speech about the "Little Russians" and the lenient critique of Comrade Khvyl´ovyi's mistakes. I consider the criticism of these mistakes, as well as the criticism of my position in general, as presented in the decisions of the Central Committee of the CP(b)U and the Comintern, to be correct.[27]

Shums´kyi did not write the statement of his own free will. It is hard to say what or who directly prompted Shums´kyi to write the statement, but it is safe to assume it was at the request of Lazar Kaganovich who at that time was in Moscow as secretary of the Central Committee of the ACP(b). Shums′kyi, still a politician, was no doubt disingenuous in his apology. As with other politicians, Shums′kyi's apology was strategic in its purposes; in this case, it was likely a precondition for Shums′kyi's relocation to and further employment in Moscow.

In February 1930, Shums′kyi was transferred to work in Moscow. Initially, he worked as deputy head of the Propaganda Department of the Central Committee of the ACP(b). In February 1931, he was elected chairman of the Central Committee of the Union of Educators of the USSR and a member of the Presidium of the All-Union Central Committee of Education. He worked there until his arrest in May 1933. In addition, he was a member of the editorial board of the newspaper *Za kommunisticheskoe prosveshchenie* (For communist enlightenment).[28] No detailed information has been preserved about this period of Shums′kyi's life and activity in Moscow. However, we know that in 1932, he traveled abroad and spent some time in Germany. From a transcript of Roman Turians′kyi's testimony of 1 April 1933, we learn that former Borotbysts and representatives of the CPWU who were in Moscow at the time gathered at the apartments of Petro Solodub and Shums′kyi to discuss issues of concern. Turians′kyi testified:

> After Shums′kyi's return from Berlin, a meeting took place in his apartment, which was attended by Shums′kyi, Solodub, Maksymovych, Turians′kyi [referring to himself in the third person], and Bei[-Orlovs′kyi]. The main issue of discussion was collectivization. Shums′kyi shared his impressions of his trip abroad. The general opinion was that collectivization accelerated the failure of the entire party policy. In the autumn of 1932, we regarded the situation as even more acute.[29]

Even if we take into account the typical Chekist rhetoric (Chekists themselves often wrote the interrogation protocols and forced the suspects to sign them), we still have reason to believe that Shums′kyi was politically active in this Moscow period as well. He was clearly worried about what was happening in Ukraine and discussed his concerns with his comrades. Of prime concern was the massive famine of 1932–33, which developed partly out of the chaos and destruction of the Soviet policy of collectivization.

During Shums′kyi's stay in Leningrad and Moscow, he was not forgotten in the UkrSSR. The Bolshevik press worked hard to sustain the negative image of him and other "nationalist-evaders" in his absence. For example, in February 1928 the magazine *Bil′shovyk Ukraïny* (Bolshevik of Ukraine) published the following in an editorial entitled "In the mire of nationalism":

> Shums′kyi supported Khvyl′ovyi, deepened his mistakes, and spread them, accusing the party of being unable to control the Ukrainian cultural process; demanding the dismantling of old party cadres who had graduated from the school of the revolution and had fought for the creation and strengthening of the Ukrainian Soviet state; substantiating the inevitability and need to fight for the proletariat in Soviet conditions along national lines; ignoring and underestimating the importance and seriousness of work among national minorities; inciting and spitting on Ukrainian communists defending Lenin's national policy. Khvyl′ovyi and Shums′kyi's views and their bias reflected the nationalist-chauvinist sentiments of the Ukrainian kulaks and bourgeoisie in the party. This bias posed a great threat to the struggle within the party itself, among the proletariat along national lines. This bias represented a capitulation to nationalist-bourgeois democracy and, in the end, led to a united national front, to a bourgeois restoration, to the strengthening of the nationalist counterrevolution and its pressure on the proletarian dictatorship.[30]

In 1932, a textbook for the Party Education and Political Education Network stated:

> In recent years, the bias toward Ukrainian chauvinism had manifested in the speeches of Khvyl′ovyi, Shums′kyi, and Volobuiev. Khvyl′ovyi spoke with the slogan "away from Moscow," preaching the orientation of Ukrainian culture to the West, to a "European psychology," no matter whether bourgeois or proletarian. Shums′kyi, who defended Khvyl′ovyi and his theory of the development of Ukrainian culture, continued Khvyl′ovyism along political lines. Underestimating the consequences achieved in Ukrainization, he demanded breaking the old party cadres—the backbone of the party—and forcibly Ukrainizing Russian workers.[31]

Late 1932 and early 1933 were marked by an attack on what was left of the achievements of Ukrainization. Terry Martin notes that the key to the implementation of hard-line Ukrainization was the active participation of the Central Committee, the symbol and embodiment of which was the work of the relevant commission of the Politburo, chaired by Lazar Kaganovich. This commission met regularly until June 1928. After that time, although the commission formally existed at least until January 1931, no traces of its activities can be found.[32] In the context of the socioeconomic and political crisis that grew in Ukraine in 1932 with the onset of mass famine and the Soviet intensification of it in the Holodomor, the Stalinist leadership began to argue that resistance to collectivization and resistance to the communist regime were generally linked to the internal and external nationalist Ukrainian counter-revolution and the agents of Piłsudski.

We have already discussed the curtailment of Ukrainization. Here we emphasize that it was exactly under these conditions that Shums′kyi was arrested in 1933, at least officially, for his alleged involvement with the so-called UMO. The Chekists soon escalated his charge from participating into leading this "widespread underground structure" in Ukraine. They alleged that, under Shums′kyi's leadership, the UMO planned an uprising against the Soviet regime in Ukraine, coordinating its activities with the UMO operating abroad under the leadership of Ievhen Konovalets′.[33] While the UMO abroad was real, its operation in Ukraine under Shums′kyi's leadership was a Chekist fantasy. This fantasy encompassed another 148 so-called UMO participants that the Chekists added to the initial list of those accused in 1933 and 1934. There were many writers and literary professionals among the accused, as well as academics and publishers.[34] The breadth of this fantasy was sufficient to encompass everyone from state employees and students involved in seemingly nonpolitical work to leading figures of Ukraine's political and cultural industry and supporters of Ukrainization.[35]

The arrest of these leading political figures was part of a more focused strategy of dismantling the remnants of the CPWU, especially its Vasyl′kivist faction, whose leadership had officially disbanded in the wake of the Shums′kyi affair in 1928. For the

Chekists, the CPWU and UMO were two sides of the same coin. All the leading political figures arrested in 1933–34 had been members of, or had links to, the CPWU, including Oleksandr Badan-Iavorenko, chief of the planning sector of the State Planning Committee of the USSR; and Klymentii Konyk, assistant to the secretary of the Central Committee of the CP(b)U. Leading CPWU activists were also targeted, including Bei-Orlovs′kyi, Baraba, Kosar, Vasyl′kiv, Maksymovych, Turians′kyi, Pavlo Ladan, Ivan Tur-Zaparyniuk, Iosyp Ersteniuk, Mykhailo Tesliuk, and Iosyp Bukshovanyi.

The People's Commissariat for Internal Affairs (NKVD) once again began making arrests or rearrests for participation in the UMO in 1937, during the Great Terror, including the rearrest of Shums′kyi himself. The Chekists implicated many of those arrested in other cases as well, charging them with participating in other organizations and plots along the lines of the UMO. Most of those arrested caved to the pressure of their interrogators to implicate Shums′kyi as their ringleader and confess to their own participation in the UMO and whatever other role the Chekists ascribed to them in these broader plots. Most of the 148 arrested in 1933 would die on the islands of the Solovki prison by the end of the 1930s, after having incriminated themselves or Shums′kyi.

Among the long list of arrestees were many who knew Shums′kyi and had long associations with him. They were precisely targeted by the Chekists to extract testimonies of Shums′kyi's counterrevolutionary activity. The Chekists gave special attention to former members of the UPSR who came back to Ukraine after emigrating in the early 1920s. In conjunction with securing the testimonies of Shums′kyi's closest and often most powerful political colleagues, that is, building their cases from the top down, the Chekists also constructed their cases from the bottom up. They molded like clay every seemingly innocuous meeting and conversation between lesser-known, or at least nonpolitical, figures and Shums′kyi over the years into more compelling evidence of his ever-increasing counterrevolutionary activity. As we make evident below, they were incredibly skilled at uncovering a web of criminal activity, which they themselves had spun, and then eliminating the evidence of their own subterfuge by executing those who confessed to the crimes.[36]

The testimony of Pavlo Khrystiuk, former general scribe of the Ukrainian Central Rada, is a case in point. He met Shums´kyi for the first time in 1922 in the Soviet mission in Vienna, where Khrystiuk worked for a short time. Shums´kyi suggested that Khrystiuk come back to Ukraine. They met by accident a second time in Kharkiv in 1925. Khrystiuk recalled: "Shums´kyi asked where I work, and, after learning that I worked in Ukrinbank, he said that it is pointless for me to stay in the bank and it would make much more sense to get a scholarly-pedagogical job."[37] Shums´kyi assisted Khrystiuk in obtaining an appointment to the board of the Derzhavne vydavnytstvo Ukraïny (State publishing house of Ukraine, DVU). Khrystiuk testified further: "Shums´kyi told me that, as a member of the board of the Publishing House, I should pay attention to the Ukrainian intelligentsia who would be dealing with the Publishing House, and ... take steps to link Ukrainian writers with the Publishing House."[38] Khrystiuk was arrested in March 1931 and was forced to confess his own "sins" under interrogation. He included in his confessed acts of "sabotage" his attempts "to promote first of all belles lettres among the reading masses, the classics of Ukrainian creative writing, etc., which were detached from the problems of socialist development."[39]

Chekists quickly worked on Khrystiuk to testify against Shums´kyi, as shown by one fragment of his testimony:

> Shums´kyi ... drew attention to the fact that there was a relatively small number of Ukrainians in the CP(b)U, that the party's national policy did not fully satisfy Borotbysts, and he also suggested that our group joined the Communist Party in order to enhance Borotbyst influence. Shums´kyi suggested that I personally switch to scholarly-pedagogical work and, while working as people's commissar for education, he appointed me as a board member of the Publishing House in 1925. By appointing me to this position, he gave me a directive to work on rallying the Ukrainian national writers around the Publishing House. I will tell you later about our connection with Shums´kyi during the blossoming of Shums´kyism in 1926.[40]

On 7 February 1932, after serving his main purpose of incriminating Shums´kyi, Khrystiuk was sentenced to five years' imprisonment. Three years later, on 21 January 1935, the Special Council (*Osoboe soveshchanie*) of the NKVD sentenced him to three years of exile in the northern territories of the USSR.[41] Later he was released, yet he did not see freedom. On 3 November 1936, the council sentenced Khrystiuk to a further eight years' imprisonment. According to prison documents, he died on 29 September 1941 in Sevvostlag (the abbreviation for the North Eastern Corrective Labor Camps, part of what later was to become the Gulag), Arkhangelsk Oblast.

More prominent figures spoke in detail about their connection to Shums´kyi during the "blossoming period" of Shums´kyism. In his testimony dated 17 July 1931, academic Matvii Iavors´kyi said that Shums´kyi was preparing "a political attack on the dictatorship of the proletariat in Ukraine."[42] Iavors´kyi, a historian whose works were considered an alternative to Mykhailo Hrushevs´kyi's scholarship, ended up in Solovki. There he renounced his previous testimonies incriminating Shums´kyi and others, becoming a resolute anti-Soviet dissident. "It seems that there was no other person who would've expressed his anger and contempt toward the NKVDists [Chekists] and everything that reminded [him of] the Soviets and Moscow the way that Iavors´kyi did," wrote Semen Pidhainyi who saw the former Marxist academic in Solovki.[43] Matvii Iavors´kyi was shot with a group of other Solovki prisoners in the fall of 1937.

According to the testimony of writer Oles´ Dosvitnii dated 29 December 1933, Shums´kyi was "an ideologist and a principal manager" of the UMO, which strove to cut off the "Ukrainian cultural front from the international influence of the all-Union socialist culture." The transcript of Dosvitnii's interrogation recorded the aim of the organization as "the separation of Ukraine from the Soviet Union and establishment of an independent bourgeois-nationalist state."[44] Despite the fact that Dosvitnii signed the false testimony—or because of it—he was shot in 1934. As a head of the "united counterrevolutionary bloc of the national forces of Ukraine," Shums´kyi also appears in testimony dated 6 September 1933 and signed by Mykola Khrystovyi, formerly a prominent Borotbyst. Khrystovyi's statement asserted: "From the words of Maksymovych and Ialovyi, I know that Shums´kyi is a leader of the center of the c[ounter]r[evolutionary] bloc."[45] Khrystovyi was executed in 1938.

Manufacturing these testimonies from both leading political figures at the top of Ukrainian social hierarchy and bureaucrats and officials at the bottom made it possible for the Chekists to squeeze Shums'kyi in an ever-tightening vise of false evidence. Many of those interrogated were marched one by one into Shums'kyi's interrogation room, forced into a seat across the table from him, and repeatedly asked to answer questions about their relationship. Their answers were predetermined by the Chekists and had been rehearsed during often-violent interrogations. All these figures implicated Shums'kyi in the crimes that the Chekists had concocted.

The most compelling face-to-face testimonies against Shums'kyi were made by the former members of the Central Committee of the CPWU Bei-Orlovs'kyi, Turians'kyi, and Maksymovych. In May and June 1933, the assistant to the head of the Secret Political Department of the OGPU, Henrikh Liushkov (who, in 1938, would flee abroad and incriminate the NKVD for its torture methods), set up these meetings. This process of face-to-face meetings, known as *ochnaia stavka* (confrontation) in Russian, was supposed to shatter Shums'kyi's remaining hopes of release by laying bare the betrayal of his closet comrades and confirming that his arrest was not a mistake by police but an order from the party. Below is an excerpt from the transcript of the face-to-face meeting of Turians'kyi and Shums'kyi, held on 27 May 1933:

> **Question to Turians'kyi:** What do you know about Shums'kyi's membership and role in the Ukrainian c[ounter]r[evolutionary] organization?
>
> **Turians'kyi:** Shums'kyi and I were part of the Ukrainian c[ounter]r[evolutionary] organization, and I belonged to the center of it, which was located in Moscow. The organization connected kulaks, Borotbysts, Shums'kyist elements, and Halychynan men who belonged to the UMO in Ukraine.
>
> **Question to Shums'kyi:** What can you say of all of this?
>
> [Shums'kyi's answer is absent.]
>
> **Question to Turians'kyi:** Give us concrete facts of your common c[ounter]r[evolutionary] activity with Shums'kyi.
>
> **Turians'kyi:** I am connected with Shums'kyi in the context of our common c[ounter]r[evolutionary] activity since the time of our membership in the leadership of the CPWU. With Shums'kyi's

consent and according to his instructions, I, along with Vasyl´kiv and others, prepared the split of the CPWU. We commenced the split under [Shums´kyi's] direct instruction, communicated through Vasyl´kiv, despite the fact that Shums´kyi did not have any formal relationship with the CPWU. We continued to receive instructions from him on how he could return to the party after our exclusion ... to engage in c[ounter]r[evolutionary] organization. ...

Question to Shums´kyi: Do you confirm all of this?

Shums´kyi: I know nothing about the point in question. All of what has been said I categorically deny.

Question to Turians´kyi: What do you know about meetings of the center of the organization and about Shums´kyi's participation in its activities?

Turians´kyi: The meetings of the center of the organization were held at Solodub's place or Shums´kyi's. More often, they were held at Solodub's. There we discussed the questions of the struggle against the party and the authorities in Ukraine. I can recall one of those meetings at Shums´kyi's place after his return from abroad in late summer in 1932. Besides Shums´kyi and me, there were present: Maksymovych, Solodub, and Bei[-Orlovskyi]. Shums´kyi shared his impressions on Germany and, afterward, a discussion about the situation in Ukraine took place. The general opinion, including Shums´kyi's, was essentially that collectivization in Ukraine certainly has failed and that Ukraine is on the verge of exploding. Questions of the future struggle against the party and authorities were discussed.

Question to Shums´kyi: Do you confirm what had been said?

Shums´kyi: I know nothing about the meetings or about the organization. I can confirm that indeed, after my arrival from Germany in 1932, there were gatherings at my place, where all people mentioned by Turians´kyi were present. I shared my impressions on Germany, but we had no talks about the situation in Ukraine or about the failure of collectivization.[46]

Maksymovych was more specific on Shums´kyi's concrete counterrevolutionary plans in their face-to-face meeting, on 22 June 1933:

Question to Maksymovych: In your testimony from 21 June 1933, you said: "After the party and Comintern liquidated Shums´kyism and [after] the split in the CPWU, Shums´kyi retained his old positions, changed his tactics, and moved to illegal forms of struggle against the party." Do you confirm this?

Maksymovych: I do.

Question to Shums´kyi: Do you confirm this?

Shums´kyi: I object.

Question to Maksymovych: Do you confirm your testimony that Shums´kyi, after he moved to Moscow, along with you, belonged to the center of the c[ounter]r[evolutionary] Ukrainian Military Organization?

Maksymovych: I confirm.

Question to Shums´kyi: What can you say on this matter?

Shums´kyi: I categorically object. I do not know of any c[ounter] r[evolutionary] organization....

Question to Maksymovych: Do you confirm your testimony of 5–6 May this year: "As a result of ... the meetings, the Moscow central group of the UMO came to the conclusion that it was necessary to prepare the uprising in the early spring of 1933. It had to be coordinated with the UMO's leadership abroad, specifically with Konovalets´. At the same time, the decision was made that in order to directly supervise the uprising and follow the plans, I had to move for permanent work to Ukraine. Vasyl´ Sirko was to assist me using his connections in the C[entral] C[ommittee of the] CP(b)U"?

Maksymovych: I confirm.

Question to Shums´kyi: Do you confirm this?

Shums´kyi: I object [to] all of this.

Question to Maksymovych: On 21 June, you testified about the execution of the projected plans for organizing the uprising in Ukraine: "At the end of 1932, after Volokh had moved from Kharkiv to Moscow and delivered information about the preparation of the uprising in the spring of 1933, during one of the meetings at Shums´kyi's place, where Shums´kyi, Solodub, and I myself were present, Solodub reported to us about the practical work in this direction." Do you confirm this?

Maksymovych: I confirm.

Question to Shums´kyi: What can you say on this matter?

Shums´kyi: I reject it categorically.[47]

Shums´kyi's former deputy in the People's Commissariat for Education, Petro Solodub, also testified against him. This did not save Solodub, who ended up a Solovki prisoner and was shot on

3 November 1937 in the Sandarmokh tract, a pine forest near the Finnish border where hundreds or possibly thousands of victims of the Great Terror were shot and buried in mass graves. Before then, in April 1934, Solodub wrote an appeal asking for his release and withdrawing his false testimonies. In this appeal, which he gave to a fellow inmate to read, Solodub confessed to giving false testimony against Shums′kyi:

> I belonged to Shums′kyi's group, it's true; the party condemned it, and I never allowed myself, even in my thoughts, to consider that the C[entral] C[ommittee] of the party would not arrest me. Prokof′ev, during the first meeting, told me, "You are being arrested with the knowledge of Com[rade] Stalin," so what was left for me to do?[48] It is not enough that I recognized my mistakes in the national question; I went further. Thinking logically, I reached the point where Shums′kyi had a far-reaching goal of creating a Ukraine of the bourgeois type that Shums′kyi never had in mind. When I was writing it, I cried. I was confident that I would be shot, because the party needed it.[49]

This testimony is only one of many that document interrogators' use of various psychological methods to pressure the arrested into providing false testimonies. Much of this history was confirmed during the Khrushchev Thaw, when survivors and witnesses from this period were found and questioned by the state and party commissions investigating Stalin's crimes. Survivors provided significant details as to how the UMO case was falsified. Here is what one of the 148 arrested in the UMO case, Mykhailo Tesliuk, stated in November 1956 in relation to his interrogation two decades earlier:

> On 20 May 1933, I was arrested by the GPU organs. During the trial, I was accused of belonging to the Ukrainian Military Organization (UMO), which was equated with the CPWU in general. ... During the investigation, I was threatened with execution. During the long interrogations [that] took place without rest and sleep, I was convinced that my confession [of] belonging to the UMO was of great significance for the struggle against nationalism.
>
> Under these circumstances, I was forced to make false testimony against Shums′kyi and myself. I said about Shums′kyi that he was one of the leaders of the UMO, that we conducted

> counterrevolutionary work under his leadership in preparing the uprising in Soviet Ukraine and other counterrevolutionary activities, which an investigator told me to say. I did not know Shums´kyi as a counterrevolutionary, I said a lot about him because of the pressure of the GPU officials.[50]

Tesliuk's testimony raises one of the major questions of our analysis. The same methods of psychological and physical pressure (threats, sleep deprivation, beating) were almost certainly applied to Shums´kyi himself. His health worsened significantly after his arrest, and he suffered nerve damage in his legs that would develop into paralysis by 1935. Yet, he categorically denied his guilt. Why and how did he manage to do so when apparently all factors worked against him, from the psychological pressure of *ochnaia stavka* to the physical pressure applied by the Chekists? No other major political figure resisted interrogations for years on end as Shums´kyi did.

To answer this question, it is worth referring to the memoirs of the former chief of the Soviet "Sabotage and Terror" Service (a special unit within the secret police), Lieutenant General Pavel Sudoplatov, who drew up the plan for Shums´kyi's assassination in 1946 with Viktor Abakumov (head of the Ministry of State Security, MGB) that eventually gained Stalin's approval (see chapter 6). Sudoplatov was arrested in 1953, soon after his boss and head of the secret police, Lavrentii Beria. Sudoplatov described in detail how he withstood his own interrogation by his former colleagues, who employed all sorts of pressure to extract a false confession from him:

> I've learned the main thing from the investigative materials of our intelligence agents who were arrested in 1937–38 (I looked through their dossiers in 1941, when I proposed to Beria the release from prison of secret agents experienced in work and struggle against enemies overseas): even if your fate is predetermined, the only way to preserve your dignity and a clean name is to deny all crimes that are attributed to you as long as you can.[51]

As to what the "work" of extracting confessions entailed, he clarified: "During interrogations, I was not beaten, but I was deprived [of] sleep. The brigades of young officers-investigators, who worked in shifts, repeated one and only one question until five o'clock in the morning: 'Do you admit your participation in treacherous plans and actions against Beria?'"[52] Sudoplatov learned these survival tactics from his mentor, the high-ranking Chekist and leading undercover operative Sergei Shpigel′glas, who organized several high-profile assassinations of Stalin's political opponents. In case of imprisonment, Shpigel′glas recommended to his intelligence agents the following:

> Stop answering questions gradually, gradually stop eating food, and reject on a daily basis a part of the meals without declaring a hunger strike: it is guaranteed that in two to three weeks you will fall prostrate. Then comes the full rejection of all food. After a while, the prison doctor will come over and pronounce a diagnosis: exhaustion, followed by hospitalization and force-feeding.[53]

Shums′kyi could not have known about Shpigel′glas's suggestions, but he employed some of the same methods of resistance when he was arrested. However, he was not silent, and he communicated his actions to his interrogators clearly. For example, he announced his intention to go on a hunger strike and wrote protests to party, state leaders, and police leaders, among others.

At first, Shums′kyi's resistance bore little fruit. By order of the Collegium of the OGPU of the USSR, the decision was made to place Shums′kyi "into the prison labor camp for ten years," beginning on 13 May 1933. "Put the case into the archive," the judgment stated, meaning that the decision was final.[54] However, something got in the way of the execution of this judgment. On 10 September 1933, it was postponed pending "a special instruction" by the court. The basis for this development was a protest from the senior assistant of the prosecutor of the Supreme Court of the USSR for Special Affairs (the supervisory body overseeing the OGPU, which later became the NKVD), Ruben Katanian.[55] Unfortunately, if the text of this protest survived, it has not been possible to locate it in the archives. This text would likely confirm the reason Shums′kyi's removal to prison was delayed in Moscow. As is evident from later delays in his case, and the eventual commutation of his prison sentence in 1935 (discussed below), the delay occurred because the court took into account the absence of a confession from Shums′kyi, as well as his broader vigorous protests on the illegality of his arrest.

On 28 September 1933, the anticipated "special instruction" was made by Iakaŭ Ahranaŭ, deputy to Genrikh Yagoda, chief of the OGPU, and on 4 October of that same year, Shums′kyi was sent with a special escort from Moscow to Suzdal for political solitary confinement. Later, he would be sent to Popov Island near Kem, before finding himself in Solovki, where he would be kept in an isolation cell in the Kremlin special detention facility reserved primarily for prominent political prisoners.

Semen Pidhainyi, who was also destined for the "land of suffering and despair," as the Solovki camps have been called, wrote in his memoirs about Shums′kyi: "I met him in 1933, actually not on the Solovki Islands themselves, but in the so-called hallway of Solovki—on Popov Island, where there was a port called Moresplav. ... Shums′kyi experienced the 'political regime,' but he was closely guarded." Other interesting details are contained in Pidhainyi's memoirs. For example, Shums′kyi could have spoken to the other prisoners, but he expressed no interest in doing so: "He barely spoke to prisoners, even to the prominent former party activists, and expressed [the] opinion that they, apparently, really were counterrevolutionaries."[56] According to Pidhainyi, Shums′kyi was sent from Moresplav to Moscow with a special escort. They never met again.

Indeed, Shums′kyi did not sign falsified confessions and did not stop making vigorous protests denouncing the inconsistent nature of the investigators' attempts to attribute to him actions that were not his. The lack of confession put a spoke in the wheel of the usual process of arrest and execution, not only through the court system but with the Chekists as well. They were forced to take it into account when further pursuing his case. Aiming to collect some additional evidence of Shums′kyi's "crimes," they took him to Ukraine, to Kharkiv, and later to Moscow. Shums′kyi complained about this in a letter to Vsevolod Merkulov, the people's commissar of state security for the USSR: "First Yagoda and Molchanov, then Balyts′kyi ... tried to set up a 'big case.' But all their investigative red tape led them nowhere, although they managed to discredit me in the eyes of the C[entral] C[ommittee] of the party and achieved my exclusion from the party."[57]

Shums'kyi appealed to the leading party bodies and separate leaders, beginning with Stalin.[58] Shums'kyi's colleagues also wrote appeals of this kind, but these were mostly ineffective. This is partly because his colleagues made their appeals either at their trial or from prison only after they had confessed to their crimes under interrogation. The Soviet leadership sometimes reviewed these appeals, but they were rarely successful. The Seliavkin affair was an exception: that case, as we will see, was reviewed in the small window in 1934 after the purge had subsided and Sergei Kirov had been assassinated, when some party and state figures had their fabricated charges dropped. For the most part, confessions under interrogation remained the strongest piece of evidence for Chekists, the courts, and the political leadership during the waves of repression in the 1930s. A confession usually established the guilt of the criminal in perpetuity, regardless of any later change of mind by the convicted person or the scaling back of repression or the reestablishment of more stringent rules of evidence in the prosecution of political suspects once the waves of repression had subsided.

Shums'kyi was able to avoid this scenario of establishing his guilt not only by employing the survival tactics of Sudoplatov and others under interrogation, but by undertaking an enduring resistance and broader protest campaign against his arrest from 1933 to his death in 1946. This campaign was successful in keeping him alive so long because he understood the type of case that was being made against him and focused his attention on identifying its weaknesses during the interrogations and in his letters to Soviet officials. We know that these officials considered his criticisms, which, as Shums'kyi anticipated, at least caused delays in his case's progress. Shums'kyi understood immediately what the Chekists were doing in escalating the charges against him. They initially sought to extract from his Borotbyst party colleagues any information on their supposed attempted sabotage or counterrevolutionary politics. Only then did they escalate to charges of attempting "to create anti-Soviet conspiratorial structures" that allegedly aimed to overthrow the Bolshevik authorities and organize foreign intervention.

A typical example of this escalation process begins with the *ochnaia stavka* between Shums´kyi and Bei-Orlovs´kyi that took place on 17 May 1933, soon after Shums´kyi's arrest. In this meeting, interrogator Henrikh Liushkov, having received confirmation of a meeting between Bei-Orlovs´kyi and Shums´kyi in Leningrad in 1929, asked Bei-Orlovs´kyi: "Did you say anything to Shums´kyi about your disagreement with the decision of the plenum of the [Central Committee of the] CPWU on the declaration of the Shums´kyist group?" The exchange proceeded:

Bei-Orlovs´kyi: I did.

Question to Shums´kyi: Do you confirm this?

Shums´kyi: I don't remember.

Question to Bei-Orlovs´kyi: What was Shums´kyi's answer to that?

Bei-Orlovs´kyi: He told me that individual appeals should be made, not group ones, and also that strong language should be used, and that the CPWU's activity should be improved through a renewal of its membership.

Question to Shums´kyi: Do you confirm this?

Shums´kyi: I do not object [to] it, but I do not remember such a conversation.

Question to Bei-Orlovs´kyi: Did you relay Shums´kyi's thoughts to the group of Turians´kyi and others?

Bei-Orlovs´kyi: I did relay them.

Question to Bei-Orlovs´kyi: Was it Shums´kyi's directive?

Bei-Orlovs´kyi: Since Shums´kyi was not a leader of the CPWU, let Shums´kyi himself comment on it.[59]

The underlying message of Liushkov's question is clear: since Shums´kyi gave a "directive," it was he who was mainly responsible for the political split in the CPWU. From Leonid Lytvyns´kyi's transcript of the interrogation from 23 August 1933, one also sees Shums´kyi playing a crucial role in the split of the CPWU. By doing so, he supposedly "cruelly stabbed [the] working class in the back, as well as all laboring people of western Ukraine in their struggle against Petliura-Polish fascism."[60]

The 5 June 1933 interrogation of Serhii Vikul provides evidence of the next escalation of charges against Shums´kyi. It contains the statement that, during Shums´kyi's diplomatic service in Poland, he allegedly contacted the Polish Socialist Party and, through it, the Polish Military Organization (PMO). He strove to "unite the forces of the Transdnieper (Zadniprovia) and Halychyna counterrevolution," and he encouraged Mykhailo Hrushevs´kyi to come back to Ukraine for the purpose of "leading the counterrevolution in Ukraine."[61]

In their attempts to discredit Shums´kyi, the Chekists repeatedly used the story of the Borotbysts joining the CP(b)U. The director of the publishing house Rukh and head of the *Ukrainian Soviet Encyclopedia*, Anton Bilen´kyi-Berezyns´kyi (who became a Chekist informant and provocateur), stated in his interrogation of 16 April 1933 that Borotbysts had joined the CP(b)U "to pursue the struggle for an independent Ukraine," and that Shums´kyi played "a leading role in it."[62] Now all the "insidious" intentions of the Borotbysts, headed by Shums´kyi, were supposed to reach their crescendo. Finally, the former secretary of the Communist Union of Youth of Western Ukraine (and, before his arrest, director of the state publishing house Molodyi bil´shovyk [Young Bolshevik]), Mykola Hrytsai, in a transcript of interrogation on 27 December 1933, accused Shums´kyi and his colleagues (Maksymovych, Turians´kyi, and others) of the creation of the "Moscow Center" of the organization. This center allegedly stayed in touch with some of the "Berlin leadership of the UMO," from which the latest instructions on organizing terror were received.[63]

The question remains, against whom would this supposed terror be directed? This climax of the Chekist escalation of the UMO fantasy was not as sophisticated as its previous elements. The Chekists proposed to Hrytsai that he sign the following confession: "Simultaneous to our preparation of terrorist acts against the leadership of the Communist Party of Ukraine—P. P. Postyshev, V. A. Balyts´kyi, and V. Ia. Chubar, the Moscow c[ounterrevolutionary] center marked Com[rade] Stalin as a target for assassination."[64]

After listening to and reading all these delusional statements, Shums´kyi behaved differently from his former allies. Unlike them, he did not protest his innocence at first only to quickly cave to the pressure of interrogation. He never cooperated with interrogators or responded to their attempts to blackmail him. Instead, he systematically and firmly required evidence be presented to him confirming his crimes. The Chekists had only the so-called queen of evidence in their arsenal: the confessions of intimidated and broken former Borotbysts (and not only Borotbysts). Some who had confessed believed, naively, that they would be able to "buy" their freedom by making false confessions; most of them were dead by 1937. Shums´kyi considered these testimonies to be insufficient proof of any wrongdoing and continued to ask for "real evidence" as he continued his struggle for freedom. In January 1934, a review of Shums´kyi's case (no. 112510) began in a court session of the Collegium of the OGPU. But the investigators did not review his case with thoughts of ending it; rather, they now tried to incriminate Shums´kyi in a new case.

In April 1934, frustrated by Shums´kyi's resistance to the UMO charges, Chekists dropped them and subjected him to a new round of interrogations to prove his guilt on new charges. He learned that he was no longer accused in the UMO case. Now, along with Mykhailo Poloz, he was made a participant in the so-called National Bloc, which was accused of planning to assassinate the head of the CP(b)U, Pavel Postyshev, and had connections with Polish-German interventionists. During this round of interrogations, Shums´kyi behaved more confidently than he had in 1933—even arrogantly at certain points. On 11 April 1934, when asked by the acting head of the Secret Political Department of the GPU (USSR), Borys Kozel´s´kyi, whether he could testify to his counterrevolutionary activities, Shums´kyi replied: "I did not commit any counterrevolutionary activities. Contrary to your claims, I did not belong to any counterrevolutionary bloc or counterrevolutionary organization, and I refuse to discuss my belonging to any of them. Please, ask me concrete questions—and I will answer them in a concrete, concise way."[65]

Later, Shums´kyi would learn that it was his former friend Poloz who had testified against him. Shums´kyi insisted on distinguishing between accusations of holding mistaken (former) political viewpoints, of which he and other proponents of

Shums´kyism could theoretically be guilty—given the criticism of Shums´kyism by the party in 1926–27—and accusations of setting up conspiratorial networks to struggle against Stalin's regime. On 13 May 1934, Shums´kyi wrote an appeal to the Central Committee of the ACP(b) in Moscow, in which he admitted his mistakes in defending Khvyl´ovyi, but underlined that he was never a counterrevolutionary. Even after August, when Shums´kyi was sent to the Solovki Islands, where he was kept in the Kremlin isolation wing, he continued his protest. On 26 November 1934, he wrote a letter to Stalin:

> Dear Comrade Stalin! I do not know if my letters reach you, but I do not lose hope of being heard and thus turn to you again. ... In April 1934, I was sent to Moscow, where I had the following conversation:
>
> "So, do you think that you are serving the sentence for no reason?"
>
> "Yes," I answered, "and I think that it is about time for the investigation to come to the same conclusion."
>
> "Well, no. We have summoned you here to 'expose' you in your crimes."
>
> This statement clearly was a shock to me: they were "exposing" me after almost a year had gone by and after my expulsion from the party and my conviction. For this purpose, I was sent to Kharkiv, where I was astounded even more to learn that I had now been accused of belonging not to the UMO, but to the National Bloc. "You are not accused of belonging to the UMO; it turns out that you were working on creating the counterrevolutionary organization National Bloc," said the investigator Comrade Sokolov. A chief of the camp, Comrade Alekseev, also told me that I was convicted not for the UMO. I asked him if I could read my sentence, and, by the way, I still have not read it. I underline this circumstance because last year I was told that I had been convicted of participating in the UMO, and I was expelled from the party because of it.[66]

This fragment of the letter shows us that, even after Shums´kyi was sentenced, there was a search for new evidence of his guilt, or at least a new fantasy of his crimes, considering his vigorous protest and desire to disprove the false accusations against him. It was done in a way bizarre yet typical for the judicial system at that time: he was convicted on charges of leading a counterrevolutionary organization. Once the charges looked unlikely to stand up to any examination, they were withdrawn, and new ones—participation in the creation of the mythical National Bloc—were put forward.

In the same letter to Stalin, Shums´kyi also showed convincingly that the evidence against him was concocted. He gave the example of Poloz, who had declared that Shums´kyi was affiliated with the National Bloc based on the fact that he allegedly had told Poloz about his connections to Germans and Poles. Refuting this statement, Shums´kyi pointed out that there was no such meeting with Poloz, since, on the day of the alleged meeting, Shums´kyi had been in Moscow, while Poloz had been in another city. Shums´kyi continued:

> At the end, Poloz's testimony was shown to me. I was sent to a camp again, where I met him. Naturally, my first question was whether he had actually given this testimony. Through his tears and hysterical moaning, I gathered that he "had signed something like this." On the same day, I wrote to the investigator about this conversation in order to remind him of the quality of the "expository" materials (a copy of the letter is attached). It is out of the question that the GPU fellows were unaware of the nature and worth of this nonsense, but it is not in their interest to defend me. After all, the GPU does not work to defend people who are devoid of the trust of the party. After the party banned me from the ordinary bodies, the GPU saw me as the enemy. And if it is about an enemy—then one has to "handle" it with the utmost "passion." Maksymovych and Poloz's slander of Shums´kyi—that was fine. The more they lied, the better.[67]

Not for the first time, Shums´kyi appealed to Stalin's own distrust of his colleagues, even in the secret police, in the hope of a sympathetic hearing:

> But I am not an enemy of the Communist Party. ... I have been charged with all these plots against the Soviet authorities, but I have never dreamed of it and I did not undertake any conspiracies against the Communist Party. ... What is happening to me makes me think that people are striving to accuse me at any price, and, moreover, they are trying to accuse me of doing horrible things. If the case with the UMO has not stuck, then—take him to the National Bloc; if there is no chance of handling the situation in the right way, then let's try to manage it by hook or by crook, but without fail, always blame [Shums´kyi].[68]

Before casting doubt on the leadership of the secret police in his letter to Stalin, Shums′kyi attempted to discredit Poloz's evidence to that same leadership. He wrote to GPU head Borys Kozel′s′kyi a few months earlier:

> You have read Poloz's testimonies—they naturally evoked a sharp indignation from my side. And, since Poloz enjoyed the reputation of an honest person among the people that knew him, I could not believe that he was involved in such a dirty and tricky provocation. In other words, I thought that the "testimonies" that were read to me were an insinuation and I was just being blackmailed. But after my meeting with Poloz, I must give you my apologies. The short conversation with him resolved my doubts: Poloz confirmed to me that he "signed something of that sort," asking me not to come to any hurried conclusions until I had listened [to] his explanations about what had happened. But his attempts to soften the abomination of what he had done by appealing to the circumstances, the conditions, the situation, and other "torments of the creative mind" [*taiemnytsi tvorchykh muk*] were unconvincing. After all, it is not so important whether the person became a scoundrel consciously and purposely—that is, according to their own inner convictions—or if they became so under the duress of external circumstances. What is important is the fact in question.[69]

Neither letter had any immediate effect. During his stay in Solovki at this time, Shums′kyi understood that he had to struggle not only for his political survival but also for his life—literally. Generally, he was not a man of robust health, and he eventually became ill, started to lose his teeth, and developed paralysis in his legs. These were only some of the difficult consequences of imprisonment in Solovki. Nevertheless, Shums′kyi continued to request that his case be reviewed, bombarding the authorities with his letters.

Shums′kyi eventually achieved a result, keeping up his faith in his protest campaign. But it would not be the result he had sought. Rather than being overturned as he had hoped, on 10 December 1935, by order of the Special Council of the NKVD of the USSR, Shums′kyi's case was reviewed and his prison sentence commuted to exile in Krasnoiarsk for the rest of the term. Shums′kyi's protest alone did not result in the commutation of his sentence. It was also the timing of his protest that mattered, in that he continued it after the purge of 1933 had subsided, in a new atmosphere where his complaints about the illegal conduct of police and ludicrous nature of the (changing) charges against him became problematic for police and prosecutors alike. Even during the height of the purge in 1933, party and state figures began to express some concern about how the secret police conducted itself, its scope of power in the system, and the effects of mass repression on society and the economy in general. Their arrest of more than half a million people, many of them ordinary peasants, for resisting collectivization or escaping its consequences (mass famine) only accelerated the crashing of the economy.

As early as May 1933, Stalin issued a secret directive to the OGPU to limit the mass arrests of peasants and those charged with minor crimes. By 1934 he had further scaled back the purge, as the catastrophe in the countryside subsided, stating in the press that he shared the concerns of state officials and issuing numerous party directives insisting that the police follow the rules of "socialist legality" in arrest procedures.[70] These included the requirement to seek judicial approval for arrests based on evidence, not simply arbitrarily imprison and shoot people. This public shift gave impetus to major political figures who had been arrested in 1933 to now write to Stalin from prison, seeking release on the basis that the OGPU had fabricated charges against them and used illegal methods (torture) to extract false confessions. Stalin and the party investigated some of these claims against the OGPU and, in some cases, cited them as examples of police misconduct in party or state directives, ordering the cases to be dropped and the convictions overturned.

The Seliavkin affair is the best example. Police initially arrested O. I. Seliavkin, the highly decorated former head of the air defense administration of the People's Commissariat for Heavy Industry, for selling state secrets to foreign powers. Stalin approved a Politburo commission to investigate Selivakin's claims against the police. The commission confirmed his claims, punished the offending Chekists, and ordered that Seliavkin's conviction and sentence of ten years' hard labor be overturned.[71] This push for "socialist legality" reached its zenith in a resolution issued by the Sovnarkom (USSR) on 17 June 1935, "On the Procedure for making arrests," which stipulated that "the NKVD [the OGPU's successor] can conduct arrests only with the consent of the relevant prosecutor" and made it much more difficult for the NKVD to arrest party and state figures, requiring it to secure permission from the relevant heads of the people's commissariats, departments, and party committees.[72]

It was common for these rules for arrest and conviction to be relaxed before the onset of a purge (the above resolution was rescinded in the Great Terror in 1937) and then to be reasserted afterward by the party as a way of slowing the arrests. The state's repressive police structures remained intact, and Stalin continued to apply them when he needed. But these rules significantly reduced the scope and slowed the pace of political repression. Mass arrests in the USSR fell from 510,000 in 1933 to 205,000 in 1934, and arrests on charges of counterrevolutionary crimes like Shums′kyi's saw a huge reduction in this same period, from 283,000 to 90,000.[73]

The assassination of the Leningrad party leader Sergei Kirov in December 1934 did not immediately alter the downward trajectory in raw arrest numbers and overall repression, but Stalin and the leadership made quick use of Kirov's murder to launch a more targeted repression against opponents and "untrustworthy" elements of the population. In 1935, Stalin began the Moscow show trials against Grigorii Zinov′ev, Lev Kamenev, and a host of other figures who were convicted of conspiring to murder Kirov. More broadly, Stalin, fearing the nexus of rising international tensions and domestic unrest, arrested members of "unreliable" ethnicities he suspected would assist their host nations in the event of a potential war (for example ethnic Poles living in western Ukraine).[74] The review of other unlawful arrests and convictions, like Seliavkin's, at the highest party levels (Politburo) were also scuttled.

This is what makes the commutation of Shums′kyi's sentence in this period (December 1935) all the more remarkable and illuminating for the understanding of this chaotic time when repression continued but—as is evident in the Sovnarkom order of June 1935—had to be conducted in a more complex environment and restrained manner. Genrikh Yagoda, the chief of the NKVD of the USSR, which succeeded the OGPU as the secret police in

1934 as part of Stalin's shift toward "socialist legality," remained concerned well into 1935 about following the rules, particularly when it came to procuring evidence and conducting proper interrogations to produce confessions. Even as repression ramped up toward the end of the year, the NKVD still had to work more closely with the judiciary to first make arrests and then produce more sufficient evidence to secure convictions. These new requirements, even when they were not widely enforced, brought some transparency to shoddy police work and fabricated cases, which were potentially embarrassing for the police.

By late 1935, Yagoda was increasingly frustrated with his regional NKVD heads for failing to follow the rules of "socialist legality," as he had instructed in a 1934 directive. Yagoda issued another directive in August 1935 to reiterate this point, four months before Shums'kyi's commutation. He was furious with the NKVD leaders in the constituent republics of the USSR for sending cases to court or special tribunals with little evidence (although, because most people confessed, such evidence-free cases were rare). A lack of confession clearly indicated to Yagoda that Chekists had failed to conduct even the most basic elements of an investigation (visiting the crime scene, taking witness statements, etc.) before arresting suspects. He was particularly concerned as Chekists were sending interrogation reports to prosecutors as evidence, sans confession, demonstrating not only their poor interrogation techniques but also the ludicrousness of the charges they had fabricated against the suspect. Yagoda was not opposed to fabrication—this remained the key tool of the secret police—but he perceived that a lack of confession underlined the poor quality of the fabrication, which was now evident to the judiciary.

Prosecutors simply returned many of these bad cases to the NKVD. Yagoda pointed to one such case in his directive. A certain Comrade Chilikindri, an "ordinary Trotskyite" accused of counterrevolutionary activity in Kazakhstan, conducted himself as Shums'kyi did under interrogation in 1934—confidently (even arrogantly) demanding concrete evidence of his crimes before commenting on the baseless accusation made against him. Yagoda reproduced fragments of the interrogation record in his directive as the most pertinent example of a clear enemy of the people, like

Shums´kyi, who could resist pressure to confess partly because of the "idiotic" interrogation style of the Chekists:

> **Chekist:** In response to the first question about a tight-knit Trotskyite counterrevolutionary group in the city of Semipalatinsk, you replied that this is "idle fantasy," but tell us about the fact, evidenced by these interrogations, of a dinner held on the anniversary of the October Revolution, which was actually held to gather monies [for counterrevolutionary activity]?
>
> **Chilikindri:** It would be useless to respond to your exceptionally idiotic question. ... Not having any evidence, you are forced to make baseless accusations about "investors" gathering for the anniversary of the Revolution. I suggest that these types of accusations only sully the reputation of the police.[75]

Like Chilikindri, Yagoda saw this as an "idiotic" interrogation, and he named and shamed the Chekist interrogator to the head of the secret police department of the Kazakhstan NKVD. But he reserved his greatest fury for the head himself, who signed the indictment against Chilikindri and passed his case on to prosecutors based on this interrogation.

Yagoda's directive helps us make sense of Shums´kyi's commutation in two ways. First, Chilikindri's case, that of an "ordinary Trotskyite," was embarrassing for police because they failed to secure a conviction from someone whom they "knew" to be an enemy. "Bad" cases like this one were sent without a confession either directly to prosecutors or to the Special Council of the NKVD. Under the new rules of "socialist legality" issued in 1935, however, prosecutors rarely progressed cases without a confession. Neither did the Special Council, which was now under scrutiny from its superior judicial body, the prosecutor of the Supreme Court of the USSR on Special Affairs. In fact, it is highly likely that the Special Council officially commuted Shums´kyi's sentence in 1935 due to the lack of a confession, based on the complaint from Ruben Katanian, a leading member of this superior body. Shums´kyi's deteriorating health (paralysis) may have also played a role in Katanian's decision, and perhaps Katanian expected that exile would placate Shums´kyi and stop him from protesting to party and state leaders about his case. Of course, Shums´kyi protested ever more loudly (see the next chapter), and the embarrassment, especially for the NKVD, only intensified.

Second, Yagoda's directive also helps us make sense of the critical importance of confession in progressing fabricated cases against high-ranking state and political figures in the 1933 purge. The year 1934 saw a small window for some of these cases to be reviewed by the party, as with the Seliavkin affair, but this window closed with Kirov's assassination in December of that year. By January 1935, reviews of other cases were discontinued.[76] In each of those cases, the defendant had confessed but subsequently retracted their confession at trial or in prison. None held out as Shums´kyi did from the beginning of his arrest. This seems to be the key distinction (at least in judicial terms) that explains Shums´kyi's commutation.

The best example of this distinction is the Markevich affair. A. M. Markevich, a deputy to the people's commissar for agriculture (USSR), and forty of his colleagues were convicted of "sabotage and spying" for Japan in 1933. The OGPU fabricated this case similarly to the UMO case in 1933. Instead of Shums´kyi's spying for the USSR's western enemy in Poland, Markevich supposedly was spying for its eastern enemy in Japan. Markevich and all forty suspects confessed to these charges under interrogation, though some claimed, at trial and later from prison in letters to Stalin, that they were innocent and only confessed to these crimes under duress, having been tortured by the police. The Markevich case, like Seliavkin's, was reviewed by a special Politburo commission under Stalin's orders. By late 1934, it looked as if the convictions might be overturned. But only two weeks after Kirov's assassination, in mid-January 1935, Stalin scuttled the review and ordered that Markevich, who was awaiting the findings of the commission in a Moscow prison cell, be returned to the prison camp where he was held previously. He was shot in 1938.

This decision was undoubtedly part of the central leadership's broader knee-jerk reaction of arrests and other measures in response to Kirov's assassination.[77] However, the key distinction between the Shums´kyi and Markevich cases remains. Because Shums´kyi never confessed, the issue was not the methods by which police gained a confession and whether these were problematic for the strength of the case against him as expectations of police conduct changed. The central leadership always understood Shums′kyi as an enemy, but his refusal to confess to any charges demonstrably tempered their conduct toward him and was the major reason why they did not kill him until 1946. The fact that the police were unable to elicit a confession from Shums′kyi reflected badly on them, which is why they kept on fabricating new cases against him in 1934 and, as we will see in the following chapters, in 1937 and 1940. The NKVD consistently sought to silence Shums′kyi in exile, especially because he outlined the shoddiness of the NKVD's police work in his case in his letters to political leaders, which, as we will see, embarrassed the NKVD terribly and complicated their attempts to progress his case.

Shums′kyi understood that his refusal to confess and his broader protest were the only things keeping him alive. His earlier experience of making the "confession" that Lazar Kaganovich demanded of him had taught him that confession, even when made strategically, only accelerated the case against a defendant. The fate of his colleagues who confessed in the UMO case must have confirmed this truth. He now launched his protest in exile with more urgency and fanaticism as he considered the commutation of his prison sentence a vindication of his resistance and proof of his innocence; thus, anything short of his release and political rehabilitation was unacceptable—including the exile order itself. So began the next stage of Shums′kyi's protest which took the form of rolling hunger strikes that, while keeping him alive, further damaged his frail health and threatened to kill him.

Oleksandr Shums´kyi before his departure for the diplomatic appointment in Warsaw, 1921. Photograph from the Shums´kyi file in the Sectoral State Archive of the Security Services of Ukraine (HDA SBU), f. 65, spr. S-4472, t. 2, konv. Reproduced by permission.

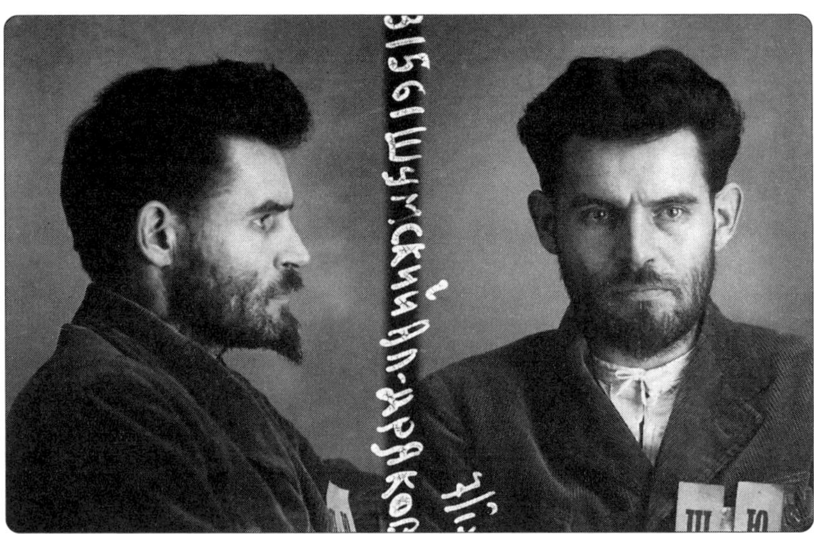

Oleksandr Shums′kyi after his arrest in Leningrad, 13 May 1933. Photograph from the Shums′kyi file in the Sectoral State Archive of the Security Services of Ukraine (HDA SBU), f. 65, spr. S-4472, t. 2, konv. Reproduced by permission.

Chapter Five

EXILE, SURVIVAL, WAR, AND "FREEDOM"

Despite his renewed protests while in exile, Shums'kyi did not succeed in having his conviction overturned or in securing his political rehabilitation before the party. Instead, he would be re-arrested in 1937 and in 1940 on new charges—just as baseless as those in 1933—in Krasnoiarsk, where he was serving his term of exile. The paradox of Shums'kyi's journey in exile from 1935 to 1946 is that he was not convicted on these new charges, and, unlike so many of his associates who were rearrested, charged, and convicted at this time, he was not shot. The key factor keeping Shums'kyi alive was the interplay of his protest campaign (his letters to Soviet leaders, hunger strikes, and refusal to confess under interrogation) with the response from both the Krasnoiarsk branch of the NKVD, which arrested him, and the superiors of the Krasnoiarsk NKVD in Moscow, who ordered the arrest. This chapter explores this interplay to understand how Shums'kyi stayed alive while so many of his associates were shot during this time, either in prison while serving their terms for their 1933 convictions in the UMO and related cases, or after being rearrested and recharged, like Shums'kyi, while in exile or in Ukraine. Shums'kyi's survival cannot be understood without understanding their deaths, and vice versa.

On the train to Krasnoiarsk, Shums'kyi went on a hunger strike, demanding full political rehabilitation and release from exile. He arrived in Krasnoiarsk on 17 December 1935, with his health deteriorating sharply. On 20 December, Shums'kyi asked the head of the Krasnoiarsk NKVD to provide him with medical treatment, but this treatment was refused, ironically, on the basis that Shums′kyi's hunger strike was illegal. Shums′kyi lived at 43 Krasnaia Armiia Street in the house of the Polennikov family. The family had not been notified before his arrival. At this family's home, he continued his hunger strike, at first taking no liquids, then a few days later drinking water. He refused to eat any food for fifty-six days. On 8 January 1936, his wife, Ievdokiia Honcharenko, came to visit him. She wrote a letter to the authorities about her husband's hunger strike and included with her submission a statement from the owner of the home:

> I, A. G. Polennikova, declare that, on the evening of 17 December 1935, in my absence, NKVD officers brought a citizen unknown to me to my apartment and placed him in a vacant room of my apartment. When I came home and learned that the emplaced resident was sick and lying in bed, I prepared food and brought it with my husband to the new resident's room. But he, in a very agitated manner, protested our offer to feed him and urged my husband and me to pick up the food we had brought and take it out of his room. After calming down a bit, he explained to us that he had been on hunger strike since 11 December, as he had gone on a hunger strike to protest his exile, and asked us not to offer him any food. Later, seeing his suffering, I offered several times at least a little milk to drink, but he flatly refused and eventually asked me not to talk to him about food at all. He only asked me to give him a mug of boiled water in the morning and in the evening, which he drank. He also asked me to take out his bladder excretions, which I did every two days, and asked me to buy him a central newspaper. Sometimes he complained that he had a bad stomachache, because he had not had a bowel movement for a few days before the hunger strike and his stomach was still not emptied. He needed an enema and a vessel to help him in this. I suggested he call a doctor. But he refused this as well as my other suggestions to help him. For example, he did not wash during this time because he could not get out of bed, and when I proposed assisting him with washing, he would refuse, saying that he did not want to trouble me. So, from the day of his arrival he lay without getting out of bed, without changing either bed linen or underwear, sometimes moaning at night and complaining of fever.[1]

On 9 January 1936, Honcharenko wrote a second submission specifically addressed to the head of the Krasnoiarsk NKVD, K. A. Pavlov, requesting assistance in placing Shums′kyi in the hospital. On 13 January, she wrote to him again, saying that she was forced to leave Krasnoiarsk, not wanting to bear the consequences of her husband's hunger strike, and that she would be returning with her son, whom she wanted to show either "a living or dead father."[2] On 14 January, she left for Moscow, and Shums´kyi continued his hunger strike.

On 17 January 1936, Shums´kyi sent a telegram to the Central Committee of ACP(b) and Stalin (along with a copy to Genrikh Yagoda), stating:

> Two arguments were put forward against my behavior. ... First: "You were free and therefore your hunger strike did not make sense." One can refer to exile as freedom only as an evil, mocking prison joke. The freedom of the exile was the freedom of a dog on a chain. But for me the point was not freedom, but rehabilitation—the removal of the slanderous accusations attached to me (of belonging to the UMO, etc.). Without the removal of these charges, I did not need any freedom. ...
>
> Second: "You considered yourself a communist and you went on a hunger strike. After all, this was a protest against the party. The party was against suicide, and the hunger strike was suicide, and so on." They said I should write and ask for a review. Yes, I wrote and asked. I had written for two and a half years and waited patiently. However, all my letters disappeared as if into a hole, and my requests went unanswered. And I was a communist—an honest man, portrayed on the basis of vile slander in the eyes of public opinion as a swindler. ... So what did I have to do: exhibit Tolstoy's nonresistance to evil or to continue to seek rehabilitation at any cost? Of course, the second. But if the requests did not work, then I had one remedy left—my life. And I had to take it. After all, with these slanderous accusations, I was thrown into the camp of the enemies of communism. Communists considered me an enemy, and enemies used my name as an instrument against communism. Of course, I had to remove my name from the list of enemies of communism, to take it away at the cost of my life, to erase it with my own blood.

At the end of the telegram, Shums´kyi addressed Stalin directly: "Only your involvement in my question will save me from ultimate death. That is why I have asked you, Comrade Stalin, to intervene in my situation and give it a moment's attention."[3]

Local Chekists were watching Shums´kyi. On 27 January 1936, the head of the Krasnoiarsk NKVD, K. A. Pavlov, sent a telegram to his superior in Moscow, G. A. Molchanov, the head of the secret political division of the Main Directorate of State Security (GUGB) in the NKVD. It stated, "Shums′kyi has been on hunger strike for 47 days, his condition is extremely serious. ... His hands are cold, blue, almost inactive. He has not taken water for two days. ... There are obvious signs of death in the coming days."[4]

On 30 January 1936, Shums′kyi sent a new telegram to Stalin and Yagoda (he dictated the text of it to an NKVD officer): "My request is for the appointment of a commission to review my case in order to drop the false accusations attributed to me and give me a hearing as soon as my health allows, and cancel the NKVD decision on repression and send me to Moscow for treatment. Everything I do will be to the benefit of the party."[5] Shums′kyi went on to tell the officer:

> I will wait for an answer to my request. Whatever the answer, that will be the end. I feel like I will live another two days. Moscow might not be able to grant my request, but the commission might issue a decision. I would agree to eat if the appropriate conditions were created for me—to be hospitalized and after two to three days of food, I would go to Moscow.[6]

Shums′kyi soon received a telegram from the Central Committee of the ACP(b) in Moscow asking him to end the hunger strike and begin working on his case for political rehabilitation. On 1 February 1936, he sent a telegram to Yagoda in which he said that he was ending his hunger strike and, like in the 30 January telegram, expressed hope that in two or three days he would be sent to Moscow for treatment. However, it soon became clear that he was not going anywhere. On 9 and 20 February, and on 11 March, he sent new telegrams to the NKVD and the Central Committee of the ACP(b) asking for progress on his move to Moscow. The answer was silence. But the silence was telling.

It is likely that those who fabricated Shums′kyi's case understood by this stage that with only a little more effort from Shums′kyi, it would become clear that he had been imprisoned, in fact, without reason. Even one of the main initiators of the UMO case, the head of the NKVD of the USSR, Vsevolod Balyts′kyi, was getting nervous. On 7 March 1936, he sent investigative materials on Shums´kyi's counterrevolutionary activities from Kyiv to Yagoda in Moscow. This evidence against Shums´kyi was extracted from often violent interrogations of suspects in 1933–34, and Shums´kyi had already been convicted on it. The list of people who gave testimony was lengthy—about thirty people—so Balyts´kyi remained defiant on Shums´kyi's guilt; there was too much evidence that Shums´kyi was dangerous and could not be granted freedom. In addition, admitting his mistakes was not at all in Balyts´kyi's repertoire, and it seemed inexpedient to analyze the previously resolved case for a second time.

On 9 April 1936, in protest of his continued detainment in Krasnoiarsk, Shums´kyi again went on a hunger strike. His health had deteriorated significantly from his previous strike, so the probability he would not survive this time was greatly increased. As a result, the NKVD ordered that he be taken to a hospital. In September of the same year, broader changes took place in the leadership structure of the security services—changes that would affect Shums´kyi's case. Nikolai Yezhov, a party official, replaced Yagoda as people's commissar for internal affairs (NKVD). The Politburo of the Central Committee of the ACP(b) decided that Yezhov would remain part-time secretary of the Central Committee and chairman of the Party Control Commission (KPK), but "nine-tenths of his time was given to the NKVD."[7] Yezhov quickly derided his predecessor, expressing dissatisfaction with Yagoda's "departmental considerations" in avoiding party control over police activities and, specifically in relation to cases like Shums´kyi's, in engaging in the widespread falsification and fabrication of criminal cases.[8]

Yezhov offered this criticism in public at the March 1937 plenum of the Central Committee of the ACP(b), where he continued:

> I must say outright that there was this practice: before the protocol was signed by the accused, it was first inspected by the investigator, then passed on to his superiors, and important protocols even reached the people's commissar. The people's commissar issued instructions, said that it was necessary to write this, instead of that, and then the protocol was allowed to be signed by the accused.[9]

For Shums´kyi, Yezhov's criticism of his predecessor signaled a new opportunity to protest, to begin a new struggle. In October, he wrote a letter to Yezhov and Lazar Kaganovich:

> I did not want to write about such things. It will work out, I thought; these are trivialities. But there was no way out. ... I was in the hospital. Polyneuritis, other complications. The doctors insisted that I should be transferred from a difficult hospital situation to sanatorium conditions with mud treatments and other things that the hospital did not have. If not this [transfer], then at least they would have me transferred to a quiet home environment. ...
>
> The question of my family's moving here was brought up. But, given living conditions in Krasnoiarsk, this meant that not only would I not get the "quiet home environment" that doctors recommended, but my family would also be deprived of their own little corner in Saratov. ... On top of that, my son got himself into trouble. The boy was expelled from school (my wife's telegram). I am writing about this because I do not think that this harassment is based on a political directive. But it cannot be resolved without your intervention.[10]

Unfortunately, the change in police leadership did not assist Shums´kyi with his family matters, treatment conditions, or political rehabilitation. In fact, this change had the opposite effect. Although Yezhov publicly condemned Yagoda's practices, he would continue—indeed, expand them—in the Great Terror, under Stalin's direction, to levels not seen in modern history. At the height of the Great Terror, from early 1937 to the end of 1938, more than 700,000 people were executed, almost all on fabricated charges, and more than that were sent to forced labor camps known as gulags.[11] The plethora of literature on the Great Terror discourages any further summary here. What is important to understand is that the Great Terror, at least in Ukraine and with regard to many Ukrainians wherever they were, was, in many ways, a continuation and an intensification of the purge of 1933. Many of those who had survived the earlier purge were targeted again in 1937 and 1938—including Shums´kyi and many of his associates. Specifically, in early 1937, the NKVD of the USSR opened a case on "underground counterrevolutionary activities among Ukrainian exiles and the connection of the Ukrainian exiles with the counterrevolutionary underground of Ukraine."[12] Among the suspects were activists from Ukraine serving sentences of prison or exile in Krasnoiarsk, Saratov, Omsk, and Kursk. Shums´kyi, of course, was again in the focus of the Chekists' gaze. In April 1937, an NKVD document addressed to Krasnoiarsk, Saratov, and Omsk stated:

> We suggest that instructions for underground work probably come primarily from O. Ia. Shums´kyi, a member of the UMO center, who is serving a term of exile in the city of Krasnoiarsk. According to our information, through Shums´kyi's wife—Honcharenko (who lives in the city of Saratov)—Shums´kyi is connected to members of the Ukrainian counterrevolutionary underground. The UNKVD [NKVD branch office] of the Saratov Oblast should establish a diligent intelligence surveillance of Honcharenko, taking it into active development, and further inform the fourth department of the Main Directorate of State Security and the interested bodies about all cases of Honcharenko's departure from Saratov.[13]

Ievdokiia Honcharenko, who was in exile in Saratov (she lived on 10 Gimnazicheskaia Street, apartment 1, and worked as a commodity expert in the Saratov branch of the Association of State Book and Magazine Publishers), was arrested on 18 October 1937 by the Saratov NKVD. Her arrest warrant was signed by the assistant to the Saratov NKVD head, major of state security Aleksandr Slavatinskii.[14]

According to the documents, Honcharenko neither pled guilty nor caved to pressure from the interrogators to implicate her husband in any criminal activity. She was accused of being a member of an "anti-Soviet Socialist-Revolutionary nationalist group," of spreading "counterrevolutionary slander," and of having ties to Ukrainian Socialist-Revolutionary nationalist elements convicted in the 1930 SVU case.[15] All this was enough for the court troika in Saratov to pass a resolution on the execution of Ievdokiia Honcharenko on 8 December 1937. On the same day, late in the evening, the sentence was carried out. Together with Honcharenko, the following people were convicted in this fabricated case: Iosyp Hermaize (who received ten years in the labor camps); and Natalia Kotsiubyns´ka, Hlib Doroshkevych, Petra Pal´ko, and Ol´ha Andriievs´ka (all shot).[16]

In the summer of 1937, another case against a so-called bourgeois-nationalist anti-Soviet organization of former Borotbysts arose in Ukraine, with Panas Liubchenko as its proclaimed leader.

In early August, the new head of the Ukrainian NKVD, Izrail′ Liapleŭski, informed Yezhov about the case in a special letter, emphasizing that the alleged organization's activities "went along the lines of creating and deploying a wide range of nationalist cadres, especially in the system of land institutions—the People's Commissariat for the Economy, the Sugar Trust... engaging in sabotage in various sectors of the economy, especially in agriculture, and creating terrorist groups to carry out terrorist attacks against party and government leaders."[17] A large number of UkrSSR party and state leaders were arrested and then repressed on charges of participating in the organization. Liubchenko, who was then head of the Ukrainian government (Sovnarkom), was accused of all sorts of counterrevolutionary crimes at the plenum of the Central Committee of the CP(b)U. He shot his wife and then himself during the break in the plenum meeting on 30 August 1937.[18] Stanisław Kosior, who chaired the plenum, saw this as confirmation that "we had dealt with the case correctly," and repressions continued.[19]

Shums′kyi was often mentioned in the forced testimonies of people who were involved in the Borotbyst case. Many of Shums′kyi's former colleagues criticized him again (and often did so in a rather brutal way) as a "nationalist-evader." Here we could mention, among others, Andrii Khvylia, longtime head of the Agitation and Propaganda Department of the Central Committee of the CP(b)U and, since 1933, deputy people's commissar for education of the UkrSSR; Oleksii Trylis′kyi, former chairman of the Odesa district executive committee and Vinnytsia district executive committee regional council, as well as former people's commissar for agriculture of the UkrSSR; and Todos Taran, editor of *Visti VUTsVK*.

Taran, for example, who was arrested on 13 August 1937, wrote a statement to Yezhov on 18 August in which he claimed that, in 1921, during the massive famine in the Soviet Union, Oleksandr Shums′kyi had gathered an "underground meeting of Borotbysts" in his apartment and proposed a plan for an armed uprising against Soviet power. Moreover, Shums′kyi "directly demanded that we disperse to the districts and begin an armed struggle against the proletarian dictatorship." According to Taran, after Shums′kyi's return from Warsaw, he, as the head of the Borotbyst underground, tried "with the help of Piłsudski to overthrow the Soviet government and to separate Soviet Ukraine from the USSR."[20]

The transcript of the *ochnaia stavka* between Oleksii Trylis′kyi and Todos Taran is preserved in the archives. Their conduct contrasts sharply with the way Shums′kyi behaved in confrontations. Trylis′kyi and Taran admitted that they took part in and even led an underground organization, which included Panas Liubchenko, Andrii Khvylia, and other former Borotbysts. They compliantly performed the roles assigned to them by their NKVD interrogators.[21] And this time, the so-called queen of evidence (confessions obtained under pressure) worked flawlessly. In addition, the testimony of Hryhorii Hryn′ko, former Borotbyst and people's commissar for finance of the USSR in 1930–37, arrested in August 1937, was used. He was convicted at the show trial of the so-called anti-Soviet right-wing Trotskyite bloc in Moscow in March 1938.

On 22 September 1937, the head of the third branch of the fourth department of the first division of the NKVD of the USSR, senior lieutenant of state security Ilia Edel′man (real name Iliushin), signed a report concerning Shums′kyi. The report stated that, according to the materials of the (fictitious) "Ukrainian Nationalist Organization," liquidated in 1937, "a number of new data were discovered on Shums′kyi's organizing role in intensifying the activities of the counterrevolutionary Borotbyst nationalist underground."[22] Based on a telegraph order of the NKVD of the USSR sent to the Krasnoiarsk NKVD dated 9 October 1937, Oleksandr Shums′kyi was arrested again on 15 October. He was transferred at that time to the Krasnoiarsk Prison Hospital from the Voskresensk Hospital, where he had been held since his previous hunger strike. When Moscow demanded that Shums′kyi be brought to the capital, the Krasnoiarsk NKVD reported that "due to illness (paralysis), [Shums′kyi] could not be interrogated and transferred to Moscow."[23]

Bogdan Kobulov, the head of the Operations Department in the Main Directorate of State Security (GUGB) of the NKVD in Moscow and a main driver in reopening Shums′kyi's case, was not deterred.[24] On 23 September 1938, he asked the deputy people's commissar for internal affairs, Lavrentii Beria, to present Shums′kyi's case at a meeting of the Military Collegium of the Supreme Court of the USSR—one of the highest judicial bodies in the Soviet Union, usually reserved for hearing cases of political figures. Beria's permission is dated 26 September. In October, the Collegium issued an indictment (one of the signatories of which was the USSR prosecutor Andrei Vyshinskii) that stated:

> The NKVD exposed and liquidated the Ukrainian anti-Soviet fascist organization that was preparing Ukraine's secession from the Soviet Union in a bloc with the right, the Trotskyites, and a military-fascist organization. O. Ia. Shums'kyi was arrested as one of the organizers and leaders of the Ukrainian anti-Soviet fascist organization. Based on these data, O. Ia. Shums'kyi, who was serving a term of exile in the Krasnoiarsk Krai, was arrested in October 1937. ... Shums'kyi pleaded not guilty. It was exposed by the testimonies of members of the UMO ... convicted in 1933, and core members of the Ukrainian nationalist organization arrested in 1937.
>
> Based on the above:
>
> O. Ia. Shums'kyi is subject to a court trial by the Military Collegium of the Supreme Court of the USSR under the law of 1 December 1934.

The authors of this Collegium order were not perplexed at how the paralyzed and ill Oleksandr Shums'kyi could have led a nationalist organization from the Krasnoiarsk Prison Hospital. It did not bother them that he was going to be tried again for crimes for which he had already been imprisoned. Most striking of all was the small footnote included at the very end of the order: "The arrested Shums'kyi had been detained in the Krasnoiarsk prison since October 1937. There is no material [physical] evidence [*veshchestvennye dokazatel'stva*] in this case."[25]

* * *

The Krasnoiarsk NKVD failed to assist the Moscow NKVD in fulfilling this order. Indeed, it had refused to assist Moscow in progressing Shums'kyi's case at pivotal points from 1937 until 1943, impeding Moscow's attempts to convict and execute him. This seemingly strange behavior of the Krasnoiarsk NKVD in regard to Shums'kyi had as much to do with the specifics of the case as it did with the broader problems with the relationship between the NKVD center in Moscow and its peripheries, especially Krasnoiarsk. The key factor in both regards was the footnote in the

Collegium order. Strangely, at a time when hundreds of thousands of innocent people were being executed on fabricated charges without real evidence, including a fair share in Krasnoiarsk, the lack of material evidence in Shums′kyi's case provided a basis for the Krasnoiarsk NKVD to stall.[26] That NKVD leaders in Krasnoiarsk pursued this course over a period of massive social upheavals, when it seemed there was little reason for doing so, requires explanation

In the space of three years, from 1936 to 1939, the leadership of the NKVD in Krasnoiarsk changed six times, and three of these leaders would be executed by the state by 1940. This was a common rate of attrition among the NKVD leadership during the Great Terror and its slowdown in late 1938, when Moscow pulled back massively on the rate of arrest and execution and began to purge the NKVD itself. At the start, in late 1936 and early 1937, leaders with reservations about ramping up the Great Terror were often replaced by those with no reservations. At the height of the Terror, leaders were changed for whatever failings their superiors ascribed to them, or treated as pawns in broader changes in the command structure of the NKVD. Finally, leadership and many middle- and lower-rung agents were replaced during the slowdown in 1938–39, with some arrested and shot for their own exuberance in the very arrests and executions for which they had been promoted in the past.

Continuities in the behavior of NKVD leaders across this changing landscape were less common. Yet, each of the six NKVD leaders in Krasnoiarsk behaved cautiously in relation to Shums′kyi, both when their superiors in Moscow were pressing for his head and when they were not. They struck a fine balance between stalling his case and not antagonizing Moscow. For instance, they arrested Shums′kyi in October 1937 on orders from Moscow, but left him in the prison hospital without interrogating him for two years. They did not interrogate him until late 1939, after their failure to do so earlier had been revealed to Moscow. When they did interrogate him, they did so perfunctorily, not directly in relation to the alleged crimes for which he was arrested in 1937, and thus found no cause to progress his case. That NKVD leaders on the periphery were successful in using such tactics to stall the progression of Shums´kyi's timeline from arrest to trial and execution speaks volumes about their capacity to operate independently from the center on certain cases.

Successive NKVD leaders in Krasnoiarsk continued the stalling policy toward Shums´kyi despite their different leadership styles and the starkly different circumstances of their tenures. The longest-serving NKVD head of the six, I. P. Semenov (1939–45), behaved remarkably similarly to the inaugural head of the Krasnoiarsk NKVD, Pavlov (1935–36) with regard to their treatment of Shums´kyi, although there is no evidence that the two leaders were ever in contact. Indeed, these were very different Chekists: Pavlov was an experienced Chekist when he assumed control of Krasnoiarsk in 1934, whereas Semenov took the role as a fresh recruit from the NKVD academy in 1939.[27] Pavlov—who was sacked in 1936 and transferred to work in the gulag system for failing to show the necessary enthusiasm for the emerging Great Terror—took a "great interest in Shums´kyi" from the latter's arrival in Krasnoiarsk in late 1935 and was initially unsure about how to deal with his extended hunger strike and letter-writing campaigns.[28] In the end, Pavlov obstructed Shums´kyi's protest campaign while complaining to his superiors in Moscow that their orders regarding Shums´kyi were unrealizable because of it.[29] Later leaders also employed such doublespeak to deflect pressure from Moscow to progress Shums´kyi's case.

At first glance, the overall continuum in behavior toward Shums´kyi makes little sense. The NKVD leaders in Krasnoiarsk had significant impetus to deal with Shums´kyi differently at the various stages of the Great Terror: upon his arrest in 1937, when the Great Terror was at its height; during the slowdown of the Great Terror over the winter of 1938–39; and during the resumption of more normal, pre-Terror NKVD operations. There was every indication that the NKVD in Siberia, including Krasnoiarsk, should have helped progress Shums´kyi's interrogation, trial, and execution upon his arrest in late 1937, at the height of the Great Terror, just as their comrades had done in relation to Shums´kyi's co-accused. Krasnoiarsk and, broadly, the Siberian NKVD had well-established credentials in fabricating false charges against exiles and producing confessions to prove them. It "discovered," for instance, a massive counterrevolutionary plot among tens of thousands of exiles in Siberia in 1937—members of the so-called Russian Social-Military Union (Russkii obshche-voinskii soiuz) who were supposedly working to overthrow the Soviet government.[30] Shums′kyi was charged as a ringleader of counterrevolutionary exiles in Siberia and, at the same time, as someone working toward the same goal in relation to Ukraine. He seemed a perfect candidate for the Krasnoiarsk NKVD to bring to trial, but the case stalled when every factor should have encouraged it to proceed.

The Krasnoiarsk NKVD stalled again, more understandably, when factors discouraged it from progressing Shums′kyi's case in October 1938. There were already signs of the impending slowdown of the Terror, and the purge of NKVD agents had begun by the time they received the Collegium order.[31] The massive scale of arrest and execution radically declined in late 1938 under orders from Stalin, who also removed Yezhov as head of the NKVD (and later had him executed). These signals from above encouraged the Krasnoiarsk NKVD to adopt a wait-and-see approach after receiving the Collegium order. Though Beria, the incoming head of the NKVD, had assented to the Collegium order, the Krasnoiarsk NKVD leaders did not know this at the time and so were clearly fearful of being held responsible by the new leadership at the NKVD for implementing an order of the previous one in relation to Shums′kyi.[32] They might have to pay with their own lives if they were to take Shums′kyi's.

Shums′kyi was lucky. In some areas of the Soviet Union, this same fear drove NKVD agents to clean house by executing prisoners who could have testified against them for their use of torture and fabrication of charges—that is, for fulfilling Yezhov's directives (though Stalin, who was now punishing them, had initially encouraged torture in the Great Terror).[33] But mostly, it seems, this fear encouraged NKVD agents to stall operations, as they were unsure of how to proceed. Sensing this change in course, prisoners began to rebel against their detainment, and thousands were released. Shums′kyi was not released in 1938 amid this wave of clemency, but was released and cleared of all charges at the end of 1939—at precisely the moment when Moscow resumed its pressure on Krasnoiarsk to advance Shums´kyi's case, and the purge of the NKVD had ended. By the end of 1939, the agency had begun to resume more normal operations and extrajudicial killings, albeit on a much smaller scale than during the Great Terror.[34] Semenov thus released Shums´kyi when he had the least impetus to do so.

The declassification of Shums´kyi's files in the Ukrainian security archives (HDA SBU) now enables us to explain the apparent illogicality of Shums´kyi's release at this time and to more accurately understand the broader role of the Krasnoiarsk NKVD in the Great Terror. The files include those on the agency's internal operations and its correspondence with superiors in Moscow, which, as leading historians of the Great Terror in Siberia know well, have rarely been accessible. The enduring lack of access to these types of files for researchers, even after the collapse of the Soviet Union, particularly in Russia, has significantly limited our understanding of center-periphery relations in the NKVD during the Great Terror.[35]

The head of the Krasnoiarsk NKVD as of October 1938, A. P. Alekseenko, was the last of the three NKVD heads to be shot by 1940. By August 1938, as signs of a central leadership shake-up in the NKVD were becoming apparent, even from Siberia, Alekseenko became desperate for any clarification on Shums´kyi's case from Moscow.[36] He sent a telegram to Yezhov's deputy, M. P. Frinovskii, complaining that he had heard nothing from Moscow about Shums´kyi since the original order to arrest him: "We arrested Shums´kyi in line with your order no. 12374 of 9 October 1937. I am asking you for the sixth time for instructions on his case."[37]

Alekseenko's predecessor, D. D. Grechukhin, who had arrested Shums´kyi, also made numerous requests for instructions before he was removed, in February 1938 (he would be shot in 1939).[38] Neither Grechukhin nor Alekseenko ever received a response, and it is clear that Alekseenko inherited Grechukhin's frustration—which may be why he misread Frinovskii's silence as a loss of interest in Shums´kyi on the part of Moscow. On 15 October 1938, with support from his deputies A. S. Khaluimov and A. P. Strel´nik, Alekseenko decided to stop Shums´kyi's case from proceeding: "Given that Shums´kyi is severely ill and thus cannot be questioned, I order that the criminal case against him be stopped until after he has recovered his health [*po ego vyzdorovleniiu*]."[39]

Unbeknownst to Alekseenko, Beria had assented to the order to bring Shums´kyi before the Military Collegium weeks earlier, on 26 September 1938.[40] The Krasnoiarsk NKVD received the Collegium order only on 20 October, five days after they had stopped Shums´kyi's case.[41]

Alekseenko was likely taken aback by his miscalculation. The Krasnoiarsk NKVD's next communication to Moscow after receiving the Collegium order came nine days later. Alekseenko did not offer to assist in fulfilling the order, as one would expect, particularly by gathering evidence against Shums´kyi, which clearly was necessary. The evidence given in support of the Collegium order consisted mainly of testimony from Shums´kyi's former colleagues on the crimes for which he had already been convicted in 1933 and hearsay testimony of Shums´kyi's possible criminal activity in exile—no real evidence. As mentioned earlier, often the only evidence that resulted in imprisonment or execution in fabricated counterrevolution and espionage cases was the confession of the accused.[42] This was especially the case when dealing with prominent political figures such as Shums´kyi, who was famous for his political "failures" and diversion from the party line in 1926–27. A confession from Shums´kyi would also make the testimonial evidence that the NKVD possessed "real." The Krasnoiarsk NKVD would have to produce this confession, or at least try to, by interrogating Shums´kyi, as its leaders claimed he was too ill to travel to Moscow for this purpose. But they had not questioned him since his arrest, refused to do so now given his illness, and conducted no surveillance of him in the prison hospital that could be used as further evidence of his anti-Soviet activities.

Instead, Alekseenko and his deputies continued the approach of seeking further instructions from Moscow on the next steps to be taken in relation to Shums´kyi, while also reiterating the two major problems with his case that discouraged the taking of any steps: Shums´kyi was too ill for questioning, and they had not been provided any real evidence by Moscow on which they could build a case. It was one of Alekseenko's deputies, in his role as representative of the fourth department (*otdel*) of the NKVD on counterrevolutionary activity who most clearly utilized this approach in his correspondence with Moscow. By December 1938, after receiving no further instructions in relation to the Collegium order that had been received on 20 October, Strel′nik wrote to Kobulov, whose department was responsible for producing the order:

> A long time has elapsed since October 1938 and we have yet to receive any information from you on this matter. Shums′kyi is ill and has been detained in the Krasnoiarsk [prison] hospital since the beginning of his arrest. Taking into account that the period of his detainment elapsed long ago and the lack of any evidence against him, we have not taken any investigatory measures in his case. We ask that you inform us immediately on measures to take in relation to Shums′kyi.[43]

The Krasnoiarsk NKVD was not formally required to do anything to help fulfill the Collegium order apart from sending Shums′kyi to Moscow. But Shums′kyi's case could also be heard in his absence. As mentioned earlier, Kobulov was made aware of Shums′kyi's inability to be transported (*etapirovan*) to Moscow for trial and reported this to Beria in his original report seeking approval for the Collegium order.[44] By refusing to at least try to provide the key piece of evidence to advance the case—Shums′kyi's confession—while continuing to seek instruction from Moscow on how to move forward, Strel′nik and Alekseenko performed a subtle doublespeak, first pioneered by Pavlov in 1936, that successfully stalled the case. This doublespeak was perhaps the best approach to dealing with pressure to pursue a weak case against a big fish like Shums′kyi in this chaotic period (October–December 1938), when the entire NKVD was undergoing massive change and the Great Terror was subsiding. In fact, in one of his slowdown orders in November 1938, Stalin chastised NKVD agents for fabricating cases and extracting forced confessions from suspects to prove them. Stalin now forbade, or at least discouraged, what the Moscow NKVD was asking the Krasnoiarsk NKVD to do to Shums′kyi. Stalin would backtrack on this message at the beginning of 1939, but confession would remain the key evidence in Soviet jurisprudence.[45] For now, as far as Alekseenko was concerned, it was probably best to stall Shums′kyi's case.

Alekseenko's inaction, and his use of doublespeak to justify it, did not, as he had probably hoped, save his skin. One of Alekseenko and Strel′nik's final pieces of correspondence with Moscow, this time to Beria, on 20 December 1938, was to ask whether a verdict had been handed down in Shums′kyi's case in the Military Collegium (assuming the case had been heard). The handwritten note on the telegram to Beria from Alekseenko's deputy Khaluimov indicates that Alekseenko was requesting a discussion with Beria on this point by telephone.[46] Alekseenko, it seems, sought a discussion and decision on his own fate as much as Shums′kyi's, with Beria now officially in control of the agency. Alekseenko did not get a discussion, let alone a reply from Beria on this question. The general response he received came in the form of his removal from his position and demotion in late December and early January. He was initially sent to fill a deputy NKVD post in the Mari Autonomous Republic, but was arrested in March 1940 and shot in July of that year.[47]

It is more difficult to trace the middle- and lower-level agents who were involved in Shums′kyi's case to find out whether they met the same fate as Alekseenko and if so, whether their conduct toward Shums′kyi had anything to do with it. We know that Strel′nik survived, as he remained involved, albeit less so, in Shums′kyi's case. All the other agents who had been involved in 1938 were no longer involved in 1939.[48] Their positions had been filled by other agents as part of the broader purge of these ranks, in line with Beria's reconfiguration of the NKVD and removal of Yezhov's appointments and their subordinate networks. Some agents were arrested and others committed suicide, but most were probably reassigned to police or other work within or beyond Krasnoiarsk and survived the purge.[49] Recent scholarship has found that fewer agents were shot in this purge than previously thought.[50]

Immediately after Alekseenko's removal, Moscow renewed its push for Krasnoiarsk to advance Shums′kyi's case by interrogating him and producing "real" evidence. To provide the new leadership of the Krasnoiarsk NKVD under Semenov a basis for doing so, Kobulov's department sent "new" evidence to Krasnoiarsk on 22 January 1939—the same evidence Alekseenko and Strel′nik had been asking for since the previous year. Though some of this evidence was new in that it came from the interrogation of Shums'kyi's colleagues in 1936–37, the accusations made against Shums'kyi still concerned the pre-1933 crimes for which he had already been convicted. The evidence thus gave the new Krasnoiarsk NKVD leadership little useful information on the basis of which to interrogate him.[51] The new leadership responded to this evidence in the same way as the old leadership had, complaining that it contained no information pertaining to his crimes after 1933. They needed evidence from his period of exile in their region beginning in 1935, on which his 1937 arrest was based.[52] They asked for such evidence numerous times but never received it, because it did not exist.

There was one exception to the lack of new evidence: a claim from 1936–37 that UMO operations in Ukraine were being directed by its old leaders in Siberian exile. Even at this stage, Moscow only suspected that Shums'kyi was the one giving instructions from Krasnoiarsk. The assumption was that Shums'kyi had communicated instructions via his wife, Honcharenko, who had regularly traveled between Krasnoiarsk, Saratov, and Moscow before her December 1937 execution. But this assumption was not supported by the surveillance of Shums'kyi and Honcharenko, which failed to identify any counterrevolutionary communications between Shums'kyi, his wife, and suspects in Saratov, Moscow, Ukraine, or anywhere else.[53] As far as the Krasnoiarsk NKVD was concerned, the allegations against Shums'kyi had not been confirmed by any corroborating evidence as of 1939.[54]

The Krasnoiarsk NKVD came to this decision through the "proper" channels. In response to Kobulov's January 1939 communication, it immediately reopened Shums'kyi's case, which had lapsed under the previous leadership. By June, this investigation, based on the "new" evidence sent from Moscow, had stalled and was being passed around from one investigator to another.[55] No one was particularly interested in pursuing this case, and all were happy to let Shums'kyi rot in the prison hospital. He might have done so, had he not intervened in his own case in July 1939, which ultimately led Semenov to drop it and release him.

Shums'kyi sent numerous letters to local and central police and political leaders protesting his detainment from October

1937, though it seems a July 1939 letter addressed to Beria (and other Soviet leaders) attracted the most attention in Moscow. In it, Shums′kyi complained that the Krasnoiarsk NKVD had held him without charge or questioning for two years, which was clearly in contravention of the law (as Strel′nik conceded). The failure to charge and question Shums′kyi was less problematic for its illegality than it was for the way it contradicted the purpose of his arrest, the Collegium order, and, indeed, common police practice. Shums′kyi exacerbated this contradiction by refuting the claims made by the Krasnoiarsk NKVD to Moscow that he was too ill to be questioned, arguing that, although he was paralyzed, he could still write and speak. Indeed, he welcomed questioning as an opportunity to demonstrate his innocence, the fear of which, Shums′kyi claimed, was the key reason that the Krasnoiarsk NKVD had stalled his case in the first place:

> My illness does not preclude me from being questioned. I have informed [them] of this orally and by letter, as although I cannot walk, I can speak and even write. The real reasons why the investigative agencies will not undertake any investigation are quite clear—[it is] because they cannot charge someone with a crime they did not commit and keep them in prison at the same time.[56]

The Krasnoiarsk NKVD prison division responsible for the hospital sent this letter, dated 29 July 1939, to the investigatory department of the NKVD in Moscow on 4 August.[57] It was common practice for Semenov or his deputies to approve any such transmissions to Moscow, though Semenov's behavior suggests that he only became aware of this letter after it was sent. He then clearly became concerned about Moscow's response. Despite receiving no communication from Moscow about the letter until 1940, he quickly moved to preempt any criticism from Moscow by interrogating Shums′kyi on 23 October. On 2 November, he wrote to a deputy in Kobulov's department, Izraïl Pinzur, asserting that the Krasnoiarsk NKVD had now addressed all the concerns raised in Shums′kyi's letter.[58]

In his letter to Pinzur, Semenov justified his inaction toward Shums′kyi in 1939, and that of his predecessors since 1937, by accepting the veracity of Shums′kyi's criticisms but deflecting responsibility for them to other agencies. Here, Semenov revealed his thinking behind the decision to drop Shums′kyi's case (and "release" him only three weeks later, on 22 November), as well as the rationale behind the continuity in the conduct of different NKVD leaders toward Shums′kyi since his arrival in Krasnoiarsk. Shums′kyi's case had indeed been delayed, Semenov agreed, but he argued that this was because of Shums′kyi's illness and the lack of evidence. Kobulov's division, he claimed, had not sent any materials on Shums′kyi's case—either with the order to arrest him on 9 October 1937 or with the Military Collegium order in October 1938—that would enable the Krasnoiarsk NKVD to proceed. Semenov ended the letter claiming that he had no update on the results of Shums′kyi's trial in the Military Collegium and that "we don't even know what Shums′kyi has been charged with."[59]

Semenov's claims were at best half true, and at worst outright false. First, Shums′kyi could not possibly have been questioned, Semenov had argued, because his paralysis meant that any bodily movement caused him "severe pain."[60] He was only questioned on 23 October 1939, accordingly, because his health had now improved (since Shums′kyi's letter of 29 July). If anything, however, Shums′kyi's health had deteriorated significantly over the duration of his detainment: partly due to the poor conditions and lack of treatment in the hospital he had contracted infectious diseases, and his rolling hunger strikes in detainment compounded his poor health. Second, Shums′kyi's charge was listed in the Collegium order, which Semenov had clearly seen. Although the initial charges on which Shums′kyi was arrested in 1937 were communicated to Krasnoiarsk only by telegraph, a local NKVD agent filled out the arrest order for the internal records of the agency, stating that Shums′kyi was arrested for counterrevolutionary activities in exile under the relevant (and infamous) statute 58-10 in the Soviet criminal code, which related to "anti-Soviet and counterrevolutionary propaganda and agitation." Even if he had not seen the 1937 telegram, then, Semenov surely had access to this file in 1939, as it survives in the HDA SBU, having arrived there when the Krasnoiarsk NKVD (by then, the KGB) sent Shums′kyi's materials to Kyiv from Krasnoiarsk in 1962.[61] Kobulov had also sent investigatory materials to Semenov's deputies in January and then in June and July 1939—materials that clearly suggested Shums´kyi's crimes were of a counterrevolutionary nature. Finally, although less involved in the case, Strel´nik maintained his position in the Krasnoiarsk NKVD and, most likely, acted as a conduit between the old and new leaderships in relation to Shums´kyi.

It was certainly true, however, that these materials provided Semenov with little detail on which to advance Shums´kyi's case, and this was apparent in the eventual interrogation that took place in October 1939. This interrogation resembled none of Shums´kyi's previous ones, which were intended to extract a confession. Indeed, it could hardly be called an interrogation at all. It was clearly intended as a matter of process rather than discovery. The senior investigator who ended up with Shums´kyi's case, Senior Sergeant Boris Fraimovich, did not ask any specific questions about Shums´kyi's counterrevolutionary activities in Ukraine, to which the hundreds of pages of evidence that Kobulov had sent supposedly pertained. After establishing Shums´kyi's history in Krasnoiarsk and his time at the hospital, Fraimovich asked Shums´kyi only one question: Had he had any correspondence during exile with anyone in Ukraine, Moscow, or Leningrad (his previous places of residence)? Based on the evidence, this was the only point relevant to Shums´kyi's arrest in 1937 specifically, and his time in Krasnoiarsk generally. Shums´kyi replied honestly that he had corresponded with no one other than his wife, thus confirming the findings of the available surveillance evidence from 1937. Fraimovich quickly ended the interrogation and recommended that the case be dropped and Shums´kyi released.

Such perfunctory interrogations may have been more prominent in the wake of Stalin's new rules for the interrogation of suspects, issued in his decrees to the NKVD in November 1938. These rules, which initiated a slowdown in the Terror, outlawed the beating of suspects, a tactic that was often used to produce confessions in support of fabricated charges (without "worrying about gathering necessary supporting [real] evidence [i.e., witness statements]").[62] These rules were taken more seriously by the NKVD at the time and, given that they were accompanied by a purge in the NKVD ranks, resulted in a massive reduction in arbitrary arrests and both the severity and overall number of interrogations.[63]

But there were always exceptions to this trend, especially in other Siberian areas, such as the Novosibirsk NKVD, whose leader reprimanded his subordinates for being cowed by the November 1938 decrees and urged them to launch a new wave of arrests and (if need be) violent interrogations of new suspects.[64] By late 1939, the new interrogation rules were no longer strictly enforced by the center in any case. The NKVD had successfully worn down the political leadership with criticism of the decrees from December 1938, arguing that it was impossible to do their jobs when suspects, confident that the NKVD could no longer beat them and that agents themselves were being purged, now refused to cooperate in any questioning or even to "partake in any conversations."[65] Stalin listened to the NKVD's complaints. Although the broader purge in the NKVD continued, as early as January 1939, he made specific exceptions for NKVD agents to continue employing violent interrogation methods against uncooperative suspects, especially clear enemies of the people—that is, suspects like Shums′kyi.[66] Moreover, confession, as Andrei Vyshinskii (the chief legal officer of the USSR) had reminded his officers in 1937, remained the key piece of evidence for establishing guilt in counterrevolutionary crimes, despite the new rules concerning how to obtain it.[67]

But Fraimovich did not take up Stalin's invitation to beat Shums′kyi to obtain a confession, which would have made the witness statements (denunciations) "real." Having heard no reply from Moscow in response to his report on 2 November or to Shums′kyi's initial letter, Semenov confirmed Fraimovich's recommendation on 22 November 1939:

> Given that material incriminating Shums′kyi in any crimes after his arrest and exile is lacking, that Shums′kyi is ill (paralyzed), and that before and after his arrest he remains in the hospital, I order that the case against Shums′kyi be dropped and that he be immediately released from detainment, still subject to [the terms of his exile].[68]

Semenov informed Moscow of this decision on 13 December 1939 as an addendum to his 2 November report. He now indicated that he understood the original charges on which Shums′kyi was arrested in 1937 and reiterated that this case had been dropped due to the absence of any new evidence.[69] He released Shums′kyi to the local state hospital.

Semenov's decision to release Shums′kyi may also be understood within the broader context of reduced NKVD operations from the beginning of 1939, with the release of hundreds of thousands of prisoners across the Soviet Union. Based on the Krasnoiarsk NKVD's own figures, it arrested 18,313 people in 1938 but only 130 in 1939.[70] Semenov clearly inherited an agency that had already begun to stall its massive arrest operations during the slowdown of 1938–39. In addition to releasing hundreds of thousands of suspects arrested on more minor charges across the Soviet Union, the NKVD released approximately 110,000 suspects charged with counterrevolutionary crimes. This figure is especially pertinent to Shums′kyi's case, since, like most of those released, he had only been *charged* with counterrevolutionary crimes. He had not been convicted (at least of the 1937 charge), and thus he remained in detainment in NKVD prisons rather than in the gulag system. Those unlucky people who had entered the gulag generally remained there.

But this lull in NKVD activity in 1939 was short lived, perhaps lasting only a few months. And few of those released would have been big fish like Shums′kyi or dangerous counterrevolutionaries. By the time Shums′kyi was released in November and December 1939, the purge of the NKVD was over. The Krasnoiarsk NKVD had already begun to scale up its operations to return to its normal (pre-Terror) levels, with 377 arrests in 1940, as well as 260 people convicted for counterrevolutionary crimes that year and another 167 convicted over the first five months of 1941 in the judicial system.[71] NKVD activity was clearly increasing in Krasnoiarsk, as elsewhere, by late 1939, and it is in this context, not during the slowdown, that Shums′kyi was released.

The figures from 1939–41 are problematic for numerous reasons, none less so than the opportunities for data loss and distortion in a period of massive staff turnover and chaos. But these problems generally strengthen our argument on the context of Shums′kyi's release, as the number of arrests in 1939 was most likely higher than actually recorded. The arrest data does not include cases that were decided extrajudicially, that is, by the NKVD itself, as these did not necessitate a formal arrest. Though extrajudicial processes were outlawed in November 1938, they likely endured on a smaller scale, and certainly cleanup operations would not have been recorded officially. The rise in judicial cases for counterrevolutionary offenses, as part of the new requirement that NKVD agents seek prosecutorial approval for arrests, likely operated alongside extrajudicial processes rather than fully replacing them. And, as many historians note, these approvals were often only a rubber stamp, done for show.[72] Indeed, the NKVD saw only 7,372 of its members (22.9 percent) removed from their positions across the Soviet Union and 998 of these arrested in the purge, leaving its structure intact.[73] Under Beria's leadership, the NKVD grew in personnel and in its position within the state apparatus until the eve of the Second World War.[74] Chekists in the "new" NKVD had to do things slightly differently from 1939 onward, a bit like they had in 1935, with more caution and collaboration with other bodies compared to the Great Terror of 1937–38. But the regime itself remained committed to eradicating anti-Soviet forces through the NKVD, which used the same methods, albeit on a smaller scale.[75]

The slowdown of NKVD activity does not, then, help explain Semenov's motives for releasing Shums′kyi at this time, when it seemed to make more sense to acquiesce to Moscow and progress his case, as it had in 1937 to arrest him. But the general resumption of NKVD activity across the Soviet Union in late 1939 does help us understand Moscow's resumption of pressure for Shums′kyi's head throughout 1940 and Semenov's response to that. Semenov clearly understood his superiors' broader expectation that he resume "normal" NKVD activities after the lull and, perhaps, anticipated their renewed push when he announced the release of Shums′kyi, because he never actually released him. Semenov put Shums′kyi under surveillance in the state hospital and would not let him leave.[76] Semenov clearly needed to keep an eye on Shums′kyi in case Moscow resumed its pressure to progress his case, which they did only three weeks after the release. On 11 January 1940, Kobulov's deputy Pinzur requested that Semenov immediately interrogate and, by implication, rearrest and charge Shums'kyi based on more evidence that had come to light. This evidence consisted of testimony from Shums'kyi's former colleague in the CPWU, Roman Turians'kyi, who had confessed to conducting espionage against Soviet Ukraine on behalf of Polish and German intelligence under Shums'kyi's leadership.[77] Three days later, on 14 January, Pinzur heaped further pressure on Semenov, requesting that he immediately inform the Moscow NKVD headquarters of the state of Shums'kyi's health and thus his suitability for interrogation.[78]

Pinzur claimed that Turians'kyi's evidence was new, but, as before, neither the evidence nor the charges were new at all. These charges were new only in that they defined specific crimes of conducting espionage for Poland (and now also Germany)—crimes of which the fictitious UMO had already been accused in 1933 (that is, working with Poland to overthrow Soviet power in Ukraine by force of arms). The "new" evidence proving this crime consisted mainly of Turians'kyi's old interrogation records from 1933, in which he accused Shums'kyi of organizing armed rebellion against Soviet power, and records of others who detailed how this rebellion would take place.[79] There is no record showing that Turians'kyi implicated Shums'kyi in espionage in later interrogations, and only one indirect statement by another CPWU member about Shums'kyi's supposed espionage activity.[80] Pinzur and his colleagues were clearly unhappy that Shums'kyi's case had been dropped. They responded by searching through the older evidence at their disposal and collating sections from different confessions to create a new charge against Shums'kyi: this time of espionage for Poland and Germany, the two countries Shums'kyi had either worked in or visited.[81]

Semenov sensed Moscow's unease. His handwritten notes on Pinzur's order of 11 January 1940 indicate that he instructed his subordinates to interrogate Shums'kyi again and to send a record of it to Pinzur. However, this did not happen immediately. Semenov did not respond to Pinzur's note of 11 January and instead continued to stall Moscow on progressing the new case. On 26 January, as was common practice, Semenov's deputy and representative of the Krasnoiarsk NKVD investigative department (rather than Semenov himself) responded to Pinzur's telegram of 14 January on Shums′kyi's health by reiterating the Krasnoiarsk NKVD's justification for dropping Shums′kyi's case: his illness and a lack of evidence. Even though Moscow had now sent additional files on Shums′kyi (denunciations, etc.) to Krasnoiarsk, all of these concerned the crimes for which he had already been convicted in 1933. Not having any compromising materials on Shums′kyi's counterrevolutionary activities in exile, and thus in relation to his 1937 charge, Semenov's deputy, V. P. Aleksandrov, claimed that they were forced to let him go.[82]

The Krasnoiarsk NKVD said nothing about Pinzur's 11 January 1940 telegram until 2 April, after Pinzur had already written to them again in mid-March, increasingly frustrated, demanding another update on the status of Shums′kyi's case.[83] Semenov now informed Pinzur that he had already requested the Turians′kyi evidence from the investigative department in Moscow and that, as soon as Shums′kyi recovered his health (*po ego vyzdorovleniiu*), Semenov would charge him with espionage. Three days later, however, the Krasnoiarsk NKVD wrote an addendum to Aleksandrov's 26 January response to Pinzur, informing him that Shums′kyi had contracted typhoid in February and, as a result, could not be interrogated at this time. Again, the Krasnoiarsk NKVD asked for the Turians′kyi evidence and instructions on how to progress the new case, after stressing the factors that made progressing it unfeasible.[84]

Moscow responded quickly by sending all the remaining evidence that supposedly implicated Shums′kyi in espionage activity in Krasnoiarsk, and, in June and July, Moscow officials sent follow-up telegrams requesting updates on Shums′kyi's health and the status of his case.[85] This evidence, consisting of the more recent interrogation records of Shums′kyi's associates, made no reference to Shums′kyi's role in espionage activity as a leader of the CPWU or UMO. The only evidence that did, as Pinzur claimed, was Turians′kyi's "new" confession, on which the new charges lay. And this was the only piece of evidence that the Krasnoiarsk NKVD did not receive. As the Krasnoiarsk NKVD complained, the lack of this key evidence further impeded its ability to move forward with Shums´kyi's case. Without it, illness or not, as in 1939, there seemed to be little point in interrogating Shums´kyi.

The Krasnoiarsk NKVD interrogated Shums´kyi only on 6 September 1940, a week after Turians´kyi had been executed by the NKVD in Moscow.[86] If a lack of evidence meant that there was little point in interrogating Shums´kyi earlier, there was no point at all now, with the main subject of the interrogation and trap for Shums´kyi dead. This is probably why the Krasnoiarsk NKVD interrogated Shums´kyi at this time—to again demonstrate to Moscow the futility of pursuing Shums´kyi's case. It can be argued that the timing of the interrogation after Turians´kyi's death was coincidental; that perhaps Semenov was not aware that Turians´kyi had been shot, or that the Krasnoiarsk NKVD felt that Shums´kyi had sufficiently recovered from typhoid by this time to be interrogated. However, the available documentation suggests otherwise. Turians´kyi had been sentenced to death in late 1939, and there was every likelihood that Semenov was aware of this and could anticipate that the sentence would be carried out quickly. Shums´kyi had recovered from typhoid around 2 April, the day Semenov sent the message to Pinzur citing typhoid as the reason to delay Shums´kyi's interrogation. Though Semenov may not have known about Shums´kyi's recovery until later, his surveillance of Shums´kyi in the hospital beginning in January 1940 clearly indicated that Shums´kyi was no longer seriously ill by April but was mentally active—reading, writing, and even offering lessons on the history of the Communist Party to other patients from his bedside. By the time Krasnoiarsk received the "evidence" in June 1940, Semenov's agents had painted a picture of a man who was as capable of being questioned as he had been in 1939. If the NKVD agents chose to delay their interrogation because they were worried about Shums´kyi infecting them with typhoid, then the October date also makes little sense. Shums´kyi was infectious for other diseases he had contracted in the notoriously unsanitary infectious diseases ward of the Krasnoiarsk state hospital. He thus stayed there until 1941, despite his earlier recovery from typhoid.[87]

The record of the interrogation further indicates that the Krasnoiarsk NKVD was determined to demonstrate to Moscow the futility of progressing Shums´kyi's case, both because of the lack of sufficient evidence from Moscow and because Turians´kyi was now dead. The interrogator—not Fraimovich but another agent, Sergeant L. G. Koptev—asked Shums´kyi nothing about Turians´kyi or about his or Shums´kyi's alleged espionage, despite Pinzur's specific instructions to do so in his telegram of 11 January. Koptev asked Shums´kyi only a few questions about his relationship with a low-level political cadre in Ukraine in the 1920s. Establishing conspiratorial networks between big fish like Shums´kyi and little ones was a common first step in fabricating cases. But there was no longer any conspiratorial web to spin with Turians´kyi gone, so nothing came of this. Shums´kyi returned to the hospital.[88]

The question remains: why would Semenov drop Shums´kyi's case and release him if he clearly anticipated that Moscow might protest, especially within a context in which his superiors expected him to resume arrests at pre-Terror levels? Why continue to stall Shums´kyi's case in this way into 1940 if the previous dangers associated with advancing his case, as in October 1938, were no longer apparent? It seems that Semenov did so because, by late 1939, it was more problematic for him to continue to detain Shums´kyi than it was to release him. As long as Shums´kyi remained a prisoner awaiting trial in Krasnoiarsk, Semenov was ultimately responsible, indeed, liable, for progressing his case. He should not have been, but as long as Moscow provided only pressure and little assistance, Semenov remained in a difficult position most aptly described by Shums´kyi in his letter of July 1939. Semenov could not simply keep him in prison without charging him with a crime, or at least he could not do so without attracting further attention to the absurdity of Shums´kyi's case and of Semenov's own role in moving it forward. The only way to break out of this impossible situation was to extract a confession from Shums´kyi, but Semenov knew this was unlikely. He had all of Shums´kyi's interrogation reports at his disposal and could see that no other Chekist had managed to achieve this. Shums´kyi clearly understood that his refusal to confess was keeping him alive.[89] It must have been jarring for Semenov to see that Shums´kyi did not fear interrogation, but welcomed it, even under the new rules set by Stalin. In his July 1939 letter, Shums´kyi further compromised Semenov's position by proclaiming his good health, stripping Semenov of his main justification for resisting Moscow's pressure to pursue the case.

But Semenov did find a way to manage his dilemma, if not to break out of it. By dropping the case and releasing the prisoner, Semenov removed Shums′kyi from his direct responsibility while keeping him within his control. Since Shums′kyi was no longer a prisoner, and therefore no longer subject to the procedural processes or "care" of police, Shums′kyi could not report to Moscow to complain, as he had in July 1939. With Shums′kyi now a private citizen effectively detained in a hospital bed and under constant surveillance, Semenov was confident that he could keep him under control and intercept his protests, thus avoiding the potential problems associated with releasing an "anti-Soviet" criminal into society.[90] Despite repeated requests from both Shums′kyi and the medical board of the Krasnoiarsk hospital, Semenov denied a transfer to a nerve clinic in Tomsk where the former prisoner could receive treatment for his paralysis. Even when the Krasnoiarsk public prosecutor supported the transfer on 23 October 1940, six weeks after Shums′kyi's final interrogation, Semenov refused to let Shums′kyi go.[91]

Semenov's denials of the transfer requests throughout 1940 make sense. He needed to keep Shums′kyi within reach but beyond his responsibility if he was to deflect Moscow's enduring pressure. Most of all, he needed to keep Shums′kyi quiet—to stop him from attracting Moscow's attention, as he had done not only in his letter of July 1939, but also in his earlier letter of January 1936, when he wrote to the Central Committee of the ACP(b) about Pavlov, Semenov's predecessor. It pays to revisit Pavlov's response to Shums′kyi's hunger strike in more depth in order to trace Semenov's development of this strategy and, broadly, the growing sophistication of the Krasnoiarsk NKVD's capacity to deflect pressure from Moscow.

Shums′kyi won his first victory against Pavlov with his first hunger strike in January 1936, when the Central Committee replied to his letters on the offenses of the NKVD by advising him to end the strike and work toward his rehabilitation.[92] When Pavlov informed Molchanov, his superior in Moscow, that Shums′kyi had resumed his hunger strike in April in protest of the NKVD's meddling in his rehabilitation and detainment in Krasnoiarsk, Molchanov made it clear to Pavlov that there could be no further tolerance for Shums´kyi's "victories" in highlighting the absurdity of the NKVD's conduct. But, Molchanov added, should Shums´kyi die, Pavlov would be held responsible:

> **Pavlov:** I can't stop him from hunger striking. Shums´kyi claims he has a letter from the Central Committee telling him to stop his strike and to begin working on his rehabilitation, but he cannot do so in Krasnoiarsk. He requires transport to a Moscow hospital where he can receive treatment (he has sent a telegram to Yezhov on this point). I ask if I can confirm his passage to Moscow. So that he can begin to eat.
>
> **Molchanov:** Do not promise him anything. You are personally responsible for persuading Shums´kyi to eat. Immediately transport him to the hospital for [force-]feeding. Perhaps suggest to him that he stop his hunger strike in line with his note from 25 January. What do you think?
>
> **Pavlov:** I fear this would be a useless discussion. Based on my conversation with him in his apartment, I am certain that he will only end his hunger strike if we agree to send him to Moscow for treatment. If we take him to the hospital here and [force-]feed him, he will only resume his strike after a few days. His position is strong: he demands a review of his criminal case. He is willing to die for this position.[93]

Some historians believe that by 1936 the Chekists had developed an effective response to hunger strikes, which earlier had caused significant difficulties in detaining political opponents.[94] The response, at least in prison camps, was now to charge prisoners undertaking hunger strikes as counterrevolutionaries and shoot them. This strategy could not be applied to Shums´kyi, and Pavlov clearly felt himself to be in an impossible situation by this time. Shums´kyi's demands could only be met by Moscow, yet Molchanov made Pavlov responsible for ending Shums´kyi's strike and keeping him alive. This was, in essence, the same intractable dilemma as Semenov's in 1939–40. Semenov clearly had to keep Shums´kyi alive just as Pavlov had. The main difference was that the entire NKVD structure was embarrassed by Shums´kyi's protest in 1936 and under pressure from Central Committee of the party to deal with Shums´kyi without killing him. This is why, despite Molchanov's pressure on Pavlov, he also advised him on how to "break" Shums´kyi's hunger strike. By 1940, this was more of an internal NKVD matter.

Pavlov's and Semenov's responses to their dilemmas were thus similar and can be traced to Molchanov's initial advice to limit Shums´kyi's capacity to highlight internal NKVD failures to Moscow. In 1936, this entailed censoring, or at least limiting, Shums´kyi's communication with the party in Moscow and the outside world, putting him in a hospital but denying him medical treatment for his paralysis, establishing surveillance over him, and intimidating his wife with threats that she would be removed from Krasnoiarsk if she continued to lobby the party on behalf of her husband.[95] In 1940, the strategy was the same, save for the need to deal with Honcharenko, whom the NKVD had executed in 1937. Shums´kyi was well aware of this strategy under Pavlov and then under Semenov, pointing it out in numerous letters to political and police leaders in Moscow (though from late 1939 onward, many of his letters were intercepted by the NKVD and never reached their destination). Unlike in 1936, Shums´kyi did not win any victories in 1940–41 after his "release," as Semenov successfully employed the strategy to silence and isolate him.

Semenov still needed to tread carefully between Shums´kyi and Moscow, as Shums´kyi came close to another victory when one of his letters made it to the Military Collegium at the beginning of 1941. This letter was similar to those he sent to Semenov, requesting a move to a hospital in Tomsk where specialist treatment for his paralysis was available. This letter evaded the censorship net that the NKVD had established in the hospital, probably because Shums´kyi's doctors sent it to Moscow on his behalf; they, too, were sending similar requests at the time. Semenov continued to deny requests from Shums´kyi and his doctors for the move until it became clear to him that his superiors in Moscow, and indeed the Collegium itself, were losing interest in progressing Shums´kyi's case. The first sign of this came in early 1941, with the head of the Collegium Secretariat, V. V. Ivanov—who had long been involved in Shums´kyi's case—asking Semenov whether he felt that this move to Tomsk for medical treatment, which would require them to change Shums′kyi's exile location, was really necessary.[96] For the first time since 1939, Semenov was presented with a way to be rid of Shums′kyi, but, at the same time, Ivanov asked Semenov to provide him with any compromising material from the hospital surveillance of Shums′kyi and another assessment of Shums′kyi's health. That is, Ivanov was asking Semenov to provide him with materials so he could make up his own mind on Shums′kyi's move. Semenov had none to send.

No decision was made, as the German invasion of the Soviet Union on 22 June 1941 disrupted the process and left Shums′kyi in Krasnoiarsk. Shums′kyi was moved, against his will, to an invalid home in Eniseisk, only in September. There was always some disagreement among Shums′kyi's doctors about his treatment. Though the medical board had recommended that he be moved to Tomsk for treatment by specialists, some of its members argued that this treatment was unlikely to help and that, as a disabled person, Shums′kyi should be transferred directly to an invalid home. Semenov had been involved in these discussions in January 1941. However, the hospital board changed with the outbreak of war (some of Shums′kyi's doctors were conscripted into military service), and the new board adopted the advice to move him to a home. The board now claimed that Shums′kyi was exaggerating the extent of his paralysis, and tried to force him to walk on crutches. When Shums′kyi was still unable to walk, the new board diagnosed him as suffering from untreatable paralysis, deemed him disabled, and argued that he should be moved to an invalid home in any case. It seems that the new board had been working toward this conclusion from the beginning, as it was also "rationalizing" bed space in the hospital at a time when wounded soldiers were arriving from the front.

The invalid home in Eniseisk, though still within Krasnoiarsk Krai, was located not in the city but in the surrounding *raion* (district). This was the most isolated place in which Shums′kyi had been detained, bar the Solovki prison. With no word from Moscow about relocating Shums′kyi to Tomsk, Semenov was happy to further isolate Shums′kyi and, with Moscow's interest in Shums′kyi's case receding, was content to leave Shums′kyi to die in Eniseisk. NKVD surveillance records reveal that one of Shums′kyi's doctors who had originally suggested that he be moved to the home referred to it as a place for "living corpses"—a place where people go to die.[97] As an NKVD informant, the doctor likely communicated this impression either to Semenov or to his agents with whom she was in contact. With no treatment available for Shums′kyi's paralysis or his many ailments—or, indeed, any real medical care in Eniseisk—his health declined rapidly, and he was lucky to survive his stay there until 1944.

Much like Shums′kyi's release from the prison hospital in 1939, the end of his period of exile did not result in his liberation or repair of his political reputation. The end of his period of exile in many ways made his fight to achieve these things much more difficult, which is the subject of the next chapter.

Chapter Six

THE TRAGIC FINALE

> One of Yagoda's henchmen said to me in Krasnoiarsk: "They don't respond to you because you are undertaking a hunger strike. This is counterrevolution." For goodness' sake! The reason I went on a hunger strike in the first place was because no one responded to my requests and statements.
>
> —*Oleksandr Shums'kyi to Joseph Stalin, August 1945*

In his August 1945 letter to Stalin, Shums'kyi outlined a central problem facing his protest campaign since his arrest in 1933: he needed to behave like a counterrevolutionary to demonstrate his innocence on counterrevolutionary charges.[1] Shums'kyi had long dealt with this problem as effectively as possible, irritating authorities at pivotal points since his arrest to stall his case and win the numerous victories that kept him alive along with his hope for rehabilitation. The commutation of his hard labor sentence to exile in 1935, the recommendation from the Central Committee of the party in 1936 to work on his rehabilitation, his survival through the Great Terror, his release from arrest in 1939, and the completion of his exile in late 1943 were all major, albeit Pyrrhic, victories.

By mid-1945, it was becoming clearer to Shums'kyi that his usual tactics were losing efficacy and that he was unlikely to win any more such victories. Political and police leaders hardly responded to his letters and protests. Ironically, now that Shums'kyi was "free," having completed his exile sentence in 1943, he found himself less able to pursue political rehabilitation. He became more and more desperate in his appeals, particularly to Stalin, to whom he had long been writing about his ordeals in a comradely and respectful manner. His final letter to Stalin, in October 1945, had a changed tone. It was a suicide note, in which Shums′kyi announced that he would commit suicide in protest of Stalin's failure to rehabilitate him, as well as his failure to stop what Shums′kyi understood as a new wave of postwar Russification over Ukraine, which might eliminate whatever slim achievements remained of Ukrainization from the 1920s and 1930s:

> Now I see that I have exhausted all avenues to achieve my political rehabilitation and have accomplished nothing. I am left with only one form of protest against the injustice committed against me: suicide. I take this step not out of fear of deprivations, suffering, further humiliations and a desire to avoid them. I have survived all of this and can survive no more. ...
>
> I also take this step to protest against the new nationalities policy, the policy of Great Russian chauvinism ... against Ukraine. It is against this attempt to transform Ukraine into an amorphous political body, into Little Russia [Malorossiia]; it is against this castration of the Ukrainian people that I raise my voice of protest.[2]

Shums′kyi was aware that his suicide note had a better chance than his previous correspondence of gaining Stalin's attention. Threats like this were to Stalin criminal acts that did not go unpunished.[3] Stalin would likely kill or imprison Shums′kyi in response if his suicide attempt was unsuccessful. How can we explain Shums′kyi's descent into desperation and death, if not by his own hand then by the state's? How do we explain why Soviet leaders including Stalin, Lazar Kaganovich, Nikita Khrushchev, and incoming minister for state security Viktor Abakumov—people who were at the top of the regime, who had been victorious in war, and whose dominion in 1946 stretched from Germany in the west to Korea in the east—would consider the threats of a paralyzed exile in Siberia so seriously as to formulate an extraordinary plot to assassinate him?[4] This chapter offers the same answer to both questions: Shums′kyi and the leadership understood themselves as vulnerable to each other at this time, though for very different reasons.

Shums´kyi's final chances for political rehabilitation and whatever achievements of Ukrainization he sought to salvage, the two things that mattered most to him, were vulnerable to the leadership's complete neglect of his case by 1945, for the first time since his arrest, and to its re-Russification of Ukraine. The leadership's security interests were vulnerable to Shums´kyi's Ukrainian nationalism and alleged foreign espionage at a time when the leadership's anxieties were being realized in the massive nationalist insurgency in western Ukraine in the context of the emerging Cold War.

Shums´kyi won his numerous "victories" against the state because his refusal to confess had created a predicament for those responsible for his case, opening a space within which he could protest successfully. Shums´kyi pointed out the procedural inconsistencies in his case to political and police leaders, fermenting jurisdictional confusion and tension between or within their different agencies and thus helping stay his conviction and execution at key points. But this predicament persisted only as long as the state needed to keep him alive to stand trial—if only for the purpose of eventually convicting and executing him. When the state ceased to care about his case, probably beginning in mid-1941 with the outbreak of war and certainly once his exile was over in 1943, Shums´kyi lost leverage and thus his capacity to achieve further victories.

Shums´kyi often complained that no one replied to his requests, and he was right in that few replied to him directly. But top political and police leaders had always discussed Shums´kyi's letters among themselves and acted on them until 1943, when they lost interest in using his case to make a point. Shums´kyi was now "free," having served his term of exile, yet he remained bound to the same Krasnoiarsk hospital bed where he had been placed in 1936. He was neither permitted to leave nor capable of doing so. By 1945, authorities were still reluctant to let him leave, not because they still perceived him as a serious security threat (though they retained some concern about this), but because of the lessening of pressure on them to act on his requests. Ironically, Shums´kyi's increasing irrelevance to the state made his chances for political rehabilitation—always slim—now unobtainable. As a "free" man,

Shums´kyi now found that he was the one—not the state or the party—who was trapped in a dilemma. His suicide letter and protest can be seen as a final attempt to break out of this situation by becoming more threatening and thus relevant to the state again, even if this was to result in his death. This was an extreme act, but entirely in keeping with Shums´kyi's strategy of bringing attention to his case, to his innocence of the charges of counterrevolutionary activity, by engaging in counterrevolutionary acts such as hunger strikes. By 1945, the threat of suicide was necessary to advance this strategy, now aimed more at the only political rehabilitation, or redemption, available to him at this time: dying for the cause of protecting Ukraine from re-Russification. As always, Shums´kyi's personal and political fates were entwined.

Despite Shums´kyi's agency, a breakthrough based on this strategy would have been unlikely if not for the Soviet political and police leadership beginning to understand that the nationalist insurgency against Soviet power in western Ukraine, which had been raging since 1943, was now supported by the USSR's erstwhile allies, especially Britain and the United States, in an attempt to destabilize the Soviet Union. As recent scholarship based on US and Soviet intelligence sources notes, this support was real, if limited. Soviet security agencies had been reporting on it since 1944, but, until late 1945, the leadership had dismissed the reporting as a likely falsification or provocation by enemy agents.[5] Shums´kyi could not have been aware of this or of the evolution of the leadership's thinking on it, but his suicide note thrust him into the center of the problem in the eyes of the leadership.

The People's Commissariat for State Security (Narodnyi komissariat gosudarstvennoi bezopasnosti, NKGB), a rival secret police agency to the NKVD, intercepted Shums´kyi's October 1945 suicide note to Stalin and investigated him.[6] But the NKGB, now under the leadership of Abakumov, reported the note to Stalin and the leadership only after Shums´kyi's failed suicide attempts in the summer of 1946. (Shums´kyi also left a copy of the letter by his bedside, addressed to the police, in a folder titled "For the Investigation.") As with the original accusations against Shums´kyi and the UMO in 1933, and then again in 1940 with the Turians´kyi case, the nexus of foreign intervention and domestic insurgency or counterrevolution provided the context for the leadership to understand Shums′kyi's threat. From this perspective, Shums′kyi's letter and attempted suicide constituted his acknowledgment of his irredeemably counterrevolutionary nature, despite his refusal to confess to individual crimes. He was, as previously charged, a nationalist with Western links threatening to destabilize Soviet Ukraine in the 1930s with the Poles and Germans, and now actually doing so with the Americans and British, not only in life, but potentially in death as a martyr for the insurgents' cause. There was no real evidence that Shums′kyi had had anything to do with Western powers or local nationalist insurgents (the nationalists and Shums′kyi despised each other as enemies), but this mattered little in the thinking of the Soviet leadership. Shums′kyi's "confession" in the suicide note was the primary evidence the leadership needed. The charges against Shums′kyi thus seemed entirely logical to them, as was the special attention the leadership paid to his assassination to ensure it would be done secretly, so as not to invite any retaliation from Ukrainian nationalist forces—Shums′kyi's supposed allies.

This final chapter traces Shums′kyi's desperate descent into suicide from 1943 to 1946, ending with his assassination, within the broader context of the Soviet leadership's growing understanding of the nexus between domestic Ukrainian nationalism and foreign intervention, and Shums′kyi's place within it. This analysis provides new insight into the leadership's thinking at the beginning of the Cold War, in relation to both the insurgency in western Ukraine and, broadly, the threat of Ukrainian nationalism. The leadership perceived this threat as encompassing a wide range of activities and sentiments beyond the borders of Ukraine, and saw it as "internationalized" by Western assistance to insurgents in western Ukraine and throughout the Soviet Union, as well as to nationalists abroad.[7]

Much of the literature on the Western assistance, which is small compared to the literature on the insurgency itself, traces the flow of covert Western assistance to both insurgents fighting in western Ukraine and nationalists in displaced persons camps in Germany, most of them Soviet citizens who had fled the Soviet Union in wartime and Ukrainian émigrés. This assistance consisted mostly of moral support, but it also involved funds and direction in espionage or sabotage operations. Clearly, the Soviet leadership thought that old domestic threats like Shums′kyi could reactivate in this new nexus, and this fear influenced decisions and counterinsurgency policymaking within and beyond western Ukraine as the Cold War intensified.

* * *

Shums′kyi remained in the invalid home in Eniseisk for almost a year after his exile sentence was completed. He gained permission to leave it only in 1944, after his usual protest tactic proved successful—that is, bringing attention to his unjustified "incarceration" by writing letters to local police and political leaders and going on hunger strikes in the hospital so that his doctors would support his requests, if only to be rid of him. Though Shums′kyi sought transfers to hospitals outside of Krasnoiarsk (specifically to Tomsk) for treatment of his paralysis, he was transferred back to the Krasnoiarsk state hospital in 1944 and, as before, was not permitted to leave it.

Shums′kyi's usual protest tactics were now slower to bear fruit in Krasnoiarsk. He repeatedly failed to gain approval from either the NKVD or the NKGB for a transfer to the Tomsk hospital for treatment, or to Saratov, which was officially his former place of residence, though Shums′kyi himself had never lived there. His family was moved to Saratov after the remainder of his hard labor sentence of 1933 was commuted to exile in 1935. Shums′kyi retained ownership of the family apartment in the city, into which he was legally permitted to move, given that Saratov was not a category 1 city (category 1 cities, which encompassed the major cities in the Soviet Union, prohibited the return of exiles after they had served their terms).

These setbacks were not new for Shums′kyi, but his changed situation by late 1945 meant that they took a greater toll on his willingness to continue fighting for his relocation and political rehabilitation. His entire family was dead. He had confirmed only in 1943 that his wife had been murdered in the Great Terror in 1937 (he had suspected that she had died in prison, rather than by execution), and later confirmed that his son had died fighting in the Red Army against the Germans in the Battle of Moscow in 1942.

Shums´kyi's personal note titled "On Disease and Treatment," dated 19 September 1945, a month before his suicide note to Stalin, is most revealing of the general change in his outlook:

> My hope of recovering from this illness was shaken when I learned that I would not be permitted to go to Tomsk but would have to remain in Krasnoiarsk. I lost whatever hope remained after I was examined by a new doctor, a professor, who concluded that there was nothing seriously wrong with me. Convinced that no one here would help me, I wrote to everyone in Moscow for help. But in vain. Even though I was informed that my son had been killed at the front in 1942, I still awaited the end of the war in the hope that he was still alive; perhaps he was taken captive? There is no hope now. They cannot treat me here. Moscow does not respond. To cling to life in this situation is cowardice.[8]

The meticulous surveillance of Shums´kyi's mood and activities in the hospital confirms that he fell into depression at this time. Even in the depths of his isolation in Eniseisk, he had remained committed to his fight for political rehabilitation and stayed mentally active, reading newspapers, maintaining correspondence, and establishing relationships with other patients. As much as police informants had tried to extrapolate "anti-Soviet sentiment" from Shums´kyi's behavior or statements, this could rarely be done, even by the standards of the Chekists who evaluated the informant reports.[9] But, from September 1945, informants, in this case patients who shared Shums´kyi's ward in Krasnoiarsk, noted an angrier tone and increasingly dismissive attitude toward the achievements of the Soviet Union in the war and toward the party in general, which Shums´kyi had always defended. On 15 September, it was reported: "When military units paraded from the train station to the town center past our hospital, patients remarked, 'The soldiers look good and their horses are wonderful.' In response, Shums´kyi turned away with a very spiteful look on his face."[10] Though these informants likely exaggerated Shums´kyi's anti-Soviet demeanor to demonstrate the usefulness of their own observations to the Chekists, Shums´kyi's angrier tone is clearly reflected in his notes and, indeed, in the suicide note to Stalin written a month after this report.

By April of the following year, surveillance reports indicated that his anger had given way to a deepening, debilitating depression:

> 23 April 1946: Shums´kyi has been morose lately, does not speak, and is even reluctant to read newspapers, which he has never been before. ...
>
> 29 May 1946: Shums´kyi ... has become even more withdrawn, completely uncommunicative. He refuses newspapers, has given his headphones [away], explaining that he does not need them now. ... He avoids talking and covers his face with his hand when doing so.[11]

By all accounts, it seems Shums´kyi was preparing for death.

The NKGB agents who took over general surveillance functions from the NKVD for counterrevolutionaries such as Shums´kyi from 1943 onward acknowledged this change in tone but displayed little concern until their superiors intercepted Shums´kyi's suicide note to Stalin in November 1945.[12] The deputy head of the second division of the NKGB (countersurveillance) in Moscow, L. F. Raikhman, referred his agents in Krasnoiarsk to the note and asked them to inspect the conditions of Shums´kyi's detainment in the state hospital, ostensibly to determine his risk of suicide or escape. They acted quickly to inspect these conditions, as is evidenced by handwritten annotations by the Krasnoiarsk NKGB head, M. F. Kovshuk-Bekman, on Raikhman's request. The inspection found nothing of concern, and the agents did not advise any change to his conditions or that any action be taken against Shums´kyi at this time.[13] Their correspondence and muted responses to surveillance reports from informants in the hospital reveal that they considered Shums´kyi to be an ongoing threat, given his history, but not a clear and present danger. This would change later, when Shums´kyi attempted suicide. Abakumov, as head of the NKGB (from early 1946, Ministry of State Security [Ministerstvo gosudarstvennoi bezopasnosti, MGB]) and minister for state security, became involved and personally situated Shums´kyi at the nexus of a domestic insurgency in Ukraine and foreign intervention.[14]

Shums´kyi's threat of suicide likely did help accelerate the approval of his earlier requests for relocation, made in late 1944 and early 1945 before he fell into his depressive state. The Krasnoiarsk

MGB (formerly NKVD; from March 1946, the Ministry of Internal Affairs [Ministerstvo vnutrennikh del, MVD]) approved a transfer request belatedly, in June 1946. Frustrated by Shums′kyi's resistance in the hospital, mostly by his refusal to eat or submit to medical examination, as well as by his rancor toward the staff, his doctors wrote to the Krasnoiarsk NKGB in December 1945 requesting it either approve Shums′kyi's request to move to Saratov or, if not, then at least to send him back to Eniseisk. They did add in their note, however, that Shums′kyi was likely to engage in further hunger strikes if he were returned to Eniseisk, and that, given his frail health, these would likely kill him.[15] That is, the doctors anticipated that Shums′kyi would commit suicide by hunger strike if he was not relocated to Saratov, while the agents reading the letter were also aware of Shums′kyi's threat to commit suicide by other means. There is no direct evidence of the thinking behind the MGB's decision to approve Shums′kyi's request, though agents did underline the section in the doctors' request showing that Shums′kyi owned an apartment in Saratov that could be considered his former place of residence, suggesting, at least in practical terms, that this request could be approved and that they could place him in his apartment. The agents' correspondence with their counterparts in Saratov facilitating his relocation further suggests that they were keen to prevent Shums′kyi's suicide.[16]

Shums′kyi did not believe his doctors in June 1946 when they informed him that his request to relocate was successful—not until he boarded the train to Saratov.[17] He was accompanied by a medical orderly. Per standard practice, the Saratov MGB established surveillance over Shums′kyi in his apartment, which consisted mainly of recruiting informants who lived in the apartment building. Shums′kyi was aware and, indeed, unfazed by this. Upon his arrival, he sent a letter to the head of the Saratov NKVD, O. O. Zakusylo, to introduce himself and inform Zakusylo of his case.[18]

Shums′kyi did not count his relocation to Saratov as a victory. Although his tactic of hunger strikes and appeals had proven successful again, if the success was much delayed, he saw little prospect of using it for his political rehabilitation as he had in 1936, at least not for exoneration by the party. Importantly, his desire for exoneration had diminished with his change in mood over the winter of 1945–46, when he began to dread his potential move to Saratov. This was partly because he understood that, in Saratov, he would live alone in the home of his dead loved ones. Shums´kyi penned a short diary entry upon his arrival in Saratov expressing this fatalism, one of a series of pieces of evidence giving insight into his thinking that survive in the archives: "At last I am 'home.' Silence. Desolation. Ruin. This is everything to which I aspired. Even if I were able to cast off in some sort of boat, where would it go in the sea of life? I have no aims, no desires. Let the wind take me. May its howl be my song."[19]

His was not an unbroken depression. Upon seeing Moscow from his train carriage (the rail journey from Krasnoiarsk to Saratov went through Moscow), Shums´kyi experienced an actual heart attack from the joy of seeing one of his former home places, a city in continental Europe, after years in Siberian exile.[20] But the city of Saratov was to provide no joy. We know from Shums´kyi's notes that he dreaded coming to Saratov because he knew he would be carried closer to his suicide in this house. He had not committed suicide when he threatened it in his letter to Stalin in October 1945 because he refused to die in Siberia, which he loathed. Shums´kyi preferred to do so in the European part of the Soviet Union; he was going "home" to kill himself.[21]

In the five weeks from his arrival in Saratov to his attempted suicide, Shums´kyi lived a normal life, at least according to surveillance reports.[22] His family's former housekeeper (*ekonomka*), who had lived in the apartment looking after Shums´kyi's son after Shums´kyi's wife was arrested in 1937, continued to live there, and Shums´kyi thanked her for her support of his family by legally transferring ownership of the apartment to her in the event of his death.[23] Shums´kyi spent most of his time alone, rarely meeting with other inhabitants of the apartment block. The surveillants during this period reported nothing of consequence to the responsible MGB, neither in Shums´kyi's statements nor in the character of his associates. In everyday encounters, he discussed mostly daily life and international relations; that is, popular topics of conversation at the time.[24] One associate was a former camp inmate whom the MGB investigated, but who raised no red flags.

Apart from one of his personal notes, which Shums´kyi kept secret, there was nothing in the surveillance to suggest to the NKGB that Shums´kyi was preparing for suicide. But, on 17 July 1946, Shums´kyi wrote:

> The time has come to part with the shadows of my loved ones, my dear ones, my family. I've spent sad days and sleepless nights among your memories, my loved ones ... now the blow of a shining blade to my heart will free me from this wretched life; from the oppression of its threefold burdens: discrimination, loneliness, and disease.[25]

There was little romance in the actual suicide attempt, which failed: "It's bad. I missed. I got the blade stuck in between my ribs: it didn't reach my heart. My hand did not err, it simply did not have enough strength. Today I'll try another way."[26] Shums´kyi wrote this addendum to his note while still bleeding from the failed attempt. It seems he waited until hours later, perhaps the following day, to try "another way," by slitting his veins above his right elbow with a razor blade. This was more effective, as the report of the police officer who attended the scene in Shums´kyi's apartment on 18 July 1946 stated: "As a result of [the suicide attempt] there was a great deal of blood on the bed and the table. Shums´kyi did not lose consciousness. He was taken by ambulance to the second state hospital for treatment."[27]

Shums´kyi left notes for his *ekonomka*, who would most likely have discovered him, detailing what to do next. He assured her that his suicide was not a personal matter but a political one, in which she played no part, and asked her to direct the police to a parcel of documents he had left on his desk for their review. The attending police officer noted that Shums´kyi had written the following on this parcel: "The reason for my death will be clear from this parcel of documents intended 'for the investigation.'" Shums´kyi included sixteen documents in the parcel, among them a few excerpts from his academic manuscript "Malorossiia" (a treatise he had written but later destroyed on the history of Ukraine's Russification), a book on Shums´kyism, copies of his three letters to Stalin in 1945, and some personal notes. Shums´kyi clearly intended this parcel to remain as a testament to his political career and his fight for political rehabilitation after his death (most of it survives in the archive). Investigators were not interested in any of Shums′kyi's writings, save the October 1945 letter to Stalin that Shums′kyi had already sent. In the leadership's decision to kill Shums′kyi, only this document mattered: not the almost decade of close surveillance that failed to reveal any criminal activity or even clear anti-Soviet sentiment; not his refusal to confess; not the collapse of the case against him in 1939 for lack of any real evidence. Shums′kyi's attempted suicide and his explanation for it in the October letter made meaningless in the eyes of the leadership his years of struggle for political rehabilitation and, as importantly, the state's own understanding of him as having committed no crime. Shums′kyi made himself guilty after years of protesting his innocence—or, more accurately, in the eyes of the Soviet leadership, he revealed himself as guilty after years of pretense.

* * *

Shums′kyi's "confession" to his crimes came at a significant turning point in the central police and political leadership's understanding of the broader threat that Shums′kyi represented. He had long been seen as a Ukrainian nationalist, a leader of the UMO supported by Western powers to secretly work toward Ukraine's secession from the Soviet Union. Like other suspects, he had spent time abroad in an official capacity, in Poland in the 1920s and in Germany in the early 1930s.[28] The difference by mid-1946 was that there was an actual, not just anticipated, secessionist struggle being waged in western Ukraine. By this time, the struggle was no longer fought in open military engagements between Soviet and Ukrainian nationalist military forces, as it had been in 1943–44, when the Soviets retook control over Ukraine from the Germans. By 1946, the Soviets' massive counterinsurgency operations, and their incentives to attract nationalists to the Soviet side, had depleted the ranks of the Ukrainian Insurgent Army (UPA), the primary military force battling the Soviets. As the UPA ceased to be a viable military force by late 1944, its remnants moved away from open military engagements, which were now suicidal given the massive asymmetry of forces.[29] The UPA consolidated its covert operations against political and police representatives of Soviet power and lurched toward domestic terrorism against civilians it deemed "collaborators" with the Soviet regime. The transition of the UPA and its parent body, the Organization of Ukrainian Nationalists (Orhanizatsiia ukraïns′kykh natsionalistiv, OUN), from competitors for state authority to simple insurgents did not reduce the threat they posed in the eyes of the Soviet leadership, but instead altered the UPA's nature from an overt military force to a covert operation that was harder to fight, particularly in light of Western assistance.[30]

Winning support from the civilian population—in the form of information, service, and allegiance—was always key to winning this covert battle in western Ukraine. Also crucial was identifying and eliminating those who collaborated with the other side, which both the Soviets and the UPA did with exceptional arbitrariness and ruthlessness, accelerating the spiral of mutual suspicion and bloodletting in western Ukraine. The Soviet awareness that the West was assisting the insurgency stoked the suspicion, already deeply rooted in Soviet society, that there were nationalist agents and collaborators beyond western Ukraine, either inside other parts of the USSR or in émigré societies.[31] The Soviet leadership thus resumed its long-standing mission (interrupted by the war) of hunting down Ukrainian nationalists wherever they could be found or, indeed, imagined.[32]

Scholars agree that the Soviets generated a comprehensive picture of Western assistance to the insurgency by early 1947, after a multitude of reports written by agents from various security agencies on the ground and sent to central police and political leaders throughout 1945 offered a progressively more confident outline of this threat.[33] This progressive process accelerated in 1946, as nationalist operations ramped up along with Cold War tensions.[34] A key moment in this timeline was Winston Churchill's "Iron Curtain" speech in March 1946, which was widely interpreted within the Soviet Union and its territories as further indication of a widely anticipated war between the Western Allies and the Soviet Union, and among nationalists fighting the Soviet regime in Ukraine as a call to arms.[35] By one calculation, Ukrainian nationalists' activity in the twelve months following the speech "grew by more than 300 percent."[36] In May 1947, the deputy minister of the Ukrainian MGB, M. S. Popereka, submitted a report to Kaganovich (who had displaced Khrushchev as head of the Ukrainian Communist Party) entitled "The Struggle against Foreign Intelligence Agents (English and American Espionage)." According to historian Jeffrey Burds, this report "for the first time laid out in vivid detail the substantial evidence of the 'nefarious threat' posed by Anglo-American schemes" to Soviet Ukraine. From this moment, the threat began to clearly inform Soviet counterinsurgency policy in Ukraine and its broader security response in the Cold War.[37]

While this report may have been the first to lay out so comprehensively this "nefarious threat," there were previous attempts to do so in mid-1946—crucially, about the time that Shums′kyi reappeared on the leadership's radar with his letter and attempted suicide. Popereka's boss, minister for state security in Ukraine S. R. Savchenko, sent a detailed report to his boss, Abakumov, on 18 June 1946. This report provided detailed and devastatingly accurate information on the emerging relationship between Western intelligence agencies and the Organization of Ukrainian Nationalists (OUN), and on the networks in Europe through which Western support (money, cadres, operational instructions) was funneled into Ukraine.[38] Savchenko's report included information garnered from interrogations and intercepted correspondence of leading insurgents and communications from double and foreign agents. Abakumov took this information and positioned Shums′kyi at the nexus of domestic insurgency and Western intervention in order to secure Stalin's consent for his assassination in early August 1946, shortly after Shums′kyi's failed suicide attempts. While the periodization of reporting on this nexus established in the literature is important, clearly the leadership did not need to wait for its more comprehensive picture to develop in 1947 before it provided a new context in which to understand old ideological threats such as the one Shums′kyi posed and to inform its decision-making on how to deal with them.

Abakumov's situating of Shums′kyi at the center of all this in his reporting to Stalin—particularly with regard to Shums′kyi's (imagined) links with insurgents and nationalist émigrés supported by Western intelligence agencies—fit exceptionally well into his broader reporting to Stalin on the insurgency at this time.

Abakumov outlined the failures of the MVD, his agency's chief rival, to tackle or even to recognize the international threat, and to identify the scale of the nationalists' covert operations and the deeper implications of the struggle in Ukraine. A primary implication was that the threat posed by the insurgency was not only criminal (banditry within the confines of western Ukraine, which could be dealt with by the normal police tactics of the MVD), but also ideological, threatening the entire Soviet Union. To fight this threat, Abakumov and the MGB "revived the prewar practice of focusing on disaffected internal ideological enemies of the state who were deemed to represent a hotbed of opportunity for recruitment by foreign intelligence services."[39] The MGB uncovered many such cases around this time across the Soviet Union, particularly other nationalist groups that had collaborated with the Germans during the Second World War and had sought collaboration with the Western powers after the war to continue their struggle against Soviet power.[40] No enemy was more disaffected than Shums′kyi, who expressed this sentiment directly to Stalin. Abakumov did not even have to uncover him. Given the "evidence" of Shums′kyi's work with foreign intelligence agencies in the previous decade, he seemed a perfect candidate for international recruitment.

This strategy enabled Abakumov's and others to wrest control over counterinsurgency operations in western Ukraine and broader matters of state security across the Soviet Union from the MVD.[41] By late 1946, the MGB had acquired a great deal of the former jurisdictional power of the MVD, as well as thousands of its operatives, its equipment, and its "ever-greater influence in State affairs ... and, in some instances, its influence exceeded even that of Party and State organs."[42] Abakumov's strategy of reinterpreting ideological threats in such a way as to claw jurisdictional power from the MVD becomes evident through an analysis of his reporting to Stalin on Shums′kyi as compared to similar reporting from Sergei Kruglov, head of the MVD. These reports from late July to early September 1946 are currently located in the Central Archive of the Federal Security Service (Tsentral′nyi arkhiv FSB Rossii, TsA FSB) in Moscow. Although both were working from the same evidence base, Abakumov presented Shums′kyi as an international threat and a clear and present danger to Soviet security, whereas Kruglov reported factually and more circumspectly, in keeping with the evidence base. Neither was entirely familiar with the details of Shums´kyi's case since it began in 1933, though both had been briefed in detail by their respective subordinates in the wake of Shums´kyi's failed suicide attempts. These briefings were accurate and detailed summaries of the key points of Shums´kyi's case over the previous thirteen years. A 29 July 1946 briefing from the Krasnoiarsk MGB to Abakumov's deputy A. Ia. Gertsovskii, the head of section "A" (archives) in the MGB, noted Shums´kyi's refusal to confess to charges made against him in 1933 and 1937, the weakness of the latter charges, and the failure of police investigations (surveillance and questioning) to reveal any crimes Shums´kyi had committed since 1933 or, indeed, any suspicious activity at all:

> The case against Shums´kyi [of 1937] was dropped on 22 November 1939 due to the absence of any compromising material implicating Shums´kyi in any anti-Soviet activities after his arrest and conviction [in 1933] and during his exile period in Krasnoiarsk, as well as due to his illness (paralysis of the legs). ... We have not received any information from our agents about any operational value from his period of exile in Krasnoiarsk to the present, nor [have we] established evidence of any links [or contacts, *sviazi*] of operational interest.[43]

Unhappy with Gertsovskii's briefing on the facts of Shums´kyi's case, Abakumov ordered his MGB agents on the ground in Krasnoiarsk and Saratov to report any compromising information on Shums´kyi since his move to Saratov. The agents were instructed to phone Moscow at 10 pm on 20 August with this information.[44] They had little to report, but this did not stop Abakumov from using what information they did provide to invert Gertsovskii's briefing in his report to Stalin, declaring that Shums´kyi had *always* been guilty of all (evidenced) charges against him, which were dropped *only* because of his paralysis, and that he was certainly guilty. The new reporting allowed Abakumov to spin this interpretation in two ways. First, he focused on the reporting that argued, based on Shums´kyi's suicide note to Stalin, that "Shums'kyi had never changed his anti-Soviet views"—that is, the charges against him of counter-revolutionary activity in 1937 and his espionage activity were accurate despite being unproven.[45] Shums'kyi thus *always* maintained connections with local insurgents in Ukraine and nationalists abroad backed by Western intelligence agencies. Second, Abakumov tied together loose references in the reporting to argue that Shums'kyi's real destination in lobbying to leave Krasnoiarsk was not (and had never been) Saratov, as Shums'kyi had claimed, but was (and had always been) Ukraine.[46] In fact, Shums'kyi demanded passage to Ukraine from the hospital and the MGB only after his suicide attempts were unsuccessful, not before.[47] Claiming that Shums'kyi had always been a nationalist working toward undermining Soviet power, Abakumov rearranged the timeline of Shums'kyi's lobbying efforts to argue that he had always planned to go to Ukraine, rather than deciding on this course after he failed to kill himself. This rearrangement allowed Abakumov and his agents to conclude that Shums'kyi's suicide attempts were only a tactic to force the state to allow him to return to Ukraine to partake in the insurgency, which he had always supported, now with the assistance of Western intelligence agencies.[48] Abakumov and his agents on the ground thus used the suicide note to rewrite Shums'kyi's criminal history and project its future.

The greatest insight into Abakumov's thinking can be found in operational documents in the FSB archive, which include the detailed operational plan to assassinate Shums'kyi, signed by Abakumov, and the testimony of Pavlo Sudoplatov, one of the assassins who helped carry it out. (His testimony was submitted to the Central Committee of the CPSU in 1960, after Sudoplatov's arrest.) Sudoplatov's career as one of Stalin's leading assassins and his later travails during de-Stalinization are well know from his sensationalist memoir published soon after the collapse of the Soviet Union.[49] It contains some unsubstantiated claims about the real motivations of Soviet leaders, which Sudoplatov could not have known, and asserts that all the leading scientists in the Manhattan Project were Soviet informants.[50] Like Sudoplatov's testimony from 1960, which he provided while working on his release from prison, his recollections were influenced by political considerations and are often self-justifying. Nevertheless, his testimony and memoir regarding Shums´kyi are closely aligned, and we can now substantiate many of his claims using the declassified documentation we have on Shums´kyi's case and assassination (permitting some errors in Sudoplatov's dates and timeline). In his October 1960 testimony on Shums´kyi's assassination, Sudoplatov claimed:

> On 23 August 1945 [*sic*; correct year was 1946], Abakumov sent a report to Stalin seeking his permission to assassinate Shums´kyi, O. Ia., noting that Shums´kyi was a clear Ukrainian nationalist. ... In 1933 he was convicted as one of the leaders of the Ukrainian Military Organization. He was arrested again in 1937 while in exile in Krasnoiarsk for anti-Soviet activities; however, he was released in 1939 due to his serious illness (paralysis of the legs) and the case against him was dropped.[51]

In his report to Stalin, Abakumov again ignored the two major factors reported to him that accounted for the NKVD dropping the case—the lack of evidence and Shums´kyi's refusal to confess—to claim falsely that Shums´kyi had always "behaved like a wicked enemy of Soviet power in exile." Sudoplatov testified further that

> [Abakumov went on] to state further in his note to Stalin [now mostly accurately] that Shums´kyi revealed his anti-Soviet views in a letter to the leaders of the CP(b) and insulted Soviet nationalities policy. Having arrived in Saratov, he demanded that he be sent to his homeland (Kyiv) and attempted suicide on 16 [*sic*; the correct date was 17–18] July 1946. Abakumov's note concluded with the instruction: Shums´kyi is subject to immediate isolation. It is essential that he is not arrested so as not to attract any attention from the Ukrainian nationalists but liquidated by poisoning.[52]

According to Sudoplatov, Abakumov claimed in his report to Stalin that he had evidence proving that Shums´kyi had established links with Western contacts:

> According to the Ukrainian MGB, Shums´kyi ... foolishly established contact with émigré circles overseas and pursued covert schemes in order to become a member of the temporary government formed

in emigration, the Ukrainian Supreme Liberation Council [Ukraïns´ka holovna vyzvol´na rada] (UHVR).

If Shums´kyi was not going back to Ukraine to flee to the West and join the UHVR (how an ill and paralyzed man could do this, no one explained), then he was clearly using the "threat of suicide," as Abakumov put it, to return to help organize the insurgency.[53]

Kruglov first reported on Shums´kyi's attempted suicide to Stalin only a few days afterward, on 20 July 1946, and attached the suicide note for Stalin to read. Whereas Abakumov drew a straight line of guilt between Shums´kyi's original conviction, his later charges in 1937, and his attempted suicide in order to present Shums´kyi as a current threat, Kruglov was less direct. He reported only that Shums´kyi had been arrested in 1933 and had his conviction commuted to exile in 1935, that his wife had been shot by the NKVD in 1937, and that he had a long history of seeking political rehabilitation. Crucially, Kruglov elected to explain Shums´kyi's attempted suicide as a protest following his failure to achieve political rehabilitation from the party, citing other correspondence from Shums´kyi ("my suicide is a protest against the situation and violence committed against me"), rather than as a protest against the Soviet policy of Ukraine's re-Russification, as Abakumov had argued.[54] Shums´kyi gave both reasons for his suicide attempt in his letter to Stalin, and it is telling that Kruglov and Abakumov chose to stress opposing explanations in their reporting.[55] For Abakumov, explaining Shums´kyi's attempted suicide as a protest against Soviet policy allowed him to extrapolate it as part of Shums´kyi's alleged counterrevolutionary plans, while Kruglov's analysis painted the attempted suicide as a result of Shums´kyi's personal misfortune—this was a depressed and paralyzed criminal who had lost his wife, his reputation, and thus his will to live. The worst that Kruglov could come up with regarding Shums´kyi's intentions in summarizing the suicide note was that it "characterizes his revolutionary and nationalist views," with no mention of the insurgency or Western links.[56] This sober summary would not position the MVD anywhere near taking control of Shums´kyi's case (the MGB did this). Kruglov may not have been as interested in Shums´kyi as Abakumov was, but this comparison reveals that Abakumov generally understood how to manufacture threats to expand his domain.

The sections of Sudoplatov's testimony available to us show that he, too, said little about Shums´kyi's Western connections in 1960. This may well be because the MGB's evidence of any ties between Shums´kyi and the insurgency or émigré nationalists who were supported by Western agencies were never confirmed by Abakumov or the political leadership at the time. Sudoplatov noted nonchalantly in his memoir: "By the way, we never actually managed to establish the existence of these foreign links."[57] Though he probably did not know it, Shums´kyi's case had been dismissed as fabricated and Shums´kyi found not guilty of the charges against him by the Military Collegium's review of his case in 1958, barely two years before Sudoplatov testified.[58] Sudoplatov's testimony, though accurate, was also part of his broader attempt to reduce or annul his prison sentence, in support of which any discussion of Shums´kyi's Western links may not have been helpful. His memoir, on the other hand, can be read as an attempt to excuse or justify his murder of numerous people, thus the discussion of these illegal connections could be seen as a legitimate reason for executing Shums´kyi, even if the connections were later disproved.

Not that proving these supposed relationships really mattered at the time. All the criminal charges against Shums´kyi—in 1933, 1937, and 1940—referred to these ties in one way or another, and, by July 1946, the leadership shared the understanding that Shums´kyi was guilty of all of them. What really mattered by this time was that Abakumov and those in Stalin's inner circle pushing for Shums´kyi's assassination (especially Khrushchev and Kaganovich) used the MGB evidence to connect Shums´kyi to the current insurgency and specifically to the UHVR, which they understood as part of the much broader threat posed by domestic insurgency and Western assistance. The UHVR was formed in 1944 by the OUN and UPA as an attempt to establish a broader political and social base for the insurgency, encompassing a wide of range of anti-Soviet groups working toward the underlying aim of establishing an independent Ukraine. As the Germans fled Ukraine, the UHVR would become a more suitable vehicle than the OUN—tainted as it was by its collaboration with Nazi Germany and its protofascist outlook—to attract assistance from Western powers in battling the Soviets. The UHVR proclaimed itself the "supreme organ of the Ukrainian people in its war of revolutionary liberation," but it existed in this sense only on paper. Though the UHVR sought to attract groups and members with different political leanings and ethnicities, the OUN and UPA remained the driving force behind it and their members filled its leadership positions.[59] Notably, however, the "government formed in the emigration" to which Sudoplatov referred did exist and did have Western connections. This was a reference to the UHVR's External Representation (*zakordonne predstavnytstvo*, ZP UHVR), formed in 1944 by leading OUN and UPA members, who fled to Western Europe to establish contacts with the Western Allies. The ZP UHVR elicited support from the Americans and British from 1945 onward, became a US Central Intelligence Agency front in the early 1950s, and continued to operate abroad in the years after the end of the insurgency in the mid-1950s.[60]

There is significant scholarship on the UHVR and a range of debates over its function and role in the insurgency and in Ukrainian history.[61] What is more important here is to understand how the Soviet leadership aligned Shums´kyi so easily with the UHVR when there was little objective evidence—indeed, little common sense—to support this alignment, and what this tells us about the leadership's broader understanding of the threat of domestic insurgency supported by Western assistance. The Soviet knowledge of UHVR activities was mostly accurate, informed by its interrogation of leading UHVR members in Ukraine and its confiscation of UHVR documentation, correspondence, and information from its vast agent networks in western Europe, where the ZP UHVR was active. The MGB did not fear the UHVR as a competitor for state authority in Ukraine, as some sort of national government, but saw it as a front for the achievement of OUN and UPA nationalist aims. The UHVR's appearance as an inclusive and at least protodemocratic polity—a pluralistic anti-Soviet organization combining different ethnicities and various political and cultural anti-Soviet groups both within and beyond Ukraine—promised to be more successful at eliciting support both in Ukraine and from the Western Allies than was the OUN, especially in the event of an Allied-Soviet conflict. Likewise, the ZP UHVR was seen as a threat because it was the conduit through which assistance would be delivered to Ukraine from both Western intelligence agencies and the large pool of Ukrainian emigrants abroad.

On 14 June 1946, just over a month before Shums´kyi's suicide attempts, the minister for state security in Ukraine, Savchenko, reported (accurately) to Abakumov that the multifaceted threat had been realized. UHVR representatives (OUN and UPA leaders) had left Ukraine in 1944 for Europe to work toward unifying the disparate émigré communities in occupied Germany, the rest of Europe, the United States, and Canada, in order to solicit support for the insurgency and aid from the British and American governments:

> The OUN had established a foreign center of operations, the so-called UHVR, which declared itself a supraparty organization, whose aim is to unite all Ukrainians living abroad, regardless of their political affiliations… [as well as to] establish ties with anti-Soviet groups in emigration also comprising other nationalities and with reactionary circles within Western governments, primarily England and the United States … in the fight for the establishment of an independent Ukrainian state. … The OUN intends to use this organization to conceal its nationalist activities among Ukrainian émigrés in all countries.[62]

The OUN pursued these aims by sending its most authoritative members, who were well known to émigré communities, to establish these ties abroad and by instructing the UPA in Ukraine to conclude pacts with its enemies, the Polish Underground Army (Armia Krajowa, AK), and various Ukrainian political forces in service of the common fight against Soviet power. The MGB claimed to possess "evidence that highlighted the successful realization of these aims by the OUN, whose actions were supported by the British and Americans, who, broadly, were taking active measures to recruit anti-Soviet cadres among Ukrainian émigrés to use against us."[63]

MGB reports at this time focused on the threat posed by a potentially close alliance among various political forces united by their anti-Soviet disposition rather than their political alignment. At least in Ukraine, the threat of a broad-based coalition was not realized, as any peace agreements between the UPA and the Armia Krajowa soon floundered and conflict between them resumed.[64] However, the MGB had good reason to take the threat of a coalition seriously in mid-1946 and to think deeply about how old "authoritative figures" among Ukrainian nationalists might pose new problems within this context, either by going abroad or by returning to Ukraine.

Shums´kyi appeared on Abakumov's radar at exactly this time, with his attempted suicides and his note to Stalin. According to Sudoplatov, when Soviet leaders discussed Shums´kyi's suicide attempts, they noted that he "foolishly established contact with Ukrainian cultural figures in Kyiv and abroad while exiled in Saratov."[65] Though inaccurate, this claim (from Abakumov) and the claim that Shums´kyi had sought to join the UHVR in Ukraine or abroad made sense to the leadership for numerous reasons. Shums´kyi had spent time in Poland in the 1920s and Germany in the early 1930s, countries that were now a base for Western assistance to the insurgency. It was primarily in the Allied occupation zones of Germany, Savchenko reported to Abakumov in June, that "the Americans and especially the British are taking active measures to recruit anti-Soviet cadres among Ukrainian émigrés to use against us."[66] The leadership likely also fixated on the 1937 charges against Shums´kyi of "maintaining connections with the Berlin center of the UMO to prepare for insurgency activities and sabotage in agriculture, as well as leading preparations for central terrorist actions," and on Shums´kyi's long history of criticizing Soviet policy and Stalin's decisions in Ukraine based on Shums´kyi's "foreign exposure." (A key piece of evidence in Shums´kyi's conviction in 1933 was that, upon returning from Germany in 1932, Shums´kyi, in conversation with his friends, criticized the Soviet Ukrainian government for its pursuit of collectivization, with its ruinous consequences.)[67] If Shums´kyi's suicide saga was a means for him to return to Ukraine either as a final destination or as a way station for going abroad, then, as the leadership understood it, it had to be that, as someone well known in nationalist circles and openly critical of the current nationalities policy, he was intending to fight against the regime with other nationalist forces.

Apparently, there was no contradiction in Shums´kyi the communist joining the broad-based coalition led mostly by protofascist forces, since Shums´kyi had supposedly never been a "real" communist, but had used his position in the party only as a cover to further his nationalist agenda. This rationale seemed solid enough and the threat posed by Shums´kyi appeared real enough for Abakumov to task Sergei Ogoltsov, deputy head of the MGB, with carrying out the assassination plan, and for Kaganovich himself, Shums´kyi's old enemy and deputy head of the government under Stalin, to travel to Saratov to identify his corpse and make sure the job had been done.[68]

We know from the visitor register at Stalin's Kremlin office, declassified in the Russian archives, that Abakumov met Stalin there on 7 September 1946, from 10:30 to 10:50 p.m.[69] Other leaders present at this time included Anastas Mikoian, Nikolai Bulganin, Aleksei Kosygin, Georgii Malenkov, and Lavrentii Beria, with Nikita Khrushchev, Konstantin Vershinin, and Ivan Serov (Kruglov's deputy and Abakumov's major rival) arriving after Abakumov had left. The purpose of Abakumov's meeting was clearly to discuss the plan for Shums´kyi's assassination with Stalin, who approved it; Abakumov signed the plan, code-named Operation *Khorek* (weasel), the following day (on 8 September).[70] It is worthwhile to quote the plan in detail to demonstrate how leading assassination teams, or "task forces" as they were called—in this case comprising ten members—eliminated their enemies, and how the leadership imagined Shums´kyi's death might affect the insurgency:

> For carrying out the operation ordered by the Minister of State Security of the USSR, the task force is established under the leadership of "Andrei" [Sudoplatov]. The task force consists of:
>
> 1. Colonel Lebedev, V. E.
> 2. Colonel of the Medical Service, Mairanovskii, G. M.
> 3. Colonel Korovin, P. A.
> 4. Sn. Lieutenant Kruglov, B. A. (driver)
> 5. Sn. Sergeant Bekhtin, A. V. (driver)
> 6. Pantiukhin, S. A. (driver)
>
> and the following agents:
>
> 1. "*Ruf*"
> 2. "*Barchukov*"
> 3. "*Gorokhov*"

Pozharov, G. F., is in reserve.

The relevant documents for each person in the task force are attached.

1. The operation is planned tentatively for execution in Sorok [code name for Saratov].
2. The task force leaves for Sorok on September 10, 1946, in Dodge and Studebaker vehicles.
3. The task force stops near Sorok, contacts Comrade Plestsov [head of Saratov MGB], finds out the whereabouts of "*Khorek*", assesses the situation, makes additional reconnaissance on its own, and decides how to conduct the operation.
4. The operation is to be conducted so as to give the impression that the "*Khorek*" died from medical complications, in order not to attract their [the nationalists'] attention and invite retaliation.
5. Special means [*spetsial'nye sredstva*] have been authorized for use against "*Khorek*."
6. The task force travels to Sorok disguised as a team of servicemen supposedly for the purpose of scouting suitable places for special construction of the USSR Ministry of the Armed Forces [Ministerstvo vooruzhennykh sil, MVS].
7. The task force is supplied with the necessary documents, civilian and military clothing, food, and money, so as to be independent of local authorities in matters of housing and food.[71]

Shums'kyi provided the task force with the perfect opportunity to conduct the operation. The day before the task force arrived in Saratov, on 9 September, the Saratov MGB reported to Moscow (specifically, to the head of the fifth division of the MGB [operational and secret-political matters], Lieutenant General P. G. Drozdetskii) that Shums'kyi had threatened to kill himself in the hospital if the MGB did not provide him with passage to Ukraine. The Saratov MGB immediately "implemented prophylactic measures to stop Shums'kyi from committing suicide, though noted advice from the doctors that there was no longer any reason to keep Shums'kyi in the hospital [his wounds had healed]."[72]

The task force resolved this stalemate by organizing Shums'kyi's departure from Saratov by train on 18 September, under the pretext of allowing him to return to his home (Kyiv). Shums'kyi's death was recorded en route in the registry office (known as Organ zapisi aktov grazhdanskogo sostoianiia, ZAGS) in Kirsanov, almost 400 kilometers (250 miles) north of Saratov, the following day. The autopsy revealed that his death occurred in his railway carriage as a result of a "hemorrhage in the cranial cavity."[73]

This was exactly the type of medical complication that the task force anticipated would be recorded in the autopsy, and was also the reason why Grigorii Mairanovskii, the physician in charge of the radioactive poison unit of the MGB's department of operational techniques (*otdel operativnoi tekhniki*), was included in the task force. Mairanovskii developed the "special means" (radioactive poison), which he injected into Shums´kyi while the other members of the task force held him down in his railway carriage, covering his mouth so he could not scream. The task force entered Shums´kyi's carriage at night, likely during the shift change of railway personnel, striking quietly and quickly. Having reconnoitered the train extensively, the task force knew exactly where Shums´kyi was, even in the dark, within the layout of his carriage. The task force's copy of the train and staff schedules is preserved in the FSB archive, along with its hand-drawn schema of the train, the location of its compartments, toilets, and so forth, recorded on the back of a Kazbek cigarette packet.[74]

This operation remained secret until Sudoplatov's memoir was published in the early 1990s (the Kirsanov MGB head was not even informed of it), as did the reason for Shums´kyi's death (most people who cared to know speculated that he had killed himself, or had been shot or died in a camp like his comrades). The task force thus avoided the feared retaliation—a fear that was unfounded, given that the Ukrainian nationalists considered Shums´kyi a communist enemy, but entirely logical, given the leadership's (skewed) understanding of Shums´kyi's threat. Ukrainian nationalists had long employed political assassination to remove their political enemies, as well as for propaganda purposes.[75] They claimed some high-profile Soviet scalps, including General Nikolai Vatutin, who had commanded the First Ukrainian Front, which had led the Soviet reoccupation of Ukraine in 1944. More broadly, nationalists killed 2,258 Soviet police, NKVD, and Red Army soldiers in 1944; 1,348 in 1945; and 696 in 1946; as well as thousands more Soviet activists, mostly party members sent to western Ukraine to form the structure of Soviet rule and to try to win support from the local population.[76]

The secrecy surrounding Shums′kyi's murder, indeed his entire case, endured long after 1946. Shums′kyi was rehabilitated secretly by the Military Collegium in 1958, after the Collegium's chief prosecutor, A. Gornyi, asked it to quash Shums′kyi's conviction as unlawful, in the midst of Krushchev's de-Stalinization drive.[77] When Shums′kyi's murder became known in the 1990s, few in Ukraine—nationalists, communists, or anyone else—hailed him as either a hero or a traitor. Shums′kyi remained on the margins of the historical and contemporary imaginations of his countrymen. Yet, in his death as in his life, Shums′kyi continues to pose uncomfortable but pressing questions for the history of Soviet Ukraine and the long shadow it casts over the contemporary Ukrainian state, a subject to which we now turn.

CONCLUSIONS

Shums'kyi: As for my "personal traditions" [my past] ... which Comrade Zatons'kyi keeps on bringing up ... I can say only that I do not have any "personal traditions" besides always fighting for the liberation of the working class and for Ukraine. Since the beginning of my revolutionary career in 1909, I have not wavered from this fight one iota.

A. V. Ivanov: That is not true.

Shums'kyi: That is only not true from your incorrect viewpoint. ... I was arrested and sentenced to death for waging a battle against nationalist counterrevolution from the first days of October [the 1917 Revolution]. I fought for Soviet power the entire time.

Ivanov: I never once saw you.

Shums'kyi: Everyone who actively fought for Soviet power saw me. That you did not is a matter for your conscience. I hardly ever saw you—you were often in Moscow during the hardest moments [of the revolution]. I do not shy away from any aspect of my past, indeed, I am proud of it, as there is nothing in my past not befitting a Bolshevik revolutionary—a Ukrainian Bolshevik.

—Politburo meeting,
Central Committee of the CP(b)U,
12 May 1926

Shums'kyi was wrong. Despite his assertion to Andrii Ivanov in this meeting, much about his past was not befitting a Bolshevik revolutionary.[1] The Bolsheviks generally regarded revolutionaries from other leftist parties who joined theirs after the revolution as *poputchiki* (literally, fellow travelers). Leon Trotsky summed up this understanding well in reflecting on his own experience in joining the Bolsheviks, many of whom looked at him as someone who was with them, but not one of them. Shums′kyi continued to believe, however, probably until this time in 1926, that he and his fellow former Borotbysts—who possessed the local authority, skill, and language that the Bolsheviks lacked in Ukraine—were still vital to the establishment of communist rule there. Many Borotbysts who joined the Bolsheviks and survived the cull of their membership in the 1920s still considered themselves if not "full" Bolsheviks, then at least equal allies on Ukrainian soil. But the Bolsheviks shattered what remained of this belief in the campaign against Shums′kyism and the later purges.

Shums′kyi's confidence in the term "Ukrainian Bolshevik" was also beginning to wane, secretly, in 1926.[2] This term would soon become oxymoronic. It was becoming increasingly difficult for so many party members like him—those committed to fulfilling the stated aims of Ukrainization—to be both Ukrainian, at least in the way they understood it, and Bolshevik at the same time. Some of Shums′kyi's opponents came to understand this contradiction earlier than he did. More importantly, they realized that this contradiction was impossible to resolve, while others—those who only ever understood Ukrainian independence as a game to be played to enable the establishment of Bolshevik rule in Ukraine—saw no contradiction at all. Shums′kyi's fundamental undoing was his enduring pursuit of this aim of Ukrainization. Despite his reservations, he long fought to see his beloved Ukraine as both a communist and an independent state in a broader union of equal Soviet republics, a vision that was still guaranteed in law by the Bolshevik party program and, after the party abandoned it, in the Constitution of the USSR.

This was a fundamental difference between Shums′kyi and the faux Ukrainizers in the party who paid lip service to the policy but often worked against it. These people had the advantage in intraparty politics. They could attack enemies in the party who opposed the policy as unappreciative of the national question or, worse, as Great Russian chauvinists; they could attack those who supported the policy wholeheartedly as dangerous nationalists. They continued to change the definitions and the policy's acceptable middle ground to push their enemies to the extremes. Lazar Kaganovich disposed of Shums′kyi in this way, and Stalin did the same to numerous opponents in the 1920s and 1930s.

Shums′kyi understood these tactics; he also understood that he, by failing to use them, was disadvantaged in the fight with Kaganovich in 1926. But Shums′kyi still did not adopt these tactics to gain an advantage for himself. Instead, he hardened his commitment to Ukrainization as a means to realize Ukrainian statehood. He derided the faux Ukrainizers, the Ukrainian Bolsheviks who saw no contradiction between Ukrainization and Bolshevism. They were dominant in the party, but Ukrainian only in name. The communist Ukraine they were building was neither communist nor independently Ukrainian, but servile to Moscow, as had been the case for Ukraine throughout its modern history. This was the essence of Shums′kyi's "Malorossiia" (Little Russia) thesis, which he expressed at the 1926 Politburo meeting just before Andrii Ivanov, a famous revolutionary clearly insulted at Shums′kyi's barely veiled description of people like him, interjected so rudely. Shums′kyi explained his thesis further when the Ukrainian party elder Hryhorii Petrovs′kyi asked him once (in Russian) why Shums′kyi did not love the term "maloross." After all, the Bolsheviks understood this term as referring only to Russified Ukrainians who were closer to them culturally than to the Ukrainian peasantry and thus a positive base for building Bolshevik rule in Ukraine. Shums′kyi understood the term differently and replied to Petrovs′kyi, whom he considered a Russified Ukrainian, thus:

> Why don't I love this despicable, selfish Little Russian [maloross]? Because he has always been equally unprincipled, hypocritical, slavishly insincere, and treacherously flattering across all historical epochs. Now he calls himself a communist and shouts a lot about "internationalism" ... but he remains the same.[3]

Sometime later, Petrovs′kyi reminded Shums′kyi of this conversation, warning him, "Always keep in mind that the party will NEVER forgive you for your 'little Russians.' You will pay for this. Mark my word, you will pay."[4]

Shums´kyi paid for this remark many times over. The absurd array of criminal charges laid against him—counterrevolutionary activities, national bias, espionage, efforts to separate Ukraine from the Soviet Union, and more—were only expressions of the original sin of this remark. Shums´kyi's "Malorossiia" thesis claimed to expose the illegitimacy of Soviet rule in Ukraine under Stalin, the hypocrisy of Ukrainization and the broader Soviet nationalities project. Stalin, Kaganovich, Khrushchev, and all the other leaders involved in Shums´kyi's case never accepted the veracity of his thesis. Indeed, their construction of Shums´kyism as a nationalist diversion helped them emasculate Ukrainization and purge its adherents. So veracity was never the point. What really stung the leadership was that Shums´kyi persisted with this dangerous thesis long after it had been "destroyed" in Ukraine, and long after his arrest, conviction, and torture, and the execution of his wife. Deploying these weapons against opponents usually silenced them, if they stayed alive, but not Shums´kyi.

Though vexed, the leadership did not respond by killing Shums´kyi, which it could have done at any point leading up to 1946. Other leaders of counterrevolutionary movements—those to whose surname the regime added the ending -ism, thus turning it into a dangerous phenomenon, a hostile movement, an aberration—generally did not survive in the Soviet Union and were lucky to escape it with their lives. What kept Shums´kyi alive for so long, it seems clear now, was his protest campaign. His refusal to confess was continually raised as the key obstacle to the progression of his case—one to which Shums´kyi further contributed by his hunger strikes and letter-writing, which irritated police, complicated political procedures, and exploited the relations between the various responsible agencies.

An experienced insider of the Soviet government, Shums´kyi knew what the sore points were in relations between these bodies—especially the party, the judiciary, and the police, as well as between central and peripheral arms of the police in times of chaos. At critical moments in his journey, Shums´kyi pressed on these points—namely, the unwillingness of officials to take responsibility for complex cases, and the antagonism Siberian Chekists felt toward their superiors for demanding action without providing support, which was returned by Moscow for the Chekists' delays. These antagonisms helped stall his case. He understood the internal bureaucratic contradictions of the Soviet system—after all, he had helped build the system in Ukraine—better than did his associates and, in some cases, better than did the political and police leaders prosecuting his case.

Shums´kyi's protest was successful also because he understood how to wage it differently in different contexts, during and after purge periods, and especially when relations between the police and the party were strained. His case reveals just how effective a tactic of embarrassing police before the party and judiciary could be in stalling cases. In the post-purge period, when the party reduced police powers by proclaiming "socialist legality," NKVD leaders were deeply concerned that the party and the judiciary might uncover how shoddily they had constructed the conspiracies against Shums´kyi and others. Of course, the party did not uncover anything new, as it had been a central player with the various police organizations in fabricating these conspiracies during the purge. Now the party used this evidence to prosecute police organizations and strip their powers as it scaled down repression. Sensing these scale-downs in repression, Shums´kyi doubled down on embarrassing police for their purge activities. His complaints about their illegal conduct and the ludicrous nature of the (changing) charges against him became hugely problematic for police and even prosecutors. Shums´kyi's deft timing in his protest campaign was the key element in securing his greatest successes: the commutation of his prison sentence to exile in 1935 and the dropping of criminal charges against him in 1939.

It is remarkable that a man who suffered from such serious medical ailments, both physical and psychological, could have conducted this protest campaign so skillfully. It is also remarkable that such an intelligent man came to understand the real Catch-22 of his situation only late in his life. As long as he waged this protest campaign in the way that he did—that is, conceding some mistakes in his political viewpoints but never absolving himself of them completely, never confessing to the regime's understanding of his errors or crimes, and never groveling to the authorities for forgiveness—he would never secure his protest's ultimate aim of political rehabilitation (if it ever was achievable). Shums´kyi remained a true believer in the Soviet project almost until the end of his life, but he lost faith in its leadership. So it was not within his character to confess and grovel to it for absolution, like so many other true believers did during the Great Terror. This list included his former deputy in the People's Commissariat for Education, Petro Solodub, who claimed to Shums´kyi that he only gave false testimony against himself and Shums´kyi under interrogation because the "party needed it."[5] Shums´kyi would not give false testimony: in his mind, the party needed him, even if, or primarily because, its leadership could not see why. Had he confessed like Solodub, he likely would have been shot alongside him and the many others who did so. The leadership's response to Shums´kyi's protest was to let him live, but only in disgrace, with his reputation torn, and only in pain, denied the medical treatment he needed to improve his condition.

By the time Shums´kyi fully understood this Catch-22, not incidentally at about the time he lost faith in the party, probably by mid-1945, he would no longer maintain it. It was only then that the leadership decided to kill him. No matter how critical Shums´kyi had been of the regime's treatment of him, how hard he had protested, his ultimate aim had remained to achieve absolution from the party itself; his entire protest was based on the shared assumption of the party's supremacy in matters of life and death. As long as Shums´kyi's protest continued based on this assumption, and with a certain amount of luck, he survived. Shums´kyi's October 1945 suicide note to Stalin represented his abandonment of his quest for absolution, and his attempted suicide in July 1946 represented his abandonment of the assumption of the party's supremacy in matters of life and death. Shums´kyi broke out of the Catch-22 that had kept him alive and went beyond the pale, so to speak, where he was no longer safe. The pressures of 1946—domestic nationalist insurgency, Western intervention in Ukraine, and rising Cold War tensions—provided the leadership with a context in which to situate the "new" threat posed by Shums´kyi. The leadership clearly suspected he was up to something, based on his history of supposed counterrevolutionary activity and his time spent abroad. This was not simply a facade. But the leadership so easily situated Shums´kyi in a new threat context only because he had finally crossed an unacceptable line. If he had always been an enemy, now, beyond absolution, he was a most dangerous one who "needed to be isolated [liquidated] immediately and secretly," per Viktor Abakumov's orders.[6]

Stalin and the leadership likely never anticipated that Shums´kyi would confess to the false charges they leveled at him. They knew of his resilience but were genuinely angered by Shums´kyi's suicide note. Shums´kyi's rude tone, his insults leveled at Soviet policy and Stalin personally, surely strengthened its resolve to kill him as soon as possible. Shums´kyi had been writing to Stalin, whom he had known personally, regularly for over twenty years, first on his dealings with Kaganovich in the mid-1920s, and later on the travails of his demotion, arrest, and exile. Shums´kyi had always done so in a respectful tone, until his suicide note. For the first time he did not ask Stalin to assist him, either in his career, life, or political rehabilitation (for which he had lost hope). Instead, he blamed Stalin directly for Khrushchev's dangerous speech on Ukraine in October 1945: "Your own speech full of compliments to the Russian people and segregation of the peoples of the Soviet Union by their intelligence and strength of character already set a dangerous precedent ... which Nikita Khrushchev, in his Little-Russian lyrical ecstasy, has applied to Ukraine."[7] Shums´kyi went on to criticize Khrushchev's speech as a "national-political castration" of the Ukrainian people, but he also warned Stalin that Khrushchev's language, reflective of Stalin's own policy of Great Russian chauvinism, threatened to fuel the Ukrainian nationalism that was raging in the insurgency. Not only was Stalin again departing from the stated aims of the Soviet revolutionary project of equality among Soviet republics (Lenin had charged Stalin with this error and Great Russian chauvinism in the 1920s), but he was now fueling the anti-Soviet nationalist insurgency the regime was fighting against.[8]

Soviet citizens did not speak to Stalin like this. Those very few who dared to do so did not escape punishment, especially in 1945, at the height of Stalin's cult of personality. Victorious in war and internationally acclaimed as one of the "Big Three" leaders, he was revered at home as a demigod, as one Russian historian notes:

> Stalin the man had by this time been so transformed into the idol of the *vozhd´* [leader] that he virtually acquired the image of a living icon. The mass consciousness, attributing mystical power to the icon ... canonized all that was identified with it, be it the authority of the system or the authority of the ideas on which the system was based.[9]

In his letter, Shums´kyi reduced the demigod to a mortal leader, and not much of one at that, and derided his creation. If Shums´kyi had managed to sting the leadership in his years of protest in different ways, his show of contempt toward it (by word in 1945 and by deed in 1946) stung the most. The leadership's irritation was palpable in the language it used when deciding to kill Shums´kyi in 1946. According to Sudoplatov, the Soviet leadership recounted that "Shums´kyi was disrespectful to Stalin in his discussions with his friends. ... Shums´kyi permitted himself to *disagree* with Stalin's opinion of him. ... Shums´kyi also sent an insolent [*derzkii*] letter to Stalin ... [in which] he slandered [*klevetal*] the Soviet nationalities policies."[10] When Abakumov met with Stalin late on the night of 7 August 1946 and likely received final approval for the assassination plan, it was certainly within his character to have pointed out to Stalin the code name they had chosen for Shums´kyi, *Khorek* (weasel). It is also likely that Abakumov referred to Shums´kyi by this name when he phoned Stalin to inform him that the assassination plan had been successfully implemented.[11] The weasel had been caught.

It is not inconsequential that Abakumov and the others referred to Shums´kyi as a rodent. Their humiliation, even dehumanization of him was not only a response to Shums´kyi's "traitorous" crimes and insults. It was a long time coming. Chekists had been informing the leadership for years of the minutiae of Shums´kyi's depredations under arrest and in exile: how he lay paralyzed in his own urine when on hunger strike, how he needed an enema, how he stank, how he had become emaciated with time, lost his teeth, and suffered from typhoid and numerous other diseases. Even then, the leadership still imagined that the rodent was lying about his paralysis. Chekists directed their informants to spy on Shums´kyi overnight, to see whether he ever stood up from his bed when no one was watching. They directed the head doctor of the Krasnoiarsk state hospital to establish a ruse to remove Shums′kyi from his ward, so that their informants could search his bed for an elusive diary they imagined he kept, to which he confessed his terrible secrets. They never found it, because the diary, like Shums′kyi's crimes, remained only a figment of the Soviet leadership's imagination.[12]

An analysis of Shums′kyi's life offers deep insights into the building of Soviet rule in Ukraine in the 1920s and the decimation of the Ukrainian political and cultural leadership in the 1930s in the machinery of repression. The leadership's language toward Shums′kyi and their perverse preoccupation with humiliating him along with his comrades remind us of the pettiness at work in the heart of the Soviet project. One of the most powerful regimes the world had ever seen, one that completely dominated 170 million souls at home and more still across its empire, obsessed desperately about whether one of its political opponents could piss standing up. It succeeded in humiliating its opponents and even more of its supporters by forcing them to confess to their own and to their comrades' imaginary sins before death, legitimating the violence and, broadly, the entire political system. But they could not do this to Shums′kyi. He clearly understood in 1945 that, because of his continuing protests, the leadership would kill him if he did not kill himself; he continued protesting until they finally did. Had Shums′kyi not sent his suicide letter to Stalin and decided to die, he might have lived out the rest of his painful life in Saratov without much trouble from the regime. But if his survival and refusal to confess had been the key elements of his protests from 1933 almost to his death, by 1945, Shums′kyi reckoned that all he had left in terms of protest was to give his life. His ultimate aim remained the same—political rehabilitation—not by the party now but, judging from the notes he left by his suicide bed, by posterity.

Ironically, Shums′kyi got his first wish in death, when he was rehabilitated by the party secretly in 1958. He was one of many victims of Stalin's repressions to be rehabilitated under Khrushchev's de-Stalinization drive, on the basis that the charges condemning them were fabricated.[13] Shums′kyi would probably not have been pleased to receive anything from Khrushchev apart from his own confession for his crimes against Ukraine and the revolution. Nor would Shums´kyi ever have understood himself as a victim—and, perhaps, neither should we. He was a committed revolutionary with some blood on his hands, and his preferred form of "national communism," a marriage of nationalism and communism, remained true to the ideals of the revolution shared by so many on the peripheries of the emerging union in the euphoria of the 1920s, but placed at risk the full realization of Stalin's empire thereafter. Shums´kyi's ideas remained dangerous, or at least irreconcilable, even long after Stalin's death, as Stalin's Soviet Union of fictitiously independent Soviet republics endured until it collapsed under the weight of this fiction in 1991, when the republics' declaration of true independence from Moscow sealed the Soviet Union's fate.

Shums´kyi's attempted marriage of nationalism and communism proved irreconcilable in post-Soviet Ukraine as well. This book was conceived by the authors in Kyiv in 2015, when a new Ukrainian government took power in the wake of the Maidan Revolution and in the midst of the Russian Federation's military aggression against eastern Ukraine. Partly in response, the Ukrainian government passed a packet of "decommunization" legislation that outlawed the veneration of Soviet communist figures in Ukrainian history and mandated the veneration of anticommunist nationalist figures who fought against Soviet power.[14] How could one now commemorate Shums´kyi and other communists who died fighting against Soviet power to realize both their nationalist and their communist ideals? What is to be done with those who died for the dream of an independent Ukrainian state in equal union with Russia, when the latter had just forcibly annexed parts of Ukrainian territory (Crimea)?

Shums´kyi and his colleagues as historical figures may thus be considered by some as passé, as people who operated in a context so different from our own as to make their ideas and examples irrelevant to the present. We argue to the contrary. Shums´kyi's example stands against monochromatic appropriations of complex pasts that seem politically useful in the contemporary moment. He reminds us that, just as Russian contempt for Ukrainian statehood remains dominant across the different political regimes and philosophies that have and will rule that country, so, too, it is the obligation and political heritage of Ukrainians affiliated with every political movement to fight that contempt. For all the historical value of Shums´kyi's work in Ukrainization, his sacrifice in defiance of Stalinist repression—which allows us to glean unique insights into the entire Soviet project—is a reminder to cultivate unity across political division and is surely his greatest, if unintended, achievement.

The reminder to strive for unity in Ukraine is even more pertinent at the time of this book's completion, with the Russian Federation having launched a full-scale invasion of the country, threatening its very existence as an independent state. For all of the contemporary speculation about Russia's military objectives in this invasion, Russia's enduring historical aims in its aggression against Ukraine lie not far beneath the surface. Shums´kyi recognized them in 1946 thinly wrapped in the postwar nationalities policy. Now, as then, Moscow seeks to make the country a constituent part once again, to force Ukraine back into the diluted identity of the "amorphous body, into little Russia [Malorossiia]." Shums´kyi's battle continues.

NOTES

INTRODUCTION

1 Nikita Petrov, "Shtatnyi gosudarstvennyi ubiitsa (reabilitirovannyi): Dva dnia iz zhizni Pavla Sudoplatova," *Novaia Gazeta*, 7 August 2013.

2 Yurii I. Shapoval, *Oleksandr Shums´kyi: Zhyttia, dolia, nevidomi dokumenty* (Kyiv: Ukraïna moderna, 2017), 35–65.

3 Terry Martin, *The Affirmative Action Empire: Nations and Nationalism in the Soviet Union, 1923–1939* (Ithaca, N.Y.: Cornell University Press, 2001), 249–60.

4 Shapoval, *Oleksandr Shums´kyi*, 156–89. For the letter that reached Stalin, see the State Archive of the Russian Federation (GARF), f. r-9401, op. 2, d. 138, ll. 258–60. For the Moscow leadership's decision to assassinate Shums´kyi, see Pavel Sudoplatov, *Spetsoperatsii: Lubianka i Kreml´ 1930–1950 gody* (Moscow: Olma-Press, 1997), 408–9, 582.

5 Shums´kyi's letter is kept in the Central Archive of the Federal Security Service (TsA FSB) in Moscow, along with the unfolded cigarette packet on which Shums´kyi's assassins wrote down the Kirsanov train station timetable and drew a schema of his rail carriage: TsA FSB, f. 4-os, op. 4, d. 32, ll, 446–48.

6 Iosif V. Stalin, "Za russkii narod," toast given on 24 May 1945, *Pravda*, 25 May 1945.

7 Shums´kyi would not have known the casualty figures, as these were not reported widely in the press and the Soviet leadership downplayed the scale of casualties, but, according to one estimate, as many as eight million Ukrainians may have died in the Second World War. See Stanislav V. Kul´chyts´kyi, *Chervonyi vyklyk: Istoriia komunizmu v Ukraïni vid ioho narodzhennia do zahybeli* (Kyiv: Tempora, 2013), 3:106.

8 GARF, f. r-9401, op. 2, d. 138, ll. 258–60 (written in Russian). Although Khrushchev was born in Ukraine, he was ethnically Russian. *Maloross* in popular usage of the time referred not to people like him but to Russified

ethnic Ukrainians. Shums´kyi clearly understood this, but he consistently used Khrushchev as a facetious example of a maloross to make his broader point.

9 GARF, f. r-9401, op. 2, d. 138, ll. 258–60.

10 Sheila Fitzpatrick, "Deaths at Two O'Clock," *London Review of Books* 33, no. 4 (17 February 2011).

11 See, e.g., Alexander Statiev, *The Soviet Counterinsurgency in the Western Borderlands* (Cambridge: Cambridge University Press, 2010); Timothy Snyder, *Bloodlands: Europe between Hitler and Stalin* (New York: Basic Books, 2010); Alexander V. Prusin, *The Lands Between: Conflict in the East European Borderlands, 1870–1992* (Oxford: Oxford University Press, 2010); John J. Kulczycki, *Belonging to the Nation: Inclusion and Exclusion in the Polish-German Borderlands, 1939–1951* (Cambridge, Mass.: Harvard University Press, 2016).

12 Sudoplatov, *Spetsoperatsii*, chap. 8.

13 Most of these compatriots were members and former members of the Communist Party of Western Ukraine (CPWU), arrested in 1933 or 1936–37.

14 See, e.g., Lynne Viola, *Stalinist Perpetrators on Trial: Scenes from the Great Terror in Soviet Ukraine* (Oxford: Oxford University Press, 2017); Lynne Viola, "New Sources on Soviet Perpetrators of Mass Repression: A Research Note," *Canadian Slavonic Papers* 60, nos. 3–4 (2018): 592–604; Hiroaki Kuromiya, *The Voices of the Dead: Stalin's Great Terror in the 1930s* (New Haven, Conn.: Yale University Press, 2016).

15 See the "Seliavkin" affair in Oleg Khlevniuk, *Khoziain: Stalin i utverzhdenie stalinskoi diktatury* (Moscow: Rosspen, 2010), 224–25.

16 Among the archives consulted were the Haluzevyi derzhavnyi arkhiv SB Ukraïny (Sectoral State Archive of the Security Services of Ukraine, HDA SBU) and the Tsentral´nyi derzhavnyi arkhiv hromads´kykh ob'iednan´ Ukraïny (Central State Archive of Public Organizations of Ukraine, TsDAHOU).

17 Chekists—the shorthand term used widely at the time for Soviet secret police agents, belonging to the Cheka, derived from VChK, the acronym for the first secret security agency established in 1917, the Vserossiiskaia chrezvychainaia komissiia (All-Russian Extraordinary Commission).

18 Joseph V. Stalin, *Works* (Moscow: Foreign Languages, 1954), 8:157–63. For the full version of the letter, see *Ocherki istorii Kommunisticheskoi partii Ukrainy. Izdanie chetvertoe, dopolnennoe* (Kyiv: Izdatel´stvo politicheskoi literatury, 1977), 385.

19 Mai Panchuk, "Zhyttia i smert´ Oleksandra Shums´koho," in *Pro mynule—zarady maibutn´oho*, ed. Yurii I. Shapoval (Kyiv: Vydavnytstvo pry Kyïvs´komu universyteti, 1989), 319–21; I. F. Kuras and P. P. Ovdiienko, "O. Ia. Shums´kyi u roky Zhovtnia i hromadians´koï viiny: Evoliutsiia pohliadiv i politychna diial´nist´," *Ukraïns´kyi istorychnyi zhurnal*, 1990, no. 12: 105–16.

20 James E. Mace, *Communism and the Dilemmas of National Liberation: National Communism in Soviet Ukraine, 1918–1933* (Cambridge, Mass.: Harvard Ukrainian Research Institute, 1983); Martin, *Affirmative Action Empire*.

21 See Ie. M. Skliarenko, "Ostannia forma protestu." In *Reabilitovani istoriieiu* (Kyiv: Ridnyi krai, 1992), 260–63; Iu. S. Shemshuchenko, ed., *Zhertvy*

repressii (Kyiv: Iurinform, 1993), 35–56; V. Verstiuk and T. Ostashko, *Diiachi Ukraïns'koï Tsentral'noï Rady: Biohrafichnyi dovidnyk* (Kyiv: Natsional'na Akademiia Nauk Ukraïny, 1998), s.v. "Shums'kyi Oleksandr Iakovych"; V. Verstiuk and T. Ostashko, "Shums'kyi Oleksandr Iakovych," in *Ukraïns'ka pedahohika v personaliiakh*, ed. O. V. Sukhomlyns'ka (Kyiv: Lybid', 2005), 2:58–63; M. Iu. Kostrytsia, "Providnyk ukraïnizatsiï," in *Reabilitovani istoriieiu: Zhytomyrs'ka oblast'*, ed. P. T. Tron'ko, vol. 7, bk. 1 (Zhytomyr: Polissia, 2006), 222–27.

22 See, e.g., V. S. Lozyts'kyi, "Polityka ukraïnizatsiï v 20–30-kh rokakh: Istoriia, problemy, uroky," *Ukraïns'kyi istorychnyi zhurnal*, 1989, no. 3: 46–55; Iaroslav Dashkevych, "Politychne oshukanstvo chy provokatsiia? Krakh ukraïnizatsiï 20-kh–30-kh rr.," *Literaturna Ukraïna*, 4 October 1990; George O. Liber, *Soviet Nationality Policy, Urban Growth, and Identity Change in the Ukrainian SSR, 1923–1934* (Cambridge: Cambridge University Press, 1992); Ia. V. Vermenych, "Diial'nist' O. Ia. Shums'koho po zdiisnenniu polityky ukraïnizatsiï," *Istoriia Ukraïny: Malovidomi imena, podiï, fakty*, no. 2, (1997): 89–103; V. A. Smolii, ed., *Ukraïnizatsiia 1920–30-kh rokiv: Peredumovy, zdobutky, uroky* (Kyiv: Instytut istoriï Ukraïny NAN Ukraïny, 2003); Elena Borisenok, *Fenomen sovetskoi ukrainizatsii: 1920–1930-e gody* (Moscow: Evropa, 2006); Matthew D. Pauly, *Breaking the Tongue: Language, Education, and Power in Soviet Ukraine* (Toronto: University of Toronto Press, 2011).

23 Shapoval, *Oleksandr Shums'kyi*. Yurii I. Shapoval's prior writings on Shums'kyi include: "Klynok ne distav sertsia. Iak kolyshnii narkom osvity Ukraïny boronyv svoie chesne im'ia," *Vitchyzna* 10 (1991): 154–61; *Ukraïna 20–50-kh rokiv: Storinky nenapysanoï istoriï* (Kyiv: Naukova dumka, 1993), 132–44; "Oleksandr Shums'kyi: His Last Thirteen Years," *Journal of Ukrainian Studies* 18, nos. 1–2 (1993): 69–84; "'Ne samohubets'!': Zlochyn, rozsekrechenyi cherez 46 rokiv," *Literaturna Ukraïna*, 25 February 1993; *Liudyna i systema (Shtrykhy do portreta totalitarnoï doby v Ukraïni)* (Kyiv: Instytut natsional'nykh vidnosyn i politolohiï NANU, 1994), 134–52; "Ioho taiemnytsi. Vypovniuet'sia 120 rokiv z dnia narodzhennia Oleksandra Shums'koho," *Den'*, 19 November 2010; "Aleksandr Shumskii: Sud'ba narkoma v imperii 'pozitivnogo deistviia,'" in *Sovetskie natsii i natsional'naia politika v 1920–1950-e gody: Materialy VI mezhdunarodnoi nauchnoi konferentsii (Kyiv, 10–12 oktiabria 2013)* (Moscow: Rosspen, 2014), 54–64. The scholarship that Shapoval's biography builds on includes a document collection that traces Shums'kyi's career as people's commissar for education: Hryhorii Hryn'ko and Oleksandr Shums'kyi, *Statti. Promovy. Dokumenty*, ed. V. O. Gaidei, O. P. Mikhno, and O. V. Sukhomlyns'ka (Kyiv: Pedahohichnyi muzei Ukraïny, 2015).

24 Some of the many works pertinent to this section are Khlevniuk, *Khoziain*; V. N. Khaustov and L. Samuel'son, *Stalin, NKVD i repressii 1936–1938 gg.* (Moscow: Rosspen, 2009); V. N. Khaustov, V. P. Naumov, and N. S. Plotnikova, eds., *Lubianka: Stalin i Glavnoe upravlenie gosbezopasnosti NKVD, 1937–1938* (Moscow: Materik, 2004); J. Arch Getty and Oleg V. Naumov, *The Road to Terror: Stalin and the Self-Destruction of the Bolsheviks, 1932–1939* (New Haven, Conn.: Yale University Press, 1999); J. Arch Getty,

"'Excesses Are Not Permitted': Mass Terror and Stalinist Governance in the Late 1930s," *Russian Review* 61, no. 1 (January 2002): 113–38; Peter Solomon, *Soviet Criminal Justice under Stalin* (Cambridge: Cambridge University Press, 1996); A. Sorokin, A. Kobak, and O. Kuvaldina, eds., *Istoriia stalinizma: Zhizn′ v terrore: Sotsial′nye aspekty repressii* (Moscow: Rosspen, 2013).

25 See Stalin's clemency considerations in the "Seliavkin" and "Markevich" affairs: Khlevniuk, *Khoziain*, 221–25, 334.

26 On these "national operations" in 1935, see Khlevniuk, *Khoziain*, 240–41; Martin, *Affirmative Action Empire*, chaps. 8 and 9; Terry Martin, "The Origins of Soviet Ethnic Cleansing," *Journal of Modern History* 70, no. 4 (December 1998): 813–61; A. E. Gur′ianov, ed., *Repressii protiv poliakov i polskikh grazhdan* (Moscow: Zven′ia, 1997), 33; I. L. Shcherbakova, ed., *Nakazannyi narod: Repressii protiv rossiiskikh nemtsev* (Moscow: Zven′ia, 1999).

27 Getty, "Excesses Are Not Permitted."

28 Khlevniuk, *Khoziain*, 287–88.

29 Solomon, *Soviet Criminal Justice under Stalin*.

30 Stephen G. Wheatcroft, "Agency and Terror: Evdokimov and Mass Killing in Stalin's Great Terror," *Australian Journal of Politics and History* 53, no. 1 (2007): 42.

31 A telegram was sent by Stalin to police and party secretaries on 10 January 1939; see Solomon, *Soviet Criminal Justice under Stalin*, 258.

32 For the specific order halting the use of troikas and establishing procuratorial control over the police, see Postanovlenie Politbiuro TsK VKP(b) "Ob arestakh, prokurorskom nadzore i vedenii sledstviia," 17 November 1938; David Shearer and Vladimir Khaustov, *Stalin and the Lubianka: A Documentary History of the Political Police and Security Organs in the Soviet Union, 1922–1953* (New Haven, Conn.: Yale University Press, 2015), 221–24. For the procuracy's rubber-stamping of police requests for arrest and the broader involvement of the procuracy in extralegal matters, see Solomon, *Soviet Criminal Justice under Stalin*, 236.

33 Getty, "Excesses Are Not Permitted," 134–35.

34 Beginning in 1937, the Collegium held sessions on circuit in various regions of the USSR to hear cases involving charges of terrorism and wrecking "especially against persons included on lists provided by Yezhov and Vyshinskii, usually with indications of the recommended punishments." Solomon, *Soviet Criminal Justice under Stalin*, 238.

35 Vyshinskii attached enormous significance to confessions as a major piece of evidence in counterrevolutionary trials. Confessions—not "objective proof," as in bourgeois courts—were the chief focus of the judge and the key factor in demonstrating guilt. For a 1937 published pamphlet on this topic, see Solomon, *Soviet Criminal Justice*, 237n14.

36 Solomon, *Soviet Criminal Justice*, 237; Khlevniuk, *Khoziain*, 366. In November 1938, Stalin set in motion a purge of the NKVD and police agencies by empowering party agencies to "cleanse" them of enemy elements. For the purge of Chekists in Ukraine, see Viola, *Stalinist Perpetrators on Trial*; Viola, "New Sources on Soviet Perpetrators of Mass Repression."

37 Solomon, *Soviet Criminal Justice*; Khlevniuk, *Khoziain*.

38 Wheatcroft, "Agency and Terror," 42.
39 TsA FSB, f. 4-os, op. 4, d. 32, ll. 446–48.

CHAPTER ONE

1 Ivan Lysiak Rudnytsky (1919–1984) was professor of history at the University of Alberta in Edmonton, Canada, where he co-founded the Canadian Institute of Ukrainian Studies (CIUS). The Ukrainian Socialist Soviet Republic (UkrSSR) was proclaimed by a decree of the Bolshevik Workers and Peasants' Government of Ukraine on 14 January 1919. According to the Constitution of the UkrSSR in 1937, the name was changed to the Ukrainian Soviet Socialist Republic. This name was preserved until the adoption of the Act of Independence of Ukraine in 1991, which enshrined the formation of an independent Ukrainian state, Ukraine.
2 Ivan Lysiak Rudnyts′kyi, *Istorychni ese* (Kyiv: Osnovy, 1994), 1:165.
3 Martin, *Affirmative Action Empire*, 1.
4 The Plenum of the Central Committee of the Russian Communist Party (RCP[b]) approved the "Political Directives of the Central Committee of the RCP(b) of the Central Committee of the CP(b)U." The Presidium of the Central Executive Committee and the People's Commissariat for Foreign Affairs of the Russian Soviet Federative Socialist Republic (RSFSR), together with the relevant bodies of what would become the Union of Soviet Socialist Republics (USSR) in 1922, were then instructed to find a new formula for interstate relations, which culminated in the treaty signed on 28 December 1920.
5 Georgii Vasil′evich Chicherin (1872–1936) was people's commissar for foreign affairs of the RSFSR and the USSR from 1918 to 1930. Christian (Khristiian or Kru˘st'o) Georgiev Rakovsky (1873–1941) remained chairman of the Council of People's Commissars of the UkrSSR until his removal in 1923.
6 M. Kyrychenko, ed., *Rezoliutsiï Vseukraïns′kykh z'ïzdiv Rad robitnychykh, selians′kykh ta chernoarmiis′kykh deputativ* (Kharkiv: Proletar, 1932), 121.
7 Kyrychenko, *Rezoliutsiï*, 121.
8 V. L′vov, *Sovetskaia vlast′ v bor′be za russkuiu gosudarstvennost″* (Berlin, 1922), 11.
9 L′vov, *Sovetskaia vlast′*, 12.
10 Martin, *Affirmative Action Empire*, 2.
11 On these debates and the formation of the Soviet Union more broadly, see Jeremy Smith, *The Bolsheviks and the National Question, 1917–1923* (London: Macmillan Press, 1999); Richard Pipes, *The Formation of the Soviet Union*, rev. ed. (Cambridge, Mass.: Harvard University Press, 1964); Ronald Grigor Suny, *The Revenge of the Past: Nationalism, Revolution, and the Collapse of the Soviet Union* (Stanford, Calif.: Stanford University Press, 1993).
12 Iosif V. Stalin, "Pis′mo V.I. Leninu 22 sentiabria 1922 g.," *Izvestiia TsK KPSS* no. 9 (1989): 198–99. The underlining appears in the manuscript document.
13 Stalin, "Pis′mo V.I. Leninu," 199.
14 Stalin, "Pis′mo V.I. Leninu," 199. The underlining appears in the manuscript.

15 Jeremy Smith, "The Georgian Affair of 1922: Policy Failure, Personality Clash or Power Struggle?" *Europe-Asia Studies* 50, no. 3 (May 1998): 519–44.

16 Valerii Vasyl′iev, *Politychne kerivnytstvo URSR i SRSR: Dynamika vidnosyn tsentr-subtsentr vlady (1917–1938)* (Kyiv: Instytut istoriï Ukraïny NAN Ukraïny, 2014), 137.

17 *Dvenadtsatyi s″ezd RKP(b), 17–25 aprelia 1923 goda: Stenograficheskii otchet* (Moskva: Izdatel′stvo politicheskoi literatury, 1968), 572 (emphasis added). Mykola Oleksiiovych Skrypnyk (1872–1933) remained people's commissar for education until he committed suicide in July 1933, after the party accused him of "nationalism" and an alliance with "foreign interventionists."

18 The Baldwin government refused to ratify the Anglo-Soviet treaty in 1924 and severed diplomatic relations with the Soviet Union in 1927.

19 Józef Klemens Piłsudski (1867–1935) was a Polish socialist, military leader, and fighter for Polish independence. From 1918 to 1922, he was the first head of state of the revived Polish state; he served as prime minister of Poland from 1926 to 1928 and in 1930. He was the minister of defense of Poland in 1918–19 and 1926–35.

20 For a broad introduction to these debates, see Ronald Grigor Suny and Terry Martin, eds., *A State of Nations: Empire and Nation-Making in the Age of Lenin and Stalin* (New York: Oxford University Press, 2002). For ethnographic considerations in *korenizatsiia*, see Francine Hirsch, *Empire of Nations: Ethnographic Knowledge and the Making of the Soviet Union* (Ithaca, N.Y.: Cornell University Press, 2002).

21 "O tak nazyvaemoi 'Sultan-Galievskoi Kontrrevoliutsionnoi Organizatsii,'" *Izvestiia TsK KPSS*, no. 10 (1990): 77.

22 On Mirsaid Sultan-Galiev, see Alexandre Benningsen and Chantal Lemercier-Quelquejay, *Sultan-Galiev: Le pére de la révolution tiers-mondiste* (Paris: Fayard, 1986).

23 Benningsen and Lemercier-Quelquejay, *Sultan-Galiev*, 77.

24 "O tak nazyvaemoi 'Sultan-Galievskoi Kontrrevoliutsionnoi Organizatsii.'"

25 *Chetvertoe soveshchanie TsK RKP(b) s otvetstvennymi rabotnikami natsional′nykh respublik i oblastei: Stenograficheskii otchet.* (Moskva: Partizdat, 1923), 67-68.

26 V. A. Smolii, ed., *Ukraïnizatsiia 1920–30-kh rokiv: Peredumovy, zdobutky, uroky* (Kyiv: Instytut istoriï Ukraïny NAN Ukraïny, 2003), 15.

27 Smolii, *Ukraïnizatsiia*, 16.

28 *Ukraïns′ka tsentral′na rada: Dokumenty i materialy* (Kyiv: Naukova dumka, 1997), 2:182.

29 German forces, still occupying Ukraine in the aftermath of the First World War and the Treaty of Brest-Litovsk, backed the coup that placed Pavlo Petrovych Skoropads′kyi (1873–1945) in power. He reclaimed the title of hetman of Ukraine from his ancestor Ivan Skoropads′kyi (1646–1722) and claimed the resurrection of the Cossack Hetmanate, which had ruled central Ukraine in the seventeenth and eighteenth centuries.

30 Bohdan Krawchenko, *Social Change and National Consciousness in Twentieth-Century Ukraine* (Edmonton: Canadian Institute of Ukrainian Studies, University of Alberta, 1987), 94.

31 "Kampaniia proty ukraïns′koï movy zrostaie vodnochas iz zrostanniam kampaniï proty ukraïns′koï derzhavnosti," *Viche,* 1994, no. 2: 150. Serhii Shelukhin (1864–1938) was minister of justice from February to April 1918 and senator under the Hetmanate, as well as acting minister of justice and prosecutor general under the Directorate. Fedir Andriiovich Lyzohub (1851–1928) headed the Council of Ministers of the UkrSSR from May to November 1918.

32 "Kampaniia proty ukraïns′koï movy...," 151, 155.

33 Iurii Shevel′ov, *Vybrani pratsi*, vol. 1, *Movoznavstvo*, ed. Larysa Masenko (Kyiv: Kyïv-Mohyla Academy, 2009), 105, 118.

34 Smolii, *Ukraïnizatsiia 1920–30-kh rokiv*, 34–35.

35 Smolii, 36. Grigorii Evseevich Zinov′ev (his real name was Ovsei-Gershen Aronovich Radomysl′skii, 1883–1936) was one of Lenin's closest associates, a key figure in the revolution, and leading Soviet state/party figure. He was executed after a show trial under Stalin's order in 1936.

36 Smolii, 37–38.

37 The decrees established a number of state/party commissions on Ukrainization to implement the policy. The Central Committee of the CP(b)U established a Commission on the National Question and a Special Commission on the Ukrainization of Trade Unions in 1923–24. The Commission for the Implementation of the Decrees of the XII Congress of the RCP(b) on the National Question worked under the Council of People's Commissars of the USSR, and the Central Commission for National Minorities worked under the auspices of the All-Ukrainian Central Executive Committee.

38 B. V. Chyrko, *Natsional′ni menshyny v Ukraïni (20–30 roky XX stolittia)* (Kyiv: Asotsiatsiia "Ukraïno", 1995).

39 Martin, *Affirmative Action Empire*, 38–40.

40 TsDAHOU, f. 263, op. 1, spr. 55475, t. 4, ark. 44.

41 TsDAHOU, f. 263, op. 1, spr. 55475, t. 4, ark. 44.

42 On the complex issue of political patronage for Soviet artists, see Mayhill Fowler, *Beau Monde on Empire's Edge: State and Stage in Soviet Ukraine* (Toronto: University of Toronto Press, 2017).

43 Oleksandr Ushkalov and Leonid Ushkalov, eds., *Arkhiv rozstrilianoho vidrodzhenia: Materialy arkhivno-slidchikh sprav ukraïnskykh pys′mennykiv 1920–1930-kh rokiv* (Kyiv: Smoloskyp, 2010), 39.

44 The prototype for the writers' organization VAPLITE was the All-Ukrainian Literary Academy, whose manifesto was written in 1924 by poet Vasyl′ Ellan-Blakytnyi: "The national revival of Ukraine coincided with its social liberation. At the same time, the young nation and the young class, the advanced social class that heads the nation, entered the historical and cultural arena. That is why the flourishing of Ukrainian literature as proletarian literature is historically inevitable today. That is why today's October Ukrainian literature should and does enter the arena of world culture as one of the first proletarian literatures in the world, paving the way that sooner or later the literatures of other nationalities will follow." Quoted in Iu. Luts′kyi, *Literaturna polityka v radians′kii Ukraïni, 1917–1934* (Kyiv: Helikon, 2000), 47. The ideas Blakytnyi expressed in the manifesto were similar to those of Mykola Khvyl′ovyi and formed the basis of VAPLITE's program of activities. Among

VAPLITE's members were Khvyl′ovyi, Mykola Bazhan, Ivan Dniprovs′kyi, Oles′ Dosvitnii, Hryhorii Epik, Maik Yohansen, Mykola Kulish, Arkadii Liubchenko, Petro Panch, Ivan Senchenko, Oleksa Slisarenko, Iurii Smolych, Volodymyr Sosiura, Pavlo Tychyna, Geo Shkurupii, Mykhailo Ialovyi, and Iurii Ianovs′kyi. Ialovyi became the first president of VAPLITE. Under pressure from party critics, VAPLITE "self-liquidated" on 12 January 1928.

45 Panas Fedenko, *Ukraïns′kyi rukh u XX stolitti* (London: Nashe Slovo, 1959), 221.

46 Stanislav V. Kul′chyts′kyi, *Istorychne mistse ukraïns′koï radians′koï derzhavnosti* (Kyiv: Instytut istoriï Ukraïny NAN Ukraïny, 2002), 29. Dmytro Pavlovych Levyts′kyi (1877–1942) was arrested by the NKVD in L′viv and died in exile in Uzbekistan.

47 George G. Grabowicz, "Sovietyzatsiia ukraïns′koï humanistyky," *Krytyka* 1, no. 1 (1997): 19.

48 See, e.g., M. V. Popovych, *Narys istoriï kul′tury Ukraïny* (Kyiv: ArtEk, 1998), 587–615; George O. Liber, *Alexander Dovzhenko: A Life in Soviet Film* (London: BFI, 2002); Myroslav Shkandrij, *Modernists, Marxists and the Nation: The Ukrainian Literary Discussion of the 1920s* (Edmonton: Canadian Institute of Ukrainian Studies Press, 1992); Serhii Trymbach, *Oleksandr Dovzhenko: Zahibel′ bohiv* (Vinnytsia: Globus-press, 2007); Iryna Makaryk, *Peretvorennia Shekspira: Les′ Kurbas, ukraïns′kyi modernizm i radians′ka kul′turna polityka 1920-kh rokiv* (Kyiv: Nika-Centre, 2010).

49 Remarkably, the Shevchenko Scientific Society (NTSh) in Lviv, then under Polish control, adopted the same orthography on 29 May of the same year.

50 *X z'ïzd KP(b)U. 20–29 lystopada 1927 r. Stenograf. zvit.* (Kharkiv: Partiine vidavnytstvo TsK KP[b]U), 526.

51 Krawchenko, *Social Change and National Consciousness in Twentieth-Century Ukraine*, 97.

52 *Ukraïna: Statystychnyi shchorichnyk na 1928* (Kharkiv: Tsentral′ne statystychne upravlinnia USRR, 1928), 24, 32.

53 M. S. Doroshko, *Nomenklatura: Kerivna verkhivka Radians′koï Ukraïny (1917–1938 rr.)* (Kyiv: Nika-Centre, 2008), 291–92.

54 For a fictionalized description of what Ukrainization looked like on the ground, see also Valer′ian Pidmohyl′nyi's 1928 novel *Misto* (The city), forthcoming from the Harvard Ukrainian Research Institute in Maxim Tarnawsky's English translation in 2025.

55 Martin, *Affirmative Action Empire*, 82. Volodymyr Petrovych Zatons′kyi (1888–1938) was one of the founders of the CP(b)U and served as people's commissar for education of the UkrSSR in 1922–23 and again in 1933–37. He was arrested in 1937 and shot in 1938. Hryhorii Fedorovych Hryn′ko (1890–1938) was a member of the Ukrainian Party of Socialist-Revolutionaries (UPSR), later a Borotbist. In 1920, he joined the CP(b)U. From 1920 to 1922, he was the people's commissar for education of the UkrSSR. He then filled a number of other important posts until, like Zatons′kyi, he was arrested in 1937 and shot in 1938.

56 Martin, *Affirmative Action Empire*, 83. Emmanuil Ionovich Kviring (1888–1937) was the general secretary of the Central Committee of the CP(b)U from 1923 to 1925. He was shot in 1937.

57 Cited in Elena Borisenok, *Fenomen sovetskoi ukrainizatsii: 1920–1930-e gody* (Moscow: Evropa, 2006), 147. Dmitrii Zakharovich Lebed′ (1893–1937) filled numerous important state and party posts in both the UkrSSR and the RSFSR, until he was shot in 1937 in Moscow.

58 Borisenok, *Fenomen*, 147.

59 Lazar′ Moiseevich Kaganovich (1893–1991) held senior positions in the party apparatus and government of the USSR until 1957. For more on Kaganovich, see Yurii I. Shapoval, "L. M. Kahanovych na Ukraïni," *Ukraïns′kyi istorychnyi zhurnal*, 1990, no. 8: 62–74; 1990, no. 10: 117–29; Yurii I. Shapoval, *Lazar Kahanovych* (Kyiv: Znannia, 1994); Roi Medvedev, *Blizhnii krug Stalina: Soratniki Vozhdia* (Moscow: Eksmo-Iauza, 2005); E. A. Rees, *Iron Lazar: A Political Biography of Lazar Kaganovich* (London: Anthem Press, 2012).

60 Iurii Mikhailovich Larin (his real name was Mikhail Aleksandrovich Lur′e, 1882–1932) was a member of the Russian revolutionary movement, a Menshevik, and, after 1917, a Bolshevik, Soviet economist, and publicist.

61 Quoted in TsDAHOU, f. 1, op. 1, spr. 160, ark. 44 and 46.

62 Ushkalov and Ushkalov, *Arkhiv rozstrilianoho vidrodzhennia*, 42.

63 "Ob ukrainskom separatizme" (Kharkiv: GPU, 1926), 3.

64 "Ob ukrainskom separatizme," 3.

65 "Ob ukrainskom separatizme," 11, 12.

66 For more details, see Yurii I. Shapoval, "'On Ukrainian Separatism': A GPU Circular of 1926," *Harvard Ukrainian Studies* 18, no. 3/4 (1994): 275–302.

67 Lazar′ M. Kaganovich, *Na putiakh stroitel′stva sotsializma* (Kharkiv: Partiinoe izdatel′stvo TsK KP[b]U, 1926), 12.

68 A. Khvylia, "Kudy vedut′ dorohy shveds′kykh mohyl?" *Komunist*, 27 September 1933.

69 For more details, see Ivan Koshelivets′, *Mykola Skrypnyk* (Munich: Modernity, 1972); V. F. Soldatenko, *Nezlamnyi: Zhyttia i smert′ Mykoly Skrypnyka* (Kyiv: Knyha pam′iati Ukraïny, 2002).

70 P. P. Liubchenko, "Vohon′ po natsionalistychnii kontrrevoliutsiï ta po natsional-ukhyl′nykakh," *Chervonyi shliakh* no. 10 (1933): 200.

71 Liubchenko, "Vohon′ po natsionalistychnii kontrrevoliutsiï," 200. Panas Petrovych Liubchenko (1897–1937) was secretary of the Central Committee of the CP(b)U beginning in 1927 and chairman of the Sovnarkom of the UkrSSR, effectively head of government, in 1934–37. He committed suicide on 30 August 1937, during a break at the plenary session of the Central Committee of the CP(b)U, at which criminal charges were to be brought against him.

72 O. Shlikhter, "Posylymo bil′shovyts′ku pyl′nist′ na fronti borot′by za zdiisnennia lenins′koï natsional′noï polityky na Ukraïni," *Bil′shovyk Ukraïny* no. 9–10 (1933): 62.

73 See, e.g., S. V. Kosior, "Pidsumky i naiblyzhchi zavdannia natsional′noï polityky na Ukraïni," *Chervonyi shliakh*, no. 8–9 (1933): 229.

74 Martin, *Affirmative Action Empire*, 219.

75 Rudnyts′kyi, *Istorychni ese*, 2:461.

76 Chapter 9 of Terry Martin's *Affirmative Action Empire* is a good introduction.

77 Iaroslav Hrytsak, *Narys istoriï Ukraïny: Formuvannia modernoï natsiï XIX–XX stolittia* (Kyiv: Heneza, 1996), 175.

78 Calculating excess mortality due to the famine in Ukraine and in other regions of the USSR where it raged is difficult for a number of reasons, particularly because many deaths in the countryside were not registered by authorities. Two current sources stand out: *Hunger by Design* (Cambridge, Mass.: Harvard Ukrainian Research Institute, 2009) and "The Great Famine Project" of the Harvard Ukrainian Research Institute's MAPA Digital Atlas of Ukraine, https://gis.huri.harvard.edu/great-famine-project, which has become a clearinghouse for the latest research on the Holodomor. Other authoritative accounts are R. W. Davies and Stephen G. Wheatcroft, *The Years of Hunger: Soviet Agriculture, 1931–1933* (New York: Palgrave Macmillan, 2004), 435; France Meslé and Jacques Vallin, eds., *Mortalité et causes de décès en Ukraine au XXe siècle* (Paris: Institut national d'études démographiques, 2003); and Stanislav V. Kul′chyts′kyi, "Skil′ky nas zahynulo vid Holodomoru 1933 roku?" *Dzerkalo tyzhnia*, 29 November 2002. On forced collectivization, see Davies and Wheatcroft, *The Years of Hunger*; Sheila Fitzpatrick, *Stalin's Peasants: Resistance and Survival in the Russian Village after Collectivization* (New York: Oxford University Press, 1994), chap. 2; Lynne Viola, *Peasant Rebels under Stalin: Collectivization and the Culture of Peasant Resistance* (New York: Oxford University Press, 1996).

79 Numerous works trace Stalin's consolidation of power in the 1920s. Some more recent ones with differing perspectives include Oleg Khlevniuk, *Stalin: New Biography of a Dictator*, trans. Nora Seligman Favorov (New Haven, Conn.: Yale University Press, 2015), chaps. 2 and 3; and Stephen Kotkin, *Stalin: Paradoxes of Power, 1878–1928* (New York: Penguin, 2014), chap. 13.

80 This was the name of the former RCP(b), adopted in 1925.

81 For more details, see Volodymyr Prystaiko and Yurii I. Shapoval, *Sprava "Spilky vyzvolennia Ukraïny": Nevidomi dokumenty i fakty* (Kyiv: Intel, 1995); Yurii I. Shapoval, "Sprava 'Spilky vyzvoleniia Ukraïny': Pohliad iz vistani 75 rokiv," *Ukraïns′kyi istorychnyi zhurnal*, 2005, no. 3: 132–43; Yurii I. Shapoval, "The 'Union for the Liberation of Ukraine' ('SVU') Trial: Fabrication, Mechanisms, Consequences," in *Political and Transitional Justice in Germany, Poland and the Soviet Union from the 1930s to the 1950s*, ed. Władysław Bułhak, Jürgen Zarusky, and Magnus Brechtken (Göttingen: Wallstein Verlag, 2019), 36–53.

82 For the telegram, see TsDAHOU, f. 1, op. 1, spr. 2038, ark. 6. Pavel Petrovich Postyshev (1887–1939) was expelled from the party in February 1938 and shot on 26 February 1939.

83 P. P. Postyshev, "Radians′ka Ukraïna—nepokhytnyi forpost velykoho SRSR," *Chervonyi shliakh*, nos. 8–9, 10, 1933, 245. Postyshev spoke about the famine as a "breakthrough."

84 "Pidsumky i naiblyzhchi zavdannia provedennia natsional′noï polityky na Ukraïni," *Chervonyi shliakh*, nos. 8–9, 1933, 267–68.

85 Iosif V. Stalin, "Ob uklonakh k natsionalizmu," *Marksism i natsial′no-kolonial′nyi vopros* (Moscow: Partizdat TsK VKP(b), 1937), 199–200. The speech was also published in *Pravda* on 28 January 1934 (issue 27) and in the proceedings of the 17th Congress: *XVII s″ezd Vsesoiuznoi Kommunisticheskoi partii (B), 26 ianvaria – 10 fevralia 1934 g.: stenograficheskii otchet* (Moscow: Partizdat, 1934).

86 Stanisław Kosior (Stanislav Vikent′evich Kosior, 1888–1939) was the first secretary of the Central Committee of the CP(b)U, beginning in 1924. Upon being displaced by Khrushchev, he served as deputy chairman of Sovnarkom (USSR) until his arrest in 1938. He was shot in February 1939.

87 TsDAHOU, f. 1, op. 6, spr. 463, ark. 2–4.

88 TsDAHOU, f. 1, op. 1, spr. 548, ark. 61 and 62.

89 TsDAHOU, f. 1, op. 1, ark. 77 and 93–97.

90 TsDAHOU, f. 1, op. 1, ark. 117–18; TsDAHOU, f. 1, op. 1, spr. 467, ark. 19.

91 TsDAHOU, f. 1, op. 1, spr. 578, ark. 199.

CHAPTER TWO

1 TsDAHOU, f. 39, op. 4, spr. 237, ark. 4.

2 State Archives of Zhytomyr Oblast (DAZhO), f. r-2275, op. 1, spr. 20, ark. 86.

3 TsDAHOU, f. 39, op. 4, spr. 237, ark. 4.

4 The RUP was founded in February 1900 in Kharkiv by student activists. It became the first active political party in central-eastern Ukraine. The RUP program began as a speech by Mykola Mikhnovs′kyi who was not a member of the RUP. He wrote the program as a draft on behalf of the RUP founders. The speech was delivered at the Shevchenko celebrations in Poltava and Kharkiv in March 1900 and was published the same year in Lviv, in a pamphlet entitled "Independent Ukraine."

5 DAZhO, f. 60, op. 1, spr. 4658, ark. 1 and 4.

6 DAZhO, f. 60, op. 1, spr. 4658, ark. 6.

7 Later, recalling the work under Biel′s′kyi, Oleksandr Shums′kyi wrote: "Working with him in the forests and swamps of Volyn [Oblast] until 1911 on land irrigation and mainly on amelioration works, I specialized in this work and became a technician. In this work of amelioration, hydraulic engineering, I worked until the revolution in the Moscow province, in the Transcaspian region, and then at the front in the engineering corps." TsDAHOU, f. 39, op. 4, spr. 237, ark. 4.

8 Quoted in DAZhO, f. 60, op. 1, spr. 4658, ark. 9–11 and 12.

9 Quoted in DAZhO, f. 60, op. 1, spr. 4658, ark. 16 and 23.

10 TsDAHOU, f. 39, op. 4, spr. 237, ark. 4.

11 TsDAHOU, f. 39, op. 4, spr. 237, ark. 4.

12 Georges Clemenceau (1841–1929) was a politician and prime minister of France.

13 Iaroslav Hrytsak, *Prorok u svoïï vitchyzni: Franko ta ioho spil′nota (1856–1886)* (Kyiv: Krytyka, 2006), 400.

14 TsDAHOU, f. 39, op. 4, spr. 237, ark. 4.

15 Oleksandr Shums′kyi, "Stara i nova Ukraïna," *Chervonyi shliakh* 2 (1923): 106.

16 Quoted in TsDAHOU, f. 39, op. 4, spr. 237, ark. 4; TsDAHOU, f. 263, op. 1, spr. 55475 FP, t. 4, ark. 34.

17 Quoted in T. A. Bevz, *Partiia natsional′nykh interesiv i sotsial′nykh perspektyv (Politychna istoriia UPSR)* (Kyiv: iPiEND, 2008), 149, 159.

18 For more details, see Bevz, *Partiia natsional′nykh interesiv*, 146–50.

19 *Narodna volia* was a daily newspaper published from May 1917 until November 1919. Mykhailo Hrushevs′kyi published multiple articles in this newspaper.

20 M. M. Kovalevs′kyi, *Pry dzherelakh borot′by: Spomyny, vrazhenniia, refleksiï* (Innsbruck: Kovalevs′ka, 1960), 273. Mykola Mykolaiovych Kovalevs′kyi (1892–1957) was a politician, publicist, poet, member of the Ukrainian Central Rada, and minister of agriculture of the Ukrainian People's Republic. He was exiled in 1920.

21 Kovalevs′kyi, *Pry dzherelakh borot′by*, 273.

22 TsDAHOU, f. 39, op. 4, spr. 237, ark. 4.

23 I. P. Mazepa, *Ukraïna v ohni i buri revoliutsiï, 1917–1921* (Dnipropetrovsk: Sich, 2002), 77. Mykhailo Mykolaiovych Poloz (real name Polozov, 1891–1937) was a leader of the Borotbists. After the transition to the CP(b)U, he was a member of the Presidium of the Ukrainian Council of National Economy, chairman of the administrative and financial commission at the Council of the People's Commissariat of the UkrSSR, representative of the UkrSSR in the RSFSR (1921–23), chairman of the State Planning Commission of the UkrSSR (1923–25), people's commissar for finance of Ukraine (1925–30), and deputy chairman of the budget commission of the Central Executive Committee of the USSR (1930–34). Arrested on 12 January 1934 and convicted in the Ukrainian Military Organization (UMO) case, he was shot on 3 November 1937 in the Sandarmokh tract. Vasyl′ Mykhailovych Ellan-Blakytnyi (real name Ellans′kyi, 1894–1925) was a poet and a leader of the Borotbists. Beginning in 1920, he was a member of the CP(b)U, editor of the central organ of the government of the USSR newspaper *Visti VUTsVK*, and founder and editor of the literary magazines *Vsesvit* and *Chervonyi perets′*. In 1934, with the clampdown on Ukrainian nationalism, his name was censored, his works banned, and his monument in Kharkiv dismantled. His works began to be published again in the UkrSSR in the 1960s.

24 *Ukraïns′ka tsentral′na rada: Documenty i materialy*, vol. 2 (Kyiv: Naukova dumka, 1997), 122.

25 V. Manilov, ed., *1917 god na Kievshchine: Khronika sobytii* (Kyiv: Gosudarstvennoe izdatel′stvo Ukrainy, 1928), 540–41. The "Kadet-Kaledin" uprising refers to the anti-Bolshevik operations of the Don Army under Ataman A. M. Kaledin, in which the Cadet Party (along with other White forces in the Civil War) were prominent.

26 On the development of the ultimatum, see "Oblastnoi s″ezd RSDRP (b-kov)," *Letopis′ revoliutsii* 5 (1926): 86.

27 Mikhail Artem′evich Murav′ev (1880–1918) was a Russian leftist Socialist-Revolutionary who commanded the Bolshevik offensive in Kyiv in January 1918, after which there were mass killings of Ukrainians in the city. In July 1918, he revolted against the Bolsheviks and was eliminated by them.

28 I. F. Kuras and P. P. Ovdiienko, "O. Ia. Shums′kyi u roky Zhovtnia i hromadians′koï viiny: Evoliutsiia pohliadiv i politychna diial′nist′," *Ukraïns′kyi istorychnyi zhurnal*, 1990, no. 12: 108.

29 Pavlo Ivanovich Mialo, "Hromads′ko-politychna diial′nist′ V. Ellana-Blakytnoho: Evoliuitsiia svitohliadu" (PhD diss., Zaporizhzhia National University), 82.

30 The Donetsk-Kryvyi Rih Soviet Republic was proclaimed on 29 January 1918 at the Fourth Regional Congress of Soviets (26 votes to 24). On 1 February 1918, the government of this republic was formed, and the Council of People's Commissars was headed by Fedor Sergeev (Comrade Artem). In fact, this caused a split in the ranks of the Bolsheviks, but they tolerated Artem as he consistently fought against the Ukrainian Central Rada. Artem and his colleagues appealed to the Russian government to accept the Donetsk-Kryvyi Rih Soviet Republic into the RSFSR, which it did. The territory of the Kharkiv and Ekaterinoslav provinces, part of the Tavriia province (to the Crimea), and the adjacent industrial districts of the Don Troops region (to the railway) were included in this republic, though only on paper, as no authority in Ukraine had agreed to this. Kharkiv became the administrative center of the Donetsk-Kryvyi Rih Soviet Republic, forced to play the role of a double capital. In March 1918, the central Moscow leadership forced Artem and his republic to join the united UkrSSR with rights of autonomy. However, Artem stubbornly refused to recognize the Bolshevik governments led by Mykola Skrypnyk and then Georgii Piatakov. Artem, who was called "little Lenin," was "tamed" only with the appointment of a new prime minister of Ukraine, Christian Rakovsky. On 17 February 1919, the Defense Council of the RSFSR decided to liquidate the Donetsk-Kryvyi Rih Soviet Republic.

31 Kuras and Ovdiienko, "O. Ia. Shums′kyi u roky Zhovtnia i hromadians′koï viiny," 108.

32 TsDAHOU, f. 39, op. 4, spr. 237, ark. 4.

33 Kuras and Ovdiienko, "O. Ia. Shums′kyi u roky Zhovtnia i hromadians′koï viiny," 109.

34 Bevz, *Partiia natsional′nykh interesiv*, 358–59.

35 Levko Borysovych Kovaliv (1894–1937) was deputy people's commissar for foreign affairs of the UkrSSR from February 1921. In March of that year, he was elected to the All-Ukrainian Central Executive Committee, but he left politics in November 1921. He was arrested in 1934 and shot in 1937. Anton Terentiiovych Prykhod′ko (1891–1938) was permanent representative of the UkrSSR to the Soviet People's Commissariat of the USSR from 1924 to 1926, plenipotentiary representative of the USSR in Czechoslovakia, and later prosecutor general of the UkrSSR. He was arrested on 31 December 1933 and shot on 29 January 1938. Andrii Ivanovych Zalyvchyi (1892–1918) died in Chernihiv during the anti-Hetman uprising.

36 Kuras and Ovdiienko, "O. Ia. Shums′kyi u roky Zhovtnia i hromadians′koï viiny," 109.

37 TsDAHOU, f. 263, op. 1, spr. 55475 FP, t. 4, ark. 44. On 22 December 1918, the newspaper *Trybuna* wrote about Oleksandr Shums′kyi's speech: "With great expression and marked oratorical talent, he attacked the 'rogues' of the Directorate parties, against whom 'Ukrainian revolutionary democracy would fight not for life but for death,' and called for the establishment of Soviet power." Quoted in Kuras and Ovdiienko, "O. Ia. Shums′kyi u roky Zhovtnia i hromadians′koï viiny," 109.

38 TsDAHOU, f. 39, op. 4, spr. 237, ark. 4.

39 TsDAHOU, f. 39, op. 4, spr. 237, ark. 5. Symon Vasyl′ovych Petliura (1879–1926) was chairman of the Directorate of the Ukrainian People's Republic (UPR) in 1919 and, in April 1920, signed the Treaty of Warsaw with Poland against Bolshevik Russia. On 25 May 1926, he was killed by an OGPU (Joint State Political Directorate, secret police) agent while in exile. Volodymyr Oleksandrovych Antonov-Ovsiienko (1883–1938) was a key figure in the organization of the Bolsheviks' armed struggle against the UPR, having been appointed people's commissar for war (for the Bolshevik campaign in Ukraine) in September 1918. He served as a prosecutor of the RSFSR from 1934 to 1935 and as people's commissar for justice (RSFSR) from 1937 until he was arrested and shot in 1938.

40 Mialo, "Hromads′ko-politychna diial′nist′ V. Ellana-Blakytnoho," 97.

41 See, e.g., *Radians′ke budivnytstvo na Ukraïni v roky hromadians′koï viiny (1918–1919): Zbirnyk dokumentiv i materialiv* (Kyiv: AN USRS, 1962), 101.

42 *Komunist* (The Communist) was founded in 1918 as an organ of the Central Committee of the Communist Party of Ukraine and the Kharkiv Provincial Committee. It was initially published in Russian and then, from April 1926, in Ukrainian. From 1943 to 1991, it was published under the title *Radians′ka Ukraïna* (Soviet Ukraine) and, after 1991, under the title *Demokratychna Ukraïna* (Democratic Ukraine).

43 *Visti VUTsVK* (News of the All-Ukrainian Central Executive Committee) was a daily newspaper published in Kharkiv from 1921 to 1934, and in Kyiv beginning in 1934. Vasyl′ Ellan-Blakytnyi was the first editor of *Visti.*

44 "V kolehiï komisariatu Osvity," *Borot′ba*, 3 August 1919.

45 Mialo, "Hromads′ko-politychna diial′nist′ V. Ellana-Blakytnoho," 99. Serhii Volodymyrovych Pylypenko (1891–1934) was the director of the Taras Shevchenko Institute of Literature before he was arrested in 1933 and shot the following year.

46 Mykhailo Iuriiovych Panchenko (1888–1938) was one of the organizers of the All-Ukrainian Association of Revolutionary Playwrights and Screenwriters, part of the All-Ukrainian Association of Revolutionary Cinematographers, before he was subjected to repression in 1938.

47 "U Kyievi: Zasidannia Tsentral′noho vykonavchoho komitetu," *Borot′ba*, 7 August 1919.

48 TsDAHOU, f. 1, op. 20, spr. 101, ark. 6. Andrei Sergeevich Bubnov (1883–1938) was the chairman of the All-Ukrainian Military Revolutionary Committee in 1918. He was arrested on 17 October 1937, sentenced to death, and executed on 1 August 1938.

49 TsDAHOU, f. 1, op. 20, spr. 101, ark. 7.

50 TsDAHOU, f. 1, op. 20, spr. 101, ark. 7.

51 "Zmazaly," *Proletars′ka borot′ba* (Zhytomyr), 11 November 1919.

52 Vladimir I. Lenin, *Neizvestnye dokumenty: 1891–1922* (Moscow: Rosspen, 1999), 306.

53 Dmytro Zakharovych Manuïl′s′kyi (1883–1959) survived the purges and served in numerous party and state posts in Ukraine and Russia until his death. He was the first secretary of the Central Committee of the CP(b)U in the early 1920s, secretary of the Executive Committee of the Comintern

in 1931–43, and people's commissar and minister of foreign affairs of the UkrSSR in 1944–52.

54 Vladimir I. Lenin, "Zakliuchne slovo v pytanni pro radians'ku vladu na Ukraïni 3 hrudnia," in Lenin, *Povne zibrannia tvoriv*, vol. 39 (Kyiv: Vydavnytstvo politychnoï literatury Ukraïny, 1974), 347–48.

55 Mialo, "Hromads'ko-politychna diial'nist' V. Ellana-Blakytnoho," 118, 120.

56 Vladimir I. Lenin, "Proekt rezoliutsii ob ukrainskoi partii borot'bistov," in Lenin, *Polnoe sobranie sochinenii*, vol. 40, *Dekabr' 1919 – aprel' 1920*, 5th ed. (Moscow: Politizdat, 1974), 122.

57 I. F. Kuras, *Torzhestvo proletarskogo internatsionalizma i krakh melkoburzhuaznykh partii v Ukraine* (Kyiv: Naukova dumka, 1978), 315.

58 Kuras, *Triumf proletars'koho internatsionalizmu*, 284.

59 TsDAHOU, f. 263, op. 1, spr. 55475, t. 1, ark. 182.

60 TsDAHOU, f. 263, op. 1, spr. 55475, t. 1, ark. 182.

61 *Arkhiv rozstrilianoho vidrodzhennia: Materialy arkhivno-slidchykh sprav ukraïns'kykh pys'mennykiv 1920–1930-kh rokiv* (Kyiv: Smoloskyp, 2010), 23.

62 Mialo, "Hromads'ko-politychna diial'nist' V. Ellana-Blakytnoho," 124–25.

63 TsDAHOU, f. 39, op. 4, spr. 237, ark. 66.

64 M. O. Frolov, "Borot'bisty u KP(b)U v 20–30-ti roky XX stolittia," *Naukovi pratsi istorychnoho fakul'tetu Zaporiz'koho Derzhavnoho Universitetu* 1, no. 13 (2001): 167.

65 Stanislav V. Kul'chyts'kyi, *Chervonyi vyklyk: Istoriia komunizmu v Ukraïni vid ioho narodzhennia do zahybeli* (Kyiv: Tempora, 2013), 1:428.

66 Vladimir I. Lenin, "Zasedanie vtoroe (30 marta, utrom)" in *Deviatyi s''ezd RKP(b) mart–aprel' 1920 g.* (Partiinoe izdatel'stvo: Moscow, 1934), 96–97.

67 Iurii Ivanovych Ozers'kyi (real name Zebnyts'kyi, 1896–1937) headed the Ukrainian state publishing house Ukrnauka before his arrest on 23 November 1933 and sentencing to ten years in prison on charges of participating in the UMO. In May 1934, he was sent to the Solovki camp. He was shot in Sandarmokh on 3 November 1937. Petro Kyrylovych Solodub (1893–1937) headed the sector of long-term planning of the People's Commissariat of Heavy Industry of the USSR before his arrest in September 1933. He was shot in 1937 among a group of Solovki prisoners. For his and others' attempts to develop the economic aspects of Ukrainian statehood, see Yurii I. Shapoval, *Nevyhadani istoriï* (Kyiv: Svitohliad, 2004), 22. Feodosii (Todos) Prokhorovych Taran (Honcharenko, 1896–1938) was the editor of the newspaper *Visti VUTsVK* before his arrest and execution in 1938. Iurii Oleksandrovych Voitsekhivs'kyi (1883–1937) was secretary of the All-Ukrainian Central Executive Committee from 1932 to 1936.

68 M. S. Doroshko, *Nomenklatura: Kerivna verkhivka Radians'koï Ukraïny (1917–1938 rr.)* (Kyiv: Nika-tsentr, 2008), 73–74.

69 Frolov, "Borot'bisty u KP(b)U v 20–30-ti roky XX stolittia," 169.

70 *Dvenadtsatyi s"ezd RKP(b), 17–25 aprelia 1923 goda: Stenograficheskii otchet* (Moscow: Izdatel'stvo politicheskoi literatury, 1968), 572.

71 Frolov, "Borot'bisty u KP(b)U v 20-30-ti roky XX stolittia," 170.

72 TsDAHOU, f. 39, op. 4, spr. 237, ark. 71 and 90.

73 Karl Avksentiiovych Savrych (pseud. Maksymovych, 1892–1934) was a politician. During the First World War, while in the Legion of Ukrainian Sich

Riflemen, he was taken prisoner by the Russians and adopted Bolshevik ideas. In the 1920s, he worked in the Communist Party of Western Ukraine (CPWU) and was its representative in the Central Committee of the CP(b)U.

74 Isai Iakovych Khurhin (1887–1925) was a politician. He was a member of the Zionist Socialist Party in 1905–18, a member of the General Jewish Labor Bund in 1918–20, and a member of the Ukrainian Central Council and the Minor Council as deputy minister of Jewish affairs in 1917–18. From 1920, he was a member of the Bolshevik Party and trade envoy of the UkrSSR in Poland, and he later worked in the trade mission of the USSR in the United States, where he died under unclear circumstances.

75 Roman Korohods′kyi, *Dovzhenko v poloni: Rozvidky ta ese pro maistra* (Kyiv: Helikon, 2000), 51.

76 G. Besedovskii, *Na putiakh k termidoru* (Moscow: Sovremennik, 1997); V. L. Genis, "Grigorii Zinovievich Besedovskii," *Voprosy istorii*, 2006, no. 7: 37–58.

77 TsDAHOU, f. 39, op. 4, spr. 237, ark. 85. Shums′kyi had apparently proposed something else (other than the previous decision).

78 *Communist Party of Ukraine: Congresses and Conferences* (Kyiv: Ukraïna, 1991), 77, 88–90. See also *Pages of the History of the Communist Party of Ukraine: Questions and Answers* (Kyiv: Lybid′, 1990), 466, 472.

79 *Chervonyi shliakh* (Red path) was a monthly sociopolitical and literary-artistic magazine, published in Kharkiv from 1923 to 1936. Pavlo Hryhorovych Tychyna (1891–1967) was a poet, translator, and politician. His early poetry is characterized by a special innovation in form, but beginning in the late 1920s, his work became increasingly formal. In the 1920s, he belonged to the literary organizations Hart and VAPLITE. He was an academic of the All-Ukrainian Academy of Sciences (VUAN) from 1929, director of the Institute of Literature of the UkrSSR Academy of Sciences (1936–39 and 1941–43), chairman of the Verkhovna Rada of the UkrSSR (1953–59), and minister of education of the UkrSSR (1943–48).

80 M. O. Frolov, *Kompartiino-radians′ka elita v Ukraïni: Osoblyvosti isnuvannia ta funktsionuvannia v 1923–1928 rr.* (Zaporizhzhia: Prem'ier 2004), 569.

CHAPTER THREE

1 TsDAHOU, f. 57, op. 2, spr. 470, ark. 166.

2 Ian Petrovych Riappo (1880–1958) served as both deputy people's commissar for education of the UkrSSR and editor in chief of the journal *Shliakh osvity* (Path of education) in the 1920s.

3 For more details, see Yurii I. Shapoval, "'Ia pomyliavsia, vziavshy na sebe provynu': Do 90-richchia M. S. Volobuieva-Artemova," *Z arkhiviv VUChK-HPU-NKVD-KHB* 1 (1994): 104–10; Yurii I. Shapoval, *Liudyna i systema (Shtrykhy do portreta totalitarnoï doby v Ukraïni)* (Kyiv: Instytut natsional′nykh vidnosyn i politolohiï NANU, 1994); Yurii I. Shapoval, "Tekst iak dolia," *Den′*, 27 February 2003.

4 TsDAHOU, f. 263, op. 1, spr. 55475 FP, t. 3, ark. 41.

5 TsDAHOU, f. 263, op. 1, spr. 55475 FP, ark. 42.

6 For more details, see Myroslav Shkandrij, *Modernists, Marxists and the Nation: The Ukrainian Literary Discussion of the 1920s* (Edmonton: Canadian Institute of Ukrainian Studies Press, 1992).

7 Mykola Khvyl'ovyi, "Apolohety Pysaryzmu," in *Tvory u dvokh tomakh* (Kyiv: Dnipro, 1990), 2:573, 575.

8 Valerii Vasyl'iev, *Politychne kerivnytstvo URSR i SRSR: Dynamika vidnosyn tsentr-subtsentr vlady (1917–1938)* (Kyiv: Instytut istorii Ukraïny NAN Ukraïny, 2014), 146.

9 Vasyl'iev, *Politychne kerivnytstvo*, 146–47.

10 Deadlines for the completion of the Ukrainization of the party apparatus were repeatedly pushed back—eventually to 1 January 1927 and later to 1 June 1929. V. A. Smolii, ed., *Ukraïnizatsiia 1920–30-kh rokiv: Peredumovy, zdobutky, uroky* (Kyiv: Instytut istorii Ukraïny NAN Ukraïny, 2003), 83.

11 A. A. Chernobaev, ed., *Na prieme u Stalina: Tetradi (zhurnaly) zapisei lits, priniatykh I. V. Stalinym (1924–1953 gg.). Spravochnik* (Moscow: Novyi khronograf, 2008), 750.

12 Mykhailo Mykolaiovych Tesliuk (party pseud. Ernst, 1899–1985) was a member of the CPWU, a member of the Politburo of its Central Committee in 1926–28, and a delegate to the Third Congress of the CPWU. In 1927–28, he opposed Moscow's nationalities policy in Ukraine and defended Oleksandr Shums'kyi. In 1932, he was recalled to the UkrSSR. He was arrested in 1933 and imprisoned until 1954, when he was released.

13 Sectoral State Archive of the Security Services of Ukraine (HDA SBU), spr. 59881 FP, t. 118, ark. 30.

14 HDA SBU, spr. 59881 FP, t. 118, ark. 30.

15 TsDAHOU, f. 1, op. 1, spr. 135, ark. 131. Isaak Kalmanovych Dashkovs'kyi (1891–1972) was an economist, a professor at Kharkiv University, rector of the Artem Communist University from 1923, and author of more than five hundred scholarly works. He was arrested in 1929 and sentenced to exile. He was sentenced for a second time in August 1949, this time to ten years in prison. He was rehabilitated in 1956. For more information on the life, scholarly legacy, and fate of Dashkovs'kyi, see V. A. Hrechenko, "I. K. Dashkovs'kyi: Narys politychnoï diial'nosti," *Ukraïns'kyi istorychnyi zhurnal*, 1991, no. 10: 87–94; V. A. Hrechenko, "Opal'nyi professor: Delo i sud'ba I. K. Dashkovskogo," *Pozitsiia: obshchestvenno-politicheskii ezhemesiachnyi zhurnal* no. 4 (1991): 66–74.

16 Chernobaev, *Na prieme u Stalina*, 24, 763.

17 V. M. Danylenko, ed., *Ukraïns'ka intelihentsiia i vlada: Zvedennia sekretnoho viddilu DPU USRR 1927–1929 rr.* (Kyiv: Tempora, 2012), 54.

18 Vasyl'iev, *Politychne kerivnytstvo URSR i SRSR*, 148.

19 Joseph V. Stalin, "Tov. Kaganovichu i drugim chlenam PB TsK KP(b)U," in Stalin, *Sochineniia*, vol. 8 (Moscow: Gosudarstvennoe izdatel'stvo politicheskoi literatury, 1948), 152.

20 Stalin, "Tov. Kaganovichu," 154.

21 Mai Panchuk, "Natsional-ukhyl'netstvo: Anatomiia problemy," in *Marshrutamy istorii*, ed. Yurii I. Shapoval (Kyiv: Politvydav Ukraïny, 1990), 224.

22 TsDAHOU, f. 1, op. 16, spr. 5, ark. 3.

23 Vasyl′iev, *Politychne kerivnytstvo URSR i SRSR*, 150.
24 TsDAHOU, f. 1, op. 6, spr. 88, ark. 116 and 117v.
25 TsDAHOU, f. 1, op. 6, spr. 88, ark. 117v. and 118.
26 TsDAHOU, f. 1, op. 6, spr. 88, ark. 119.
27 TsDAHOU, f. 1, op. 6, spr. 88, ark. 119v and 120.
28 TsDAHOU, f. 1, op. 6, spr. 88, ark. 121. Mykola Nesterovych Demchenko (1896–1937) was a member of the Central Committee of the CP(b)U (1927–37), people's commissar for agriculture of the USSR, and, in 1937, people's commissar for grain and livestock state farms of the UkrSSR, until his arrest on 22 July 1937. He was shot in October of that year.
29 TsDAHOU, f. 1, op. 6, spr. 88, ark. 122 and 123v.
30 TsDAHOU, f. 1, op. 6., spr. 88, ark. 126. Fedir Danylovych Korniushyn (1893–1938) was a candidate member of the Central Committee of the CP(b)U before being transferred to Moscow in 1928. He was arrested and executed in 1938.
31 TsDAHOU, f. 1, op. 6, spr. 88, ark. 127.
32 TsDAHOU, f. 1, op. 6, spr. 88, ark. 127.
33 TsDAHOU, f. 1, op. 6, spr. 88, ark. 129.
34 TsDAHOU, f. 1, op. 6, spr. 88, ark. 129.
35 TsDAHOU, f. 1, op. 20, spr. 2248, ark. 8–13.
36 TsDAHOU, f. 1, op. 1, spr. 210, ark. 1.
37 TsDAHOU, f. 1, op. 1, spr. 210, ark. 2.
38 TsDAHOU, f. 1, op. 1, spr. 210, ark. 2v and 4.
39 Vasyl′iev, *Politychne kerivnytstvo URSR i SRSR*, 154.
40 Oleksandr Shums′kyi, "Ideolohichna borot′ba v ukraïns′komu kul′turnomu protsesi," *Bil′shovyk Ukraïny*, no. 2 (1927): 11–25.
41 Vasyl′iev, *Politychne kerivnytstvo URSR i SRSR*, 155.
42 TsDAHOU, f. 39. op. 4, spr. 237, ark. 92.
43 Andrii Fedorovych Radchenko (1887–1938) was a member of the Politburo of the Central Committee of the CP(b)U 1925–28 and a member of the Central Committee of the ACP(b) from 1925 to 1927. He was arrested in 1937 and shot in January 1938.
44 TsDAHOU, f. 39, op. 4, spr. 237, ark. 94.
45 TsDAHOU, f. 39, op. 4, spr. 237, ark. 94.
46 TsDAHOU, f. 39, op. 4, spr. 237, ark. 94–95.
47 Chernobaev, *Na prieme u Stalina*, 769.
48 Danylenko, *Ukraïns′ka intelihentsiia i vlada*, 68.
49 Danylenko, *Ukraïns′ka intelihentsiia i vlada*, 64, 66.

CHAPTER FOUR

1 Mai Panchuk, "Zhyttia i smert′ Oleksandra Shums′koho," in *Pro mynule—zarady maibutn′oho*, ed. Yurii I. Shapoval (Kyiv: Vydavnytstvo pry Kyïvs′komu universyteti, 1989), 326.
2 Iu. Iu. Slyvka, *Storinky istoriï KPZU* (Lviv: Kameniar, 1989), 13.
3 Slyvka, *Storinky istoriï KPZU*, 23.

4 Iosyp Vasyl′ovych Krilyk (party pseud. Vasyl′kiv, 1898–1941) was a communist activist in western Ukraine, a secretary of the Central Committee of the CPWU, and a member of the Politburo of the Central Committee of the Communist Party of Poland (CPP). In 1933, he was arrested on the fabricated case of the UMO and sentenced to ten years in prison. On 11 September 1941, he was shot in a group of 157 prisoners of the Orel prison, together with the former head of the UkrSSR government Christian Rakovsky. See O. S. Rubl′ov and Ia. A. Cherchenko, *Stalinshchyna i dolia zakhidnoukraïns′koï intelihentsiï* (Kyiv: Naukova dumka, 1994), 208. Roman Volodymyrovych Kuz′ma (Turians′kyi, 1894–1940) was a member of the CPWU, and a member of the Central Committee's Polish section of the Comintern from 1926. In 1933, he was arrested in the UMO case and sentenced to five years in prison. He was rearrested in 1939 and shot the following year.

5 Terry Martin, *Affirmative Action Empire*, 226.

6 Martin, *Affirmative Action Empire*, 218–19.

7 Slyvka, *Storinky istoriï KPZU*, 27.

8 Nikolai Ivanovich Bukharin (1888–1938), who held numerous central state and party posts, reportedly retained a more nuanced position toward Shums′kyi and was against reconsidering the case against him in 1928. See Mai Panchuk, *"Bili pliamy" heroïchnoho litopysu: Iz istoriï Komunistychnoï partiï Zakhidnoï Ukraïny* (Kyiv: Politvydav Ukraïny, 1989), 28. Bukharin's loss to Stalin in the interparty struggle rendered these sentiments academic. He was arrested in 1937 and executed the following year.

9 Slyvka, *Storinky istoriï KPZU*, 28.

10 Panchuk, *"Bili pliamy" heroïchnoho litopysu*, 23.

11 Slyvka, *Storinky istoriï KPZU*, 29–62. See also I. B. Vasiuta, *Politychna istoriia Zakhidnoï Ukraïny (1918–1939)* (Lviv: Kameniar, 2006), 220–21.

12 Dmytro Ivanovych Dontsov (1883–1973) was a literary critic, publicist, philosopher, politician, and ideologue of Ukrainian integral nationalism. At the beginning of his activity (1905–13), he was a member of the Ukrainian Social Democratic Workers Party (USDRP). In 1914, he headed the pro-Austrian Union for the Liberation of Ukraine. In 1918, during the Hetmanate of Pavlo Skoropads′kyi, he was the director of the Ukrainian Telegraph Agency. He published the *Literaturno-naukovyi vistnyk* (Literary-scientific herald) in Lviv (later the *Herald*) in the 1920s and 1930s. He lived in exile after 1939. For more on Dontsov, see Trevor Erlacher, *Ukrainian Nationalism in the Age of Extremes: An Intellectual Biography of Dmytro Dontsov* (Cambridge, Mass.: Harvard Ukrainian Research Institute, 2021).

13 Oleksandr Zaitsev, *Ukraïns′kyi intehral′nyi natsionalizm (1920–1930-ti roky): Narysy intelektual′noï istoriï* (Kyiv: Krytyka, 2013), 401.

14 Frolov, *Kompartiino-radians′ka elita v Ukraïni*, 595.

15 Panchuk, *"Bili pliamy" heroïchnoho litopysu*, 22.

16 For more details, see Shapoval, *Ukraïna 20-50-kh rokiv*, 132–48. At the time of his arrest, Maksymovych was working as a senior inspector of the Grain Procurement Department (Zagotzerno) in Moscow.

17 For more details, see Slyvka, *Storinky istoriï KPZU*, 89–90; Panchuk, *"Bili pliamy" heroïchnoho litopysu*, 127–28.

18 TsDAHOU, f. 263, op. 1, spr. 55475 FP, t. 4, ark. 81. Matvii Ivanovych Iavors´kyi (1885–1937) was a government-sponsored official historian in the UkrSSR in the 1920s but was expelled from the All-Ukrainian Academy of Sciences (VUAN) and CP(b)U in 1930. He was arrested in 1931, sentenced to six years in prison in Solovki, and shot in 1937. See Shapoval, *Ukraïna 20–50-kh rokiv*, 91–96; Volodymyr Masliichuk, "Marksysts´ki skhemy ukraïns´koï istoriï: Matvii Iavors´kyi, Volodymyr Sukhino-Khomenko, Mykola Horban´," *Ukraïna Moderna* 14, no. 3 (2009): 63–77.

19 TsDAHOU, f. 263, op. 1, spr. 55475 FP, t. 4, ark. 84.

20 Oleksandr Ushkalov and Leonid Ushkalov, eds., *Arkhiv rozstrilianoho vidrodzhennia: Materialy arkhivno-slidchykh sprav ukraïns´kykh pys´mennykiv 1920–1930-kh rokiv* (Kyiv: Smoloskyp, 2010), 48.

21 Ushkalov and Ushkalov, *Arkhiv rozstrilianoho vidrodzhennia*, 48.

22 Rubl´ov and Cherchenko, *Stalinshchyna i dolia zakhidnoukraïns´koï intelihentsiï*, 266–67. Roman Hryhorovych Kupchyns´kyi (1894–1976) was a journalist, poet, novelist, composer, and Civil War commander. He emigrated to Poland and Germany in 1939, and to the United States in 1949, where he continued his literary work. Petro Ivanovych Kalnyshevs´kyi (1690–1803) was the last Kish ataman of the Zaporizhian Sich in 1762 and 1765–75. On 25 June 1776, he was arrested and sent to Solovki for life.

23 TsDAHOU, f. 263, op. 1, spr. 55475 FP, t. 4, ark. 40.

24 TsDAHOU, f. 263, op. 1, spr. 55475 FP, t. 4. ark. 41. Valerii Mykhailovych Horozhanin (1889–1938) was one of the key organizers of the purge in Ukraine against Shums´kyi and his associates. From May 1930, he was deputy chief of the Secret Department of OGPU (Joint State Political Directorate, secret police) of the USSR, and, from 1935, he was deputy head of the Foreign Department of the Main Directorate of State Security of the NKVD of the USSR. From February 1937 he was chief, and, from May of that year, deputy chief of the Special Bureau of the NKVD of the USSR. He was arrested in 1937 and executed the following year.

25 Quoted in V. M. Danylenko, ed., *Ukraïns´ka intelihentsiia i vlada: Zvedennia sekretnoho viddilu DPU USRR 1927–1929 rr.* (Kyiv: Tempora, 2012), 287, 294.

26 Danylenko, *Ukraïns´ka intelihentsiia i vlada*, 356. The rationale is uncertain for the placement of scare quotes by the GPU officer writing the report.

27 TsDAHOU, f. 1, op. 20, spr. 2894, ark. 3–4.

28 The newspaper *Za kommunisticheskoe prosveshchenie* (For communist enlightenment) was published in Moscow from 1924 to 1937 under the auspices of the Central Committee of the Union of Educators of the USSR. Later it was called *Uchitel´skaia gazeta* (Teachers' newspaper).

29 TsDAHOU, f. 263, op. 1, spr. 55475 FP, t. 4, ark. 114. Fedir Vladyslavovych Bei-Orlovs´kyi (1899–1938) was a member of the Central Committee of the CPWU. At the time of his arrest, he was attending Marxism-Leninism courses in Moscow. He was arrested in 1933 in the fabricated UMO case. He was shot on 15 September 1938.

30 "V bahni natsionalizmu," *Bil´shovyk Ukraïny* 4 (1928): 5–6.

31 M. Volin, *Istoriia KP(b)U v styslomu narysi* (Kharkiv: Proletar, 1932), 162–63.

32 Martin, *Affirmative Action Empire*, 119.

33 Ievhen Konovalets′ (1891–1938) was colonel in the army of the Ukrainian People's Republic (UPR), commander of the Sich Riflemen, commander in the actual Ukrainian Military Organization (founded in 1920 and active primarily in western Ukraine, then under Polish control), founder and the first leader of the Organization of Ukrainian Nationalists (OUN). He was assassinated in Rotterdam by an NKVD agent using an explosive device.

34 Accused writers included Borys Antonenko-Davydovych, Pavlo Hubenko (pseud. Ostap Vyshnia), Oles′ Dosvitnii, Dmytro Zahul, Myroslav Irchan-Bab'iuk, Anatolii Karabut, Mykhailo Kachaniuk, Mykhailo Kozoriz, Hryhorii Kosynka (Strilets′), Serhii Pylypenko, Valer′ian Polishchuk, Oleksa Slisarenko, and Mykhailo Ialovyi. Accused academics included Kharkiv Institute of the History of Ukrainian Culture director Ievhen Cherniak, Odesa University associate professor Volodymyr Borshchevs′kyi, Kharkiv Geographic Institute research fellow Vasyl′ Butsura, Kharkiv Institute of Red Professors professor Dmytro Vakhniak, Kyiv Art Institute rector Ivan Vrona, scholar Vasyl′ Desniak-Vasylenko, and "Ukrzernotsentr" referent Petro Zhuravel′. Publishers included *Ukraïns′ka Radians′ka Entsyklopediia* employee Iulian Bachyns′kyi (author of the book *Ukraïna irredenta*), Zhytomyr Institute for People's Education director Vasyl′ Hotsa, Kharkiv publishing house Molodyi bil′shovyk (Young Bolshevik) director Mykola Hrytsai, Central Committee of the CP(b)U publishing house Partvydav literary editor Stepan Popovych, and UkrSSR People's Commissariat of Education referent Fedir Prystupa. For more details on the tragic fate of one of these figures, Iulian Bachyns′kyi, see Yurii I. Shapoval, "'Vynnym sebe ne vyznaiu': Nevidomi storinky Iuliiana Bachyns′koho," *Rozbudova derzhavy* 1 (1996): 52–57; 2 (1996): 53–55; Yurii I. Shapoval, "The Tragic Faith of Yulian Bachynskyi," *Journal of Ukrainian Studies* 23, no. 1 (1998): 25–39; Yurii I. Shapoval, "Unknown Pages from Yulian Bachynskyi Biography," *History of Ukraine* 14 (2000): 5–7.

35 These included Bila Tserkva motor-technical station director Dmytro Fidek, Kryvyi Rih local party committee secretary Vasyl′ Sirko, Central Committee of the KP(b)U assistant secretary Vasyl′ Oliinyk, Kharkiv Transportation Institute member Potap Zaderei, Artemivs′k (Donetsk Oblast) public bank director Mykola Zaiets′, Kharkiv Electrical College teacher of German language Oleksii Ivanchevs′kyi, Kharkiv Central Scientific Library director Serhii Kaniuk, Kyiv oblast Veterinary Department chief Dmytro Klymenko, Kyiv Historical Museum scientific fellow Ihnat Koltsuniak, Dnipropetrovsk Institute of Engineers of Transportation department head Frants Kondrats′kyi, Holovlit inspector Serhii Kopach-Kholodnyi, Mariupol Pedagogical Institute professor Mykola Kuzniak, Kyiv movie screenwriter Faust Lopatyns′kyi, Sil′hospvydav editor Fedir Malyts′kyi, Kyiv painter Iukhym Mykhailiv, *Komsomolets′ Ukraïny* newspaper Department of Information head Stepan Navars′kyi-Ieleniuk, scholar Ostap Ohar, Kyiv Energy Institute research fellow Oleksandr Osiiuk, sculptor Mar′ian Panasiuk, Kharkiv Institute of Mechanization and Electrification of Agriculture student Pankrat Polishchuk, Kyiv Veterinary Institute professor Dmytro Rudyk, National Academy of Sciences of Ukraine academic Stepan Rudnyts′kyi, Yalta sanatorium Paryz′ka Komuna doctor Volodymyr Senchyn, Radio-Telegraph Agency of Ukraine referent-journalist Ostap Sorochan, schoolteacher Ivan

Tereshchenko, Kharkiv University student Mykhailo Terlets′kyi, scholar Vasyl′ Farylo, National Academy of Sciences of Ukraine research fellow and Kyiv Opera House director Mykola Khrystovyi, professor Illia Ts′okan, National Academy of Sciences of Ukraine library research fellow Oleksii Iavors′kyi, academics Matvii Iavors′kyi and Mykhailo Hrushevs′kyi, General Secretariat of the Ukrainian Central Rada former general scribe Pavlo Khrystiuk (who was working for the People's Commissariat of Finance when he was arrested), Shums′kyi's former deputy in the People's Commissariat for Education Petro Solodub, *Ukrainian Soviet Encyclopedia* fellow Antin Krushel′nyts′kyi and sons Ivan and Taras, theater director Les′ Kurbas, and many others.

36 This was a broader tactic used throughout the 1930s by the NKVD, especially during the Great Terror.

37 HDA SBU, spr. 59881 FP, t. 7, 28. No further information is available about Khrystiuk's time in Vienna.

38 HDA SBU, spr. 59881 FP, t. 7, 28. DVU was founded in Kharkiv in 1919 as the Derzhvydav. In 1930, it was rebranded as Derzhavne vydavnyche ob'iednannia Ukraïny.

39 HDA SBU, spr. 59881 FP, t. 7, ark. 87.

40 HDA SBU, spr. 55475 FP, t. 4, ark. 25.

41 The NKVD succeeded the OGPU as the main secret police body in 1934.

42 HDA SBU, spr. 55475 FP, t. 4, ark. 28.

43 Semen Pidhainyi, *Ukraïns′ka inteligentsiia na Solovkakh: Nedostriliani* (Neu Ulm: Prometheus, 1947), 56.

44 HDA SBU, spr. 55475 FP, t. 4, ark. 62–63.

45 HDA SBU, spr. 55475 FP, t. 4, ark.70.

46 HDA SBU, spr. 55475 FP, t. 4, ark. 173–74.

47 Shapoval, *Ukraïna 20–50-kh rokiv*, 135.

48 Georgii Evgenovich Prokof′ev (1895–1937) was a commissar of state security first rank, a member of the Communist Party of the Soviet Union (b) beginning in 1919 (an anarchist in 1916–19), and in the Cheka from 1920. Beginning in 1926 he was head of the economic department of the OGPU of the USSR, and from 1931, head of the special department of the OGPU of the USSR. From October 1931 he was the deputy people's commissar of the Workers' and Peasants' inspector general of the USSR, from November 1932 he was deputy chairman of the OGPU of the USSR. In July 1934 he became deputy people's commissar of internal affairs of the USSR and from September 1936, the deputy people's commissar of communications of the USSR. He was arrested in April 1937 and shot shortly thereafter.

49 *Ostannia adresa: Rozstrily solovets′kykh v′iazniv z Ukraïny u 1937–1938 rokakh*, 2nd ed., vol. 1 (Kyiv: Sfera, 2003), 446. About Petro Solodub's life, see Serhii Shevchenko, "Vypusknyk 'Solovets′koï akademiï,'" *Dzerkalo tyzhnia*, February 21, 2014.

50 Shapoval, *Ukraïna 20–50-kh rokiv*, 136.

51 Pavel Sudoplatov, *Razvedka i Kreml′: Zapiski nezhelatel′nogo svidetelia* (Moscow: TOO Geia, 1996), 438.

52 Sudoplatov, *Razvedka i Kreml′*, 440.

53 Sudoplatov, *Razvedka i Kreml′*, 441. Sergei Mikhailovich Shpigel′glas (1897–1941) was a major of state security, served in the Intelligence Service, and, from 1936, was a deputy head of the Foreign Department of the Head Office of the Security of the USSR NKVD. From February 1938, he fulfilled the duties of the head of this department. He participated in liquidating defectors, mostly former employees of the Soviet secret services. He was arrested during the purge of the NKVD in 1938 and shot in 1941.

54 Shapoval, *Ukraïna 20–50-kh rokiv*, 136.

55 Ruben Pavlovich Katanian (1880–1966) was a Soviet statesman and a lawyer by profession (he graduated from Moscow University in 1906 and had a law practice). From 1920 to 1921, he was head of the propaganda department of the Central Committee of the RCP(b). In 1921, he was head of the foreign department of the Cheka (All-Russian Extraordinary Commission, VChK). In 1922, he was a consul general of the USSR in Berlin, working for the USSR People's Commissariat of Finance. From 1923, he was assistant to the prosecutor of the RSFSR, senior assistant to the Supreme Court prosecutor of the USSR in special affairs (with supervision over the OGPU and, later, NKVD), and state prosecutor on political processes. He was arrested in 1938 and rehabilitated in 1955. He subsequently worked as a professor at Moscow University.

56 Pidhainyi, *Ukraïns′ka intelihentsiia na Solovkakh*, 48.

57 HDA SBU, spr. 55475 FP, t 5, ark. 1. Vsevolod Nikolaevich Merkulov (1895–1953) was a Communist Party member and statesman, general of the army, chief of the Headquarters of the State Security of the USSR NKVD (1938–41), and people's commissar for state security of the USSR (1941 and 1943–46). He was shot in 1953. Georgii Molchanov (1897–1937) was head of the Secret Political Department of the OGPU to the Council of People's Commissars (1931–36), chief of the Headquarters of the State Security of the USSR NKVD, and commissar second class of state security. This structure specifically persecuted all political opponents of Stalin and was responsible for fabricating charges in the show trials of 1935–36. Molchanov was shot in October 1937.

58 His appeals could be the subject of dedicated research project and, hopefully, will one day get the attention they deserve. Shums′kyi's letters clearly demonstrate his state of mind and spirit and contain, with no exaggeration, unique information on the collisions of the alleged leader of the "nationalist-evaders" in Ukraine. Svitlana I. Vlasenko made the first attempt to publish a small number of Oleksandr Shums′kyi's letters. See Vlasenko, "Lysty Oleksandra Shums′koho iz zaslannia (iz fondiv TsDAHO Ukraïny)," *Publikatsiia arkhivnykh dokumentiv*, 2011, 165–78.

59 TsDAHOU, f. 263, op. 1, spr. 55475 FP, t. 1, ark. 171.

60 TsDAHOU, f. 263, op. 1, spr. 55475 FP, t. 1, ark. 17.

61 TsDAHOU, f. 263, op. 1, spr. 55475 FP, t. 1, ark. 8–10.

62 TsDAHOU, f. 263, op. 1, spr. 55475 FP, t. 1, ark. 11.

63 TsDAHOU, f. 263, op. 1, spr. 55475 FP, t. 1, ark. 22.

64 TsDAHOU, f. 263, op. 1, spr. 55475 FP, t. 1, ark. 22.

65 TsDAHOU, f. 263, op. 1, spr. 55475 FP, t. 4, ark. 48. Borys Volodymyrovych Kozel's'kyi (Bernard Vol'fovych Holovanivs'kyi, 1902–36) was a major of state security and was in the ACP(b) from 1931 and in the Cheka from 1921. He was assistant head of the Secret Political Department of the GPU (USSR) from 1931, temporary acting head of this department from December 1933, and head of the Secret Political Department of the Office of State Security of the NKVD (USSR) beginning in November 1934. He committed suicide in 1936.

66 Shapoval, *Ukraïna 20–50-kh rokiv*, 137. "Comrade Sokolov" appears to be a reference to Petr Grigor'evich Shostak (1896–1937), who was a head in the Operative Department from 1933 to 1936, first of the GPU and then of the USSR NKVD. He was shot in 1937.

67 TsDAHOU, f. 263, op. 1, spr. 55475 FP, t. 1, ark. 2.

68 TsDAHOU, f. 263, op. 1, spr. 55475 FP, t. 1, ark. 3.

69 Quoted in Shapoval, *Ukraïna 20–50-kh rokiv*, 138.

70 Khlevniuk, *Khoziain*, 181.

71 Khlevniuk, *Khoziain*, 227–28.

72 Khlevniuk, *Khoziain*, 242.

73 Khlevniuk, *Khoziain*, 229.

74 On these "national operations" in 1935, see Khlevniuk, *Khoziain*, 240–41; Martin, *Affirmative Action Empire*, chaps. 8–9; Terry Martin, "The Origins of Soviet Ethnic Cleansing," *Journal of Modern History* 70, no. 4 (December 1998): 813–61; A. E. Gurianov, ed., *Repressii protiv poliakov i polskikh grazhdan* (Moscow: Zven'ia, 1997), 33; I. L. Shcherbakova, ed., *Nakazannyi narod: Repressii protiv rossiiskikh nemtsev* (Moscow: Zven'ia, 1999).

75 This exchange was reproduced in NKVD order no. 00321, 15 August 1932, on "the abuses of fundamental rules of investigative work."

76 Khlevniuk, *Khoziain*, 228.

77 Matthew E. Lenoe, *The Kirov Murder and Soviet History* (New Haven, Conn.: Yale University Press, 2010), chap. 7, esp. 252: "Probably on the night of December 1–2, 1934, Stalin drafted the infamous 'Law of December 1,' instructing the police and courts to try cases of terrorism without delay, reject appeals, and carry out death sentences immediately upon conviction."

CHAPTER FIVE

1 TsDAHOU, f. 263, op. 1, spr. 55475 FP, t. 1, ark. 37.

2 Shapoval, *Ukraïna 20-50-kh rokiv*, 330.

3 Shapoval, *Ukraïna 20-50-kh godov*, 139.

4 TsDAHOU, f. 263, op. 1, spr. 55475 FP, t. 1, ark. 58.

5 TsDAHOU, f. 263, op. 1, spr. 55475 FP, t. 1, ark. 59.

6 TsDAHOU, f. 263, op. 1, spr. 55475 FP, t. 1, ark. 59.

7 O. V. Khlevniuk et al., eds., *Stalinskoe Politbiuro v 30-e gody: Sbornik dokumentov* (Moscow: Rosspen, 1995), 150.

8 "Materialy fevral′sko-martovskogo plenuma TsK VKP(b) 1937 goda," *Voprosy istorii*, 1995, no. 2: 19.

9 "Materialy fevral′sko-martovskogo plenuma TsK VKP(b) 1937 goda," 16.

10 Shapoval, *Ukraïna 20–50-kh rokiv*, 140.

11 For a discussion of the figures, see Oleg Khlevniuk, *Khoziain*, 320.

12 Sectoral State Archive of the Security Services of Ukraine (HDA SBU), f. 65, spr. S-4472 FP, t. 2, ark. 2.

13 HDA SBU, f. 65, spr. S-4472 FP, t. 2, ark. 2.

14 Aleksandr Sergeevich Slavatinskii (1892–1939) was a major of state security (1935); from 1936 to 1937, he was an assistant chief of the Transport Department of the NKVD of the USSR and assistant chief of the NKVD in the Saratov oblast. He was arrested and shot as an "enemy of the people." He was rehabilitated in 1955. For more details, see A. V. Dienko, *Razvedka i kontrrazvedka v litsakh: Entsiklopedicheskii slovar′ rossiiskikh spetssluzhb* (Moscow: Russkii mir, 2002), 453.

15 Ievdokiia Borysivna Tatarenko (Honcharenko) was monitored on suspicion of ties to former Socialist-Revolutionaries, and killed, according to the denunciation, for saying that Valentin Kataev's 1936 novel *Beleet parus odinokii* (A white sail gleams), about the 1905 Revolution, "was the only book in which the children of the intelligentsia were portrayed in a positive light." Honcharenko was accused of discrediting Soviet literature. Arkhiv UFSB po Saratovskoi oblasti, f. OS-16228, 172–73.

16 Iosyp Iuriiovych Hermaize (1892–1958) was a historian, an employee of the historical institutions of the All-Ukrainian Academy of Sciences (VUAN) in Kyiv in the 1920s, and a member of the Russian Social Democratic Labor Party (RSDLP[b]) and the Ukrainian Social Democratic Workers Party (USDRP). He was arrested in July 1929 and sentenced to five years in prison in the SVU case. He was arrested again in 1937, and his sentence was extended to ten years. He died in prison. Nataliia Antonivna Kotsiubyns′ka (1896–1937) was an art critic and, in the 1920s, an employee of VUAN. She was arrested in 1924, 1934, and 1937, this last time while she was in exile in Saratov. She was sentenced to death and shot on 11 December 1937. Hlib Kostiantynovych Doroshkevych (1899–1937) was a teacher and the brother of the professor Oleksandr Doroshkevych. Ol′ha Trokhymivna Andriievs′ka (1876–1937) was a linguist and, in the 1920s, an employee of the VUAN commission to compile a dictionary of the living Ukrainian language.

17 Shapoval, *Ukraïna 20–50-kh rokiv*, 223–24. Izrail′ Maiseevich Liapleŭski (1894–1938) was head of the Special Department of the NKVD of the USSR beginning in 1936. He was appointed people's commissar for internal affairs of the UkrSSR in June 1937, demoted to head of the Transport Department of the NKVD in January 1938, arrested in April 1938, and executed in July of the same year.

18 For more details, see R. Ia. Pirog, "Kak pogib predsedatel′ Sovnarkoma Ukrains′koi SSR P. P. Liubchenko," *Izvestiia TsK KPSS*, no. 10, 1990, 140–41; Shapoval, *Ukraïna 20–50-kh rokiv*, 223–40; V. A. Smolii, ed., *Politychnyi*

teror i teroryzm v Ukraïni XIX–XX stolittia. Istorychni narysy (Kyiv: Naukova dumka, 2002), 400–495.

19 Shapoval, *Ukraïna 20–50-kh rokiv*, 240.

20 HDA SBU, spr. 38834 FP, ark. 17.

21 HDA SBU, spr. 38834 FP, ark. 207–12.

22 TsDAHOU, f. 39, op. 4, spr. 237, ark. 37.

23 Shapoval, *Ukraïna 20–50-kh rokiv*, 141–42.

24 Bogdan Zakharovich Kobulov (1904–53) was a member of State Security and one of the key organizers of the Great Terror. In 1938–39, he was head of the investigative unit of the NKVD of the USSR and a member of Lavrentii Beria's inner circle. He was shot in 1953. The Operations Department was one of two departments (*otdely*) in the office (*upravlenie*) of State Security.

25 Shapoval, *Ukraïna 20-50-kh rokiv*, 142.

26 The Krasnoiarsk NKVD arrested 31,942 people in 1937 and 1938. O. Mozokhin, *Repressii v tsifrakh i dokumentakh: Deiatel'nost'' organov VChK-OGPU-NKVD-MGB (1918–1953 gg.)* (Moscow: Veche, 2018), 194–98.

27 Ivan Pavlovich Semenov (1905–72) was younger than Karl Aleksandrovich Pavlov (1895–1957), though he had a longer career in the party and military before entering the NKVD. Pavlov had been in the NKVD (Cheka-OGPU) since 1918, steadily rising in its ranks. Pavlov killed himself in 1957 after he retired. N. V. Petrov and K. V Skorkin, *Kto rukovodil NKVD: 1934–1941* (Moscow: Memorial, 1999), 378–79, 443.

28 HDA SBU, f. 65, spr. 4772 FP, ch. 2, ark. 11.

29 TsDAHOU, f. 263, op. 1, spr. 55475 FP, t. 1, ark. 108–9.

30 A. G. Tepliakov, "Organy NKVD Zapadnoi Sibiri v 'kulatskoi operatsii,'" in *Stalinizm v sovetskoi provintsii: 1937–1938 gg., Massovaia operatsiia na osnove prikaza No. 00447*, ed. M. Iunge, B. Bonvech, and R. Binner (Moscow: Rosspen, 2009), 543–44.

31 Khlevniuk, *Khoziain*, 338–48.

32 Anatolii Il'in, "Oprichniki Berii v Krasnoiarske," *Vechernii Krasnoiarsk*, August 12, 1997; S. A. Papkov, *Obyknovennyi terror: Politika stalinizma v Sibiri* (Moscow: Rosspen, 2012), 254.

33 Stephen G. Wheatcroft, "Agency and Terror: Evdokimov and Mass Killing in Stalin's Great Terror," *Australian Journal of Politics and History* 53, no. 1 (2007): 42.

34 Papkov, *Obyknovennyi terror*, 255, 257–61, 271; Tepliakov, "Organy NKVD Zapadnoi Sibiri," 565. See, more broadly, J. Arch Getty, "'Excesses Are Not Permitted': Mass Terror and Stalinist Governance in the Late 1930s," *Russian Review* 61, no. 1 (January 2002): 113–38.

35 Tepliakov, "Organy NKVD Zapadnoi Sibiri," 537.

36 Stephen Kotkin, *Stalin: Waiting for Hitler, 1929–1941* (New York: Penguin, 2017), 543–44.

37 TsDAHOU, f. 263, op. 1, spr. 55475 FP, t. 1, ark. 132.

38 Dmitrii Dmitrievich Grechukhin was the Krasnoiarsk NKVD head from 13 September 1937 until 26 February 1938.

39 TsDAHOU, f. 263, op. 1, spr. 55475 FP, t. 1, ark. 132.

40 TsDAHOU, f. 39, op. 4, spr. 237, ark. 33.

41 TsDAHOU, f. 263, op. 1, spr. 55475 FP, t. 1, ark. 133.

42 TsDAHOU, f. 263, op. 1, spr. 55475 FP, t. 1, ark. 189.
43 TsDAHOU, f. 263, op. 1, spr. 55475 FP, t. 1, ark. 133.
44 TsDAHOU, f. 39 op. 4, spr. 237, ark. 33.
45 Postanovlenie Politbiuro TsK VKP(b) "Ob arestakh, prokurorskom nadzore i vedenii sledstviia," 17 November 1938.
46 TsDAHOU, f. 263, op. 1, spr. 55475 FP, t. 1, ark. 134, 136.
47 Petrov and Skorkin, *Kto rukovodil NKVD*, 54–55. Semenov took over as head of Krasnoiarsk NKVD, probably in practice at the end of December 1938 and officially on 17 January 1940; see Petrov and Skorkin, 443.
48 HDA SBU, f. 65, spr. S-4472 FP, t. 1, ark. 1.
49 Papkov, *Obyknovennyi terror*, 254.
50 Khlevniuk, *Khoziain*, 365–66.
51 TsDAHOU, f. 263, op. 1, spr. 55475 FP, t. 1, ark. 190.
52 TsDAHOU, f. 263, op. 1, spr. 55475 FP, t. 5, ark. 19.
53 HDA SBU, f. 65, spr. S-4472 FP, t. 2, ark. 1–2.
54 TsDAHOU, f. 263, op. 1, spr. 55475 FP, t. 5, ark. 10–12.
55 TsDAHOU, f. 263, op. 1, spr. 55475 FP, t. 1, ark. 138–39.
56 TsDAHOU, f. 263, op. 1, spr. 55475 FP, t. 5, ark. 25.
57 TsDAHOU, f. 263, op. 1, spr. 55475 FP, t. 5, ark. 24.
58 TsDAHOU, f. 263, op. 1, spr. 55475 FP, t. 5, ark. 22.
59 TsDAHOU, f. 263, op. 1, spr. 55475 FP, t. 5, ark. 23.
60 TsDAHOU, f. 263, op. 1, spr. 55475 FP, t. 5, ark. 22.
61 HDA SBU f. 65 op. 2 spr. 4472, t. 2 ark. 162.
62 Postanovlenie Politbiuro TsK VKP(b) "Ob arestakh, prokurorskom nadzore i vedenii sledstviia," 17 November 1938.
63 Khlevniuk, *Khoziain*, 349–66; O. B. Mozokhin, *Pravo na repressii: Vnesudebnye polnomochiia organov gosudarstvennoi bezopasnosti* (Moscow: Kuchkovo Pole, 2011), 214–18.
64 The head of the Novosibirsk NKVD, Ivan Aleksandrovich Mal′tsev, chided his subordinates for "shying away" (*sharakhanie*) and for undue caution (*perestrakhovka*) in response to Stalin's November 1938 decree on the disbandment of troikas and the ending of arrest without sanction from the prosecutor. He advised them to continue the Great Terror but to change course, focusing not on "interrogations of old prisoners [those already in custody]," but on the testimony (*pokazania*) of newly arrested prisoners: A. G. Tepliakov, "Portrety sibirskikh chekistov," *Vozvrashchenie pamiati: Istoriko-arkhivnyi al′manakh*, 1997, no. 3: 99. Mal′tsev was arrested at the end of January 1939, sentenced to eight years' imprisonment, and died in the Gulag (Petrov and Skorkin, *Kto rukovodil NKVD*, 323).
65 Papkov, *Obyknovennyi terror*, 255.
66 Khlevniuk, *Khoziain*, 359–60.
67 Solomon, *Soviet Criminal Justice under Stalin*, 237n14.
68 TsDAHOU, f. 263, op. 1, spr. 55475 FP, t. 1, ark. 193.
69 HDA SBU, f. 65, spr. S-4472 FP, t. 2, ark. 9.
70 Mozokhin, *Repressii v tsifrakh i dokumentakh*, 198, 201.
71 Mozokhin, *Repressii*, 210; Papkov, *Obyknovennyi terror*, 255–56. Papkov (257) notes that these data refer only to those cases that passed through

the Krasnoiarsk court, and that the number of arrests made by the Krasnoiarsk NKVD and sentences passed out-of-court by police organs (*Osoboe soveshchanie*) is unknown.

72 Stephen G. Wheatcroft, "The Great Terror in Historical Perspective: The Records of the Statistical Department of the Investigative Organs of OGPU/NKVD," in *The Anatomy of Terror: Political Violence under Stalin*, ed. James Harris (Oxford: Oxford University Press, 2013), 288.

73 Khlevniuk, *Khoziain*, 366. Also, the influx of new members into the NKVD came mostly from the party. Of the 14,500 who joined the NKVD in 1939, over 11,000 came from the party and the Komsomol.

74 Tepliakov, "Organy NKVD Zapadnoi Sibiri v 'kulatskoi operatsii,'" 571.

75 Papkov, *Obyknovennyi terror*, 256–57.

76 HDA SBU, f. 65, spr. S-4472 FP, ch. 1, ark. 1; TsDAHOU, f. 263, op. 1, spr. 55475 FP, t. 1, ark. 37.

77 TsDAHOU, f. 263, op. 1, spr. 55475 FP, t. 1, ark. 28.

78 TsDAHOU, f. 263, op. 1, spr. 55475 FP, t. 1, ark. 36.

79 TsDAHOU, f. 263, op. 1, spr. 55475 FP, t. 4, ark. 78–80, 113–15.

80 TsDAHOU f. 37 op. 4. spr. 237 ark. 38.

81 For Shums′kyi's time as Ukrainian consul to Poland in the early 1920s and his visit to Germany in 1932 as a trade union representative, see Shapoval, *Oleksandr Shums′kyi*, 98–101, 157.

82 TsDAHOU, f. 263, op. 1, spr. 55475 FP, t. 5, ark. 12.

83 TsDAHOU, f. 263, op. 1, spr. 55475 FP, t. 5, ark. 15.

84 TsDAHOU, f. 263, op. 1, spr. 55475 FP, t. 5, ark. 10.

85 TsDAHOU, f. 263, op. 1, spr. 55475 FP, t. 5, ark. 41–42.

86 TsDAHOU, f. 263, op. 1, spr. 55475 FP, t. 5, ark. 46–48. Turians′kyi had already been sentenced at the end of 1939 to death for espionage and was shot on 29 August 1940: Shapoval, *Oleksandr Shums′kyi*, 200.

87 HDA SBU, f. 65, spr. S-4472 FP, t. 2, ark. 28.

88 There is no record of the Krasnoiarsk NKVD's having received the Turians′kyi evidence, even after the Krasnoiarsk officials requested it again in March 1940: TsDAHOU, f. 263, op. 1, spr. 55475, t. 5, ark. 9. In July and August 1939, Kobulov's department had sent copies of the interrogations of other suspects, including Oleksii Trylis′kyi, Oleksandr Lisovyk, Volodymyr Lohynov, Semen Krupko, and Iurii Voitsekhivs′kyi. On the well-honed police tactic of arresting major political figures by starting with minor persons from their family circles, such as housekeepers and cooks, see David R. Shearer and Vladimir Khaustov, *Stalin and the Lubianka: A Documentary History of the Political Police and Security Organs in the Soviet Union, 1922–1953* (New Haven, Conn.: Yale University Press, 2015), doc. 99.

89 A. Iu. Vatlin, "Soprotivlenie na etape sledstviia: Po materialam 'nemetskikh del' Moskovskogo upravleniia NKVD 1937–1938 gg.," in *Istoriia stalinizma: Zhizn′ v terrore. Sotsial′nye aspekty repressii*, ed. A. Sorokin, A. Kobak, and O. Kuvaldina (Moscow: Rosspen, 2013), 413. This is a case study of ethnic Germans in the Great Terror, but it provides important general information on the role of resistance under questioning as a method of delaying the "conveyor belt of death" from arrest, to charge, to execution.

90 TsDAHOU, f. 263, op. 1, spr. 55475 FP, t. 5, ark. 37.
91 TsDAHOU, f. 263, op. 1, spr. 55475 FP, t. 5, ark. 8.
92 TsDAHOU, f. 263, op. 1, spr. 55475 FP, t. 1, ark. 76.
93 TsDAHOU, f. 263, op. 1, spr. 55475 FP, t. 1, ark. 84, and see ark. 72 and 83. The reference to the 25 January note shows that Yagoda had received Shums´kyi's letter.
94 A. Iu. Morozova, "Golodovki politzakliuchennykh v 1920–30-e gody: Mesto v tiuremnom soprotivlenii i opyt klassifikatsii," in Sorokin, Kobak, and Kuvaldina, *Istoriia stalinizma*, 364–73.
95 TsDAHOU, f. 263, op. 1, spr. 55475 FP, t. 1, ark. 87.
96 HDA SBU, f. 65, spr. S-4472 FP, t. 2, ark. 29.
97 HDA SBU, f. 65, spr. S-4472 FP, t. 2, ark. 22.

CHAPTER SIX

1 HDA SBU, f. 65, spr. S-4472 FP, t. 2, ark. 113–13v.
2 HDA SBU, f. 65, spr. S-4472 FP, t. 2, ark. 109–9v.
3 Fitzpatrick, "Deaths at Two O'Clock." On Stalin and the leadership interpreting the suicide of other party members (particularly Mikhail Tomskii who, in 1936, committed suicide in anticipation of his arrest and, like Shums´kyi, left a note to Stalin protesting his innocence) as deceitful, threatening, and even "part of a plot ... to cast discredit on the regime." See Sheila Fitzpatrick, *On Stalin's Team: The Years of Living Dangerously in Soviet Politics* (Princeton, N.J.: Princeton University Press, 2015), 123.
4 Viktor Semenovich Abakumov (1908–54) was the head of Soviet military counterintelligence (SMERSH) during the Second World War, and from 1946 to 1954, head of the Ministry of State Security (MGB).
5 Jeffrey Burds, *The Early Cold War in Soviet West Ukraine, 1944–1948,* The Carl Beck Papers in Russian and East European Studies, no. 1505 (Pittsburgh: Center for Russian and East European Studies, University of Pittsburgh, 2001); Myroslav Shkandrij, *Ukrainian Nationalism: Politics, Ideology, and Literature, 1929–1956* (New Haven, Conn.: Yale University Press, 2015), 73; Taras Kuzio, "U.S. Support for Ukraine's Liberation during the Cold War: A Study of Prolog Research and Publishing Corporation," *Communist and Post-Communist Studies* 45, no. 1–2 (2012): 51–64; O. A. Rzheshevskii, "Sekretnye voennye plany U. Cherchillia protiv SSSR v mae 1945 g.," *Novaia i noveishaia istoriia*, 1999, no. 3: 98–123.
6 HDA SBU, f. 65, spr. S-4472 FP, t. 2, ark. 63.
7 On local Soviet security concerns about Ukrainian exiles "activating" in Siberia—specifically insurgents, their families, and, broadly, anyone suspected of supporting them or "Ukrainian nationalism" (i.e., anyone deported there from western Ukraine from 1944 onward)—see E. L. Zberovskaia, "Spetsposelentsy iz Zapadnoi Ukrainy v Krasnoiarskom krae (1945 g.–nachalo

1960-kh gg.): Protsess sotsiokul'turnoi adaptatsii," *Vestnik KrasGAU*, 2014, no. 5: 250–54.

8 HDA SBU, f. 65, spr. S-4472 FP, t. 2, ark. 114 (130).

9 HDA SBU, f. 65, spr. S-4472 FP, t. 1, ark. 9–9v.

10 HDA SBU, f. 65, spr. S-4472 FP, t. 2, ark. 61–61v.

11 HDA SBU, f. 65, spr. S-4472 FP, t. 2, ark. 73 and 74.

12 A. I. Kokurin and N. V. Petrov, *Lubianka: VChK–OGPU–NKVD–NKGB–MGB–MVD–KGB, 1917–1960, Spravochnik* (Moscow: Mezhdunarodnyi fond "Demokratiia," 1997), 34–37.

13 HDA SBU, f. 65, spr. S-4472 FP, t. 2, ark. 63–64.

14 Aaron Bateman, "The KGB and Its Enduring Legacy," *Journal of Slavic Military Studies* 29, no. 1 (2016): 34.

15 HDA SBU, f. 65, spr. S-4472 FP, t. 2, ark. 66–66v. For Shums'kyi's own declarations on resisting any move back to Eniseisk in April 1946, see HDA SBU, f. 65, spr. S-4472 FP, t. 2, ark. 73–74.

16 HDA SBU, f. 65, spr. S-4472 FP, t. 2, ark. 145.

17 HDA SBU, f. 65, spr. S-4472 FP, t. 2, ark. 74 and 77.

18 HDA SBU, f. 65, spr. S-4472 FP, t. 2, ark. 104–104v.

19 HDA SBU, f. 65, spr. S-4472 FP, t. 2, ark. 137–137v.

20 HDA SBU, f. 65, spr. S-4472 FP, t. 2, ark. 93–93v.

21 HDA SBU, f. 65, spr. S-4472 FP, t. 2, ark. 103–103v (119–119v).

22 HDA SBU, f. 65, spr. S-4472 FP, t. 2, ark. 78–78v, 79, 80, 97, 132.

23 HDA SBU, f. 65, spr. S-4472 FP, t. 2, ark. 105 (121).

24 HDA SBU, f. 65, spr. S-4472 FP, t. 2, ark. 93–93v.

25 HDA SBU, f. 65, spr. S-4472 FP, t. 2, ark. 102 (118).

26 HDA SBU, f. 65, spr. S-4472 FP, t. 2, ark. 102 (118).

27 HDA SBU, f. 65, spr. S-4472 FP, t. 2, ark. 101 (117).

28 Shapoval, *Oleksandr Shums'kyi*, 98–101, 157.

29 Soviet forces killed 123,782 guerrilla fighters and "other anti-Soviet elements" in western Ukraine in 1944, suffering 2,058 fatalities (police, NKVD, and Red Army soldiers): Alexander Statiev, *The Soviet Counterinsurgency in the Western Borderlands* (Cambridge: Cambridge University Press, 2010), 110, 125.

30 Mark Edele and Filip Slaveski, "Violence from Below: Explaining Crimes against Civilians across Soviet Space, 1943–1947," *Europe-Asia Studies* 68, no. 6 (2016): 1027; Burds, *Early Cold War*, 27. There is a wealth of literature on the OUN and UPA. A good start is Stanislav V. Kul'chyts'kyi, *Orhanizatsiia ukraïns'kykh natsionalistiv i Ukraïns'ka povstans'ka armiia* (Kyiv: Instytut istoriï Ukraïny NAN Ukraïny, 2005).

31 For a general history of wartime collaboration in the Second World War, see M. I. Semiriaga, *Kollaboratsionizm: Priroda, tipologiia i proiavleniia v gody Vtoroi mirovoi voiny* (Moscow: Rosspen, 2000). On Ukraine, see David R. Marples, *Heroes and Villains: Creating National History in Contemporary Ukraine* (Budapest: Central European University Press, 2007); Karel C. Berkhoff, *Harvest of Despair: Life and Death in Ukraine under Nazi Rule* (Cambridge, Mass.: Belknap Press of Harvard University Press, 2004); Filip

Slaveski, *Remaking Ukraine after World War II: The Clash of Local and Central Soviet Power* (Cambridge: Cambridge University Press, 2021).

32 Statiev, *Soviet Counterinsurgency*, 105–23.

33 Burds, *Early Cold War*; Shkandrij, *Ukrainian Nationalism*; Kuzio, "U.S. Support for Ukraine's Liberation."

34 Alexander Statiev, "The Strategy of the Organisation of Ukrainian Nationalists in Its Quest for a Sovereign State, 1939–1950," *Journal of Strategic Studies* 43, no. 3 (2020): 461. Many Soviet interrogation records of OUN and UPA members are located in the State Archive of the Russian Federation (GARF), f. r-9478.

35 For the spread of the "war myth" in Soviet-occupied Germany, see Filip Slaveski, *The Soviet Occupation of Germany: Hunger, Mass Violence and the Struggle for Peace, 1945–1947* (Cambridge: Cambridge University Press, 2016), 83–84. For Ukraine, see Burds, *Early Cold War*, 20–21.

36 Burds, *Early Cold War*, 27.

37 Burds, *Early Cold War*, 39.

38 A. N. Artizov, ed., *Ukrainskie natsionalisticheskie organizatsii v gody Vtoroi mirovoi voiny*, vol. 2, *1944–1945* (Moscow: Rosspen, 2012), 876–84.

39 Burds, *Early Cold War*, 37.

40 V. N. Khaustov, V. P. Naumov, and N. S. Plotnikova, *Lubianka: Stalin i MGB SSSR, mart 1946–mart 1953* (Moscow: Materik, 2007), 20–21, 27–28, 32–33.

41 This broader expansion extended to Soviet-occupied territories in Europe. For Germany, see Nikita Petrov, *Pervyi predsedatel´ KGB Ivan Serov* (Moscow: Materik, 2005), 64–72.

42 Kuznetsov, "Stalin's Minister," 158.

43 HDA SBU, f. 65, spr. S-4472 FP, t. 2, ark. 94–95v

44 HDA SBU, f. 65, spr. S-4472 FP, t. 2, ark. 149.

45 HDA SBU, f. 65, spr. S-4472 FP, t. 2, ark. 91.

46 TsA FSB, f. 4-os, op. 4, d. 32, ll. 446–48 (Shums´kyi section).

47 HDA SBU, f. 65, spr. S-4472 FP, t. 2, ark. 97, 149.

48 TsA FSB, f. 4-os, op. 4, d. 32, ll. 446–48.

49 Sudoplatov, *Spetsoperatsii*.

50 Robert Legvold, review of *Special Tasks: The Memoirs of an Unwanted Witness—A Soviet Spymaster*, by Pavel Sudoplatov and Anatoli Sudoplatov, with Jerrold L. and Leona P. Schechter, *Foreign Affairs*, July/August 1994; Brian Cathcart, review of *Special Tasks*, *Independent*, July 3, 1994.

51 TsA FSB, f. 4-os, op. 4, d. 32, ll. 446–48.

52 TsA FSB, f. 4-os, op. 4, d. 32, ll. 446–48.

53 Sudoplatov, *Spetsoperatsii*, 409.

54 TsA FSB, f. 4-os, op. 4, d. 32, ll. 446–48.

55 HDA SBU, f. 65, spr. S-4472 FP, t. 2, ark. 109–9v

56 TsA FSB, f. 4-os, op. 4, d. 32, ll. 446–48.

57 Sudoplatov, *Spetsoperatsii*, 408–409.

58 HDA SBU f. 65, spr. S-4472, t. 2, ark. 163–66.

59 The OUN had divided into two factions by this point, OUN-B (following Stepan Bandera) and OUN-M (following Andrii Mel´nyk). Only OUN-B leaders

filled UHVR positions—not those of the OUN-M. On the distinction, see Marples, *Heroes and Villains*, chap. 3.

60 Shkandrij, *Ukrainian Nationalism*, 73–76; Kuzio, "U.S. Support for Ukraine's Liberation during the Cold War"; Per Anders Rudling, *The OUN, the UPA and the Holocaust: A Study in the Manufacturing of Historical Myths*, Carl Beck Papers in Russian and East European Studies, no. 2107 (Pittsburgh: Center for Russian and East European Studies, University of Pittsburgh, 2011), 18–19; CIA Position Paper for Ukrainian Discussion with SS in London, 23–25 April 1951, declassified 2007.

61 Ie. Shtendera, ed., *Litopys Ukraïns'koi Povstans'koï Armiï*, vol. 8, *Ukraïns'ka Holovna Vyzvol'na Rada, 1944–1945* (Toronto: Litopys UPA, 1992); Yurii I. Shapoval, "'Buv i zalyshaiet'sia ideinym ukraïns'kym natsionalistom': Povernennia Kyryla Os'maka," *Voienna istoriia* 5, no. 41 (2008), http://warhistory.ukrlife.org/5_08.html; Per Anders Rudling, "Historical Representation of the Wartime Accounts of the Activities of the OUN–UPA (Organization of Ukrainian Nationalists—Ukrainian Insurgent Army)," *East European Jewish Affairs* 36, no. 2 (2006): 163–89.

62 Artizov, *Ukrainskie natsionalisticheskie organizatsii*, 2:880.

63 Artizov, *Ukrainskie natsionalisticheskie organizatsii*, 2:884.

64 Ihor Il'iushyn, *Ukraïns'ka Povstans'ka Armiia i Armiia Kraiova: Protystoiannia v Zakhidnii Ukraïni (1939–1945 rr.)* (Kyïv: Kyievo-Mohylians'ka Akademiia, 2009).

65 Sudoplatov, *Spetsoperatsii*, 409.

66 Artizov, *Ukrainskie natsionalisticheskie organizatsii*, 2:880.

67 TsDAHOU, f. 263, op. 1, spr. 55475 FP, t. 5, ark 113–15.

68 TsA FSB, f. 4-os, op. 4, d. 32, ll. 446–48.

69 See A. A. Chernobaev, ed., *Na prieme u Stalina: Tetradi (zhurnaly) zapisei lits, priniatykh I. V. Stalinym (1924–1953 gg.). Spravochnik* (Moscow: Novyi khronograf, 2008), 478.

70 Sudoplatov devised this plan and dated it 6 September 1946. Shapoval, *Oleksandr Shums'kyi*, 186.

71 TsA FSB, f. 4-os, op. 4, d. 32, ll. 446–48.

72 HDA SBU, f. 65, spr. S-4472 FP, t. 2, ark. 145.

73 TsA FSB, f. 4-os, op. 4, d. 32, ll. 446–48.

74 TsA FSB, f. 4-os, op. 4, d. 32, ll. 446–48.

75 Timothy Snyder, "A Fascist Hero in Democratic Kiev," *New York Review of Books*, February 24, 2010.

76 Statiev, *Soviet Counterinsurgency*, 108, 125.

77 HDA SBU f. 65, spr. S-4472, t. 2, ark. 166.

CONCLUSION

1 Central State Archive of Public Organizations of Ukraine (TsDAHOU), f. 1, op. 6, spr. 88, ark. 127–29v. Andrii Vasyl'ovych Ivanov (1888–1927), Shums'kyi's interlocutor, was a Russian-Ukrainian Communist Party activist and politician.

2 Sectoral State Archive of the Security Services of Ukraine (HDA SBU), f. 65, spr. S-4472 FP, t. 2, ark. 109–9v (125–25v).

3 TsDAHOU, f. 39, op. 4, spr. 237, ark. 34.

4 TsDAHOU, f. 39, op. 4, spr. 237, ark. 34.

5 *Ostannia adresa: Rozstrily solovets´kykh v´iazniv z Ukraïny u 1937–1938 rokakh*, 2nd ed., vol. 1 (Kyiv: Sfera, 2003), 446.

6 Central Archive of the Federal Security Service (TsA FSB), f. 4-os, op. 4, d. 32, ll. 446–48.

7 HDA SBU, f. 65, spr. S-4472 FP, t. 2, ark. 109–9v

8 David R. Marples, "Stalin: Authoritarian Populist or Great Russian Chauvinist?" *Nationalities Papers* 38, no. 5 (2010): 751.

9 Elena Zubkova, *Russia after the War: Hopes, Illusions, and Disappointments, 1945–1957*, trans. Hugh Ragsdale (Armonk, N.Y.: M. E. Sharpe, 1998), 33.

10 Sudoplatov, *Spetsoperatsii*, 408–409; TsA FSB, f. 4-os, op. 4, d. 32, ll. 446–48 (emphasis added).

11 TsA FSB, f. 4-os, op. 4, d. 32, ll. 446–48.

12 HDA SBU, f. 65, spr. S-4472 FP, t. 2, ark. 18, 32.

13 Albert P. van Goudoever, *The Limits of Destalinization in the Soviet Union: Political Rehabilitations in the Soviet Union since Stalin*, trans. Frans Hijkoop (New York: St. Martin's Press, 1986).

14 David R. Marples, "Decommunization, Memory Laws, and 'Builders of Ukraine in the 20th Century,'" *Acta Slavica Iaponica* 39 (2018): 1–22.

BIBLIOGRAPHY

Arkhiv Rozstrilianoho Vidrodzhennia: Materialy arkhivno-slidchykh sprav ukraïns'kykh pys'mennykiv 1920–1930-kh rokiv. Kyiv: Smoloskyp, 2010.

Artizov, A. N., ed. *Ukrainskie natsionalisticheskie organizatsii v gody Vtoroi mirovoi voiny.* Vol. 2, *1944–1945.* Moskva: Rosspen, 2012.

Bateman, Aaron. "The KGB and Its Enduring Legacy." *Journal of Slavic Military Studies* 29, no. 1 (2016): 23–47.

Bennigsen, Alexandre, and Chantal Lemercier-Quelquejay. *Sultan Galiev: Le père de la révolution tiers-mondiste.* Paris: Fayard, 1986.

Berkhoff, Karel C. *Harvest of Despair: Life and Death in Ukraine under Nazi Rule.* Cambridge, Mass.: Belknap Press of Harvard University Press, 2004.

Besedovskii, G. *Na putiakh k termidoru.* Moskva: Sovremennik, 1997.

Bevz, T. A. *Partiia natsional'nykh interesiv i sotsial'nykh perspektyv (Politychna istoriia UPSR).* Kyiv: iPiEND, 2008.

Borisenok, Elena. *Fenomen sovetskoi ukrainizatsii: 1920–1930-e gody.* Moskva: Evropa, 2006.

Burds, Jeffrey. *The Early Cold War in Soviet West Ukraine, 1944–1948.* The Carl Beck Papers in Russian and East European Studies, no. 1505. Pittsburgh: Center for Russian and East European Studies, University of Pittsburgh, 2001.

Cathcart, Brian. Review of *Special Tasks: The Memoirs of an Unwanted Witness—A Soviet Spymaster,* by Pavel Sudoplatov and Anatoli Sudoplatov with Jerrold L. and Leona P. Schechter. *Independent,* 3 July 1994.

Central Archive of the Federal Security Service (TsA FSB), f. 4-os, op. 4, d. 32, ll, 446–48 (Shums'kyi section).

Chernobaev, A. A., ed. *Na prieme u Stalina: Tetradi (zhurnaly) zapisei lits, priniatykh I. V. Stalinym (1924–1953 gg.). Spravochnik.* Moscow: Novyi khronograf, 2008.

Chetvertoe soveshchanie TsK RKP(b) s otvetstvennymi rabotnikami natsional'nykh respublik i oblastei: Stenograficheskii otchet. Moscow: Partizdat, 1923.

Chyrko, B. V. *Natsional'ni menshyny v Ukraïni (20–30 roky XX stolittia)*. Kyiv: Asotsiatsiia "Ukraïno", 1995.

CIA Position Paper for Ukrainian Discussion with SS in London. 23–25 April 1951. Declassified 2007.

Danylenko, V. M., ed. *Ukraïns'ka intelihentsiia i vlada: Zvedennia sekretnoho viddilu DPU USRR 1927–1929 rr.* Kyiv: Tempora, 2012.

Danylenko, V. M., Ia. V. Vermenych, P. M. Bondarchuk, L. V. Grynevych, O. O. Koval'chuk, V. V. Masnenko, and B. M. Chumak. *"Ukraïnizatsiia" 1920–30-kh rokiv: Peredumovy, zdobutky, uroky*. Edited by V. A. Smolii. Kyiv: Instytut istoriï Ukraïny NAN Ukraïny, 2003.

Dashkevych, Iaroslav. "Politychne oshukanstvo chy provokatsiia? Krakh ukraïnizatsiï 20-kh–30-kh rr." *Literaturna Ukraïna*, 4 October 1990.

Davies, R. W., and Stephen G. Wheatcroft. *The Years of Hunger: Soviet Agriculture, 1931–1933*. New York: Palgrave Macmillan, 2004.

Dienko, A. V. *Razvedka i kontrrazvedka v litsakh: Entsiklopedicheskii slovar' rossiiskikh spetssluzhb*. Moscow: Russkii mir, 2002.

Doroshko, M. S. *Nomenklatura: Kerivna verkhivka Radians'koï Ukraïny (1917–1938 rr.)*. Kyiv: Nika-tsentr, 2008.

Dvenadtsatyi s"ezd RKP(b), 17–25 aprelia 1923 goda: Stenograficheskii otchet. Moscow: Izdatel'stvo politicheskoi literatury, 1968.

Edele, Mark, and Filip Slaveski. "Violence from Below: Explaining Crimes against Civilians across Soviet Space, 1943–1947." *Europe-Asia Studies* 68, no. 6 (2016): 1020–35.

Fedenko, Panas. *Ukraïns'kyi rukh u XX stolitti*. London: Nashe Slovo, 1959.

Fitzpatrick, Sheila. "Deaths at Two O'Clock." *London Review of Books* 33, no. 4 (17 February 2011).

———. *On Stalin's Team: The Years of Living Dangerously in Soviet Politics*. Princeton, N.J.: Princeton University Press, 2015.

———. *Stalin's Peasants: Resistance and Survival in the Russian Village after Collectivization*. New York: Oxford University Press, 1994.

Fowler, Mayhill. *Beau Monde on Empire's Edge: State and Stage in Soviet Ukraine*. Toronto: University of Toronto Press, 2017.

Frolov, M. O. "Borot'bisty u KP(b)U v 20–30-ti roky XX stolittia." *Naukovi pratsi istorychnoho fakul'tetu Zaporiz'koho Derzhavnoho Universitetu* 1, no. 13 (2001): 122-29.

———. *Kompartiino-radians'ka elita v Ukraïni: Osoblyvosti isnuvannia ta funktsionuvannia v 1923–1928 rr.* Zaporizhzhia: Prem'ier, 2004.

Genis, V. L. "Grigorii Zinovievich Besedovskii." *Voprosy istorii*, 2006, no. 7: 37–58.

Getty, J. Arch. "'Excesses Are Not Permitted': Mass Terror and Stalinist Governance in the Late 1930s." *Russian Review* 61, no. 1 (January 2002): 113–38.

Getty, J. Arch, and Oleg V. Naumov. *The Road to Terror: Stalin and the Self-Destruction of the Bolsheviks, 1932–1939*. New Haven, Conn.: Yale University Press, 1999.

Goudoever, Albert P. van. *The Limits of Destalinization in the Soviet Union: Political Rehabilitations in the Soviet Union since Stalin*. Translated by Frans Hijkoop. New York: St. Martin's Press, 1986.

Grabowicz, George G. [Hryhorii Hrabovych]. "Sovietyzatsiia ukraïns'koï humanistyky." *Krytyka* 1, no. 1 (1997)): 18–23.

Gur'ianov, A. E., ed. *Repressii protiv poliakov i polskikh grazhdan*. Moskva: Zven'ia, 1997.

Hirsch, Francine. *Empire of Nations: Ethnographic Knowledge and the Making of the Soviet Union*. Ithaca, N.Y.: Cornell University Press, 2002.

Hrechenko, V. A. "I. K. Dashkovs'kyi: Narys politychnoï diial'nosti." *Ukraïns'kyi istorychnyi zhurnal*, 1991. no. 10: 87–94.

———. "Opal'nyi professor: Delo i sud'ba I. K. Dashkovskogo." *Pozitsiia: obshchestvenno-politicheskii ezhemesiachnyi zhurnal*, 1991, no. 4: 66–74.

Hryn'ko, Hryhorii, and Oleksandr Shums'kyi. *Statti. Promovy. Dokumenty*. Edited by V. O. Gaidei, O. P. Mikhno, and O. V. Sukhomlyns'ka. Kyiv: Pedahohichnyi muzei Ukraïny, 2015.

Hrytsak, Iaroslav. *Narys istoriï Ukraïny: Formuvannia modernoï natsiï XIX–XX stolittia*. Kyiv: Heneza, 1996.

———. *Prorok u svoïi vitchyzni: Franko ta ioho spil'nota (1856–1886)*. Kyiv: Krytyka, 2006.

Il'in, Anatolii. "Oprichniki Berii v Krasnoiarske." *Vechernii Krasnoiarsk*, 12 August 1997.

Il'iushyn, Ihor. *Ukraïns'ka Povstans'ka Armiia i Armiia Kraiova: Protystoiannia v Zakhidnii Ukraïni (1939–1945 rr.)*. Kyiv: Kyievo-Mohylians'ka Akademiia, 2009.

Kaganovich, Lazar' M. *Na putiakh stroitel'stva sotsializma*. Kharkiv: Partiinoe izdatel'stvo TsK KP(b)U, 1926.

Kampaniia proty ukraïns'koï movy zrostaie vodnochas iz zrostanniam kampaniï proty ukraïns'koï derzhavnosti." *Viche*, 1994, no. 2: 150–62.

Khaustov, V. N., V. P. Naumov, and N. S. Plotnikova, eds. *Lubianka: Stalin i Glavnoe upravlenie gosbezopasnosti NKVD, 1937–1938*. Moscow: Materik, 2004.

———, eds. *Lubianka: Stalin i MGB SSSR, mart 1946–mart 1953*. Moscow: Materik, 2007.

Khaustov, V. N., and L. Samuel'son. *Stalin, NKVD i repressii 1936–1938 gg*. Moscow: Rosspen, 2009.

Khlevniuk, Oleg. *Khoziain: Stalin i utverzhdenie stalinskoi diktatury*. Moskva: Rosspen, 2010.

———. *Stalin: New Biography of a Dictator*. Translated by Nora Seligman Favorov. New Haven, Conn.: Yale University Press, 2015.

Khlevniuk, O. V. [Oleg], A. V. Kvashonkin, L. P. Kosheleva, and L. A. Rogovaia, eds. *Stalinskoe Politbiuro v 30-e gody: Sbornik dokumentov*. Moscow: Rosspen, 1995.

Khvylia, A. "Kudy vedut' dorohy shveds'kykh mohyl?" *Komunist*, 27 September 1933.

Khvyl'ovyi, Mykola. "Apolohety Pysaryzmu." In *Tvory u dvokh tomakh*, 2: 925. Kyiv: Dnipro, 1990.

Kokurin, A. I., and N. V. Petrov. *Lubianka: VChK–OGPU–NKVD–NKGB–MGB–MVD–KGB, 1917–1960, Spravochnik*. Moscow: Mezhdunarodnyi fond "Demokratiia," 1997.

Korohods'kyi, Roman. *Dovzhenko v poloni: Rozvidky ta eseï pro maistra*. Kyiv: Helikon, 2000.

Koshelivets', Ivan. *Mykola Skrypnyk*. Munich: Suchasnist', 1972.

Kosior, S. V. "Pidsumky i naiblyzhchi zavdannia natsional'noï polityky na Ukraïni." *Chervonyi shliakh*, nos. 8–9 (1933): 205–44.

Kostrytsia, M. Iu. "Providnyk ukraïnizatsiï." In *Reabilitovani istoriieiu: Zhytomyrs'ka oblast'*, edited by P. T. Tron'ko, book 1, 222–27. Zhytomyr: Polissia, 2006.

Kotkin, Stephen. *Stalin: Paradoxes of Power, 1878–1928*. New York: Penguin, 2014.

———. *Stalin: Waiting for Hitler, 1929–1941*. New York: Penguin, 2017.

Kovalevs'kyi, M. M. *Pry dzherelakh borot'by: Spomyny, vrazhennia, refleksiï*. Innsbruck: Kovalevs'ka, 1960.

Krawchenko, Bohdan. *Social Change and National Consciousness in Twentieth-Century Ukraine*. Edmonton: Canadian Institute of Ukrainian Studies, University of Alberta, 1987.

Kul'chyts'kyi, Stanislav V. *Chervonyi vyklyk: Istoriia komunizmu v Ukraïni vid ioho narodzhennia do zahybeli*. 3 vols. Kyiv: Tempora, 2013.

———. *Istorychne mistse ukraïns'koï radians'koï derzhavnosti*. Kyiv: Instytut istoriï Ukraïny NAN Ukraïny, 2002.

———. *Orhanizatsiia ukraïns'kykh natsionalistiv i Ukraïns'ka povstans'ka armiia*. Kyiv: Instytut istoriï Ukraïny NAN Ukraïny, 2005.

———. "Skil'ky nas zahynulo vid Holodomoru 1933 roku?" *Dzerkalo tyzhnia*, 29 November 2002.

Kulczycki, John J. *Belonging to the Nation: Inclusion and Exclusion in the Polish-German Borderlands, 1939–1951*. Cambridge, Mass.: Harvard University Press, 2016.

Kuras, Ivan. *Torzhestvo proletarskogo internatsionalizma i krakh melkoburzhuaznykh partii na Ukraine*. Kyiv: Naukova dumka, 1978.

Kuras, I. F., and P. P. Ovdiienko. "O. Ia. Shums'kyi u roky Zhovtnia i hromadians'koï viiny: Evoliutsiia pohliadiv i politychna diial'nist'." *Ukraïns'kyi istorychnyi zhurnal*, 1990, no. 12: 105–16.

Kuromiya, Hiroaki. *The Voices of the Dead: Stalin's Great Terror in the 1930s*. New Haven, Conn.: Yale University Press, 2016.

Kuzio, Taras. "U.S. Support for Ukraine's Liberation during the Cold War: A Study of Prolog Research and Publishing Corporation." *Communist and Post-Communist Studies* 45, nos. 1–2 (2012): 51–64.

Kuznetsov, I. I. "Stalin's Minister, V.S. Abakumov 1908–54." *Journal of Slavic Military Studies* 12, no. 1 (1999): 149–65.

Kyrychenko, M., ed. *Rezoliutsiï Vseukrains'kykh z'ïzdiv Rad robitnychykh, selians'kykh ta chervonoarmiis'kykh deputativ*. Kharkiv: Proletar, 1932.

Legvold, Robert. Review of *Special Tasks: The Memoirs of an Unwanted Witness—A Soviet Spymaster*, by Pavel Sudoplatov and Anatoli Sudoplatov with J. and L. Schechter. *Foreign Affairs*, July/August 1994.

Lenin, Vladimir I. *Neizvestnye dokumenty: 1891–1922.* Moscow: Rosspen, 1999.

———. "Proekt rezoliutsii ob ukrainskoi partii borot′bistov." In *Polnoe sobranie sochinenii.* Vol. 40, *Dekabr′ 1919 – aprel′ 1920*, 5th ed. Moscow: Politizdat, 1974.

———. "Zakliuchne slovo v pytanni pro radians′ku vladu na Ukraïni 3 hrudnia." In *Povne zibrannia tvoriv*, by V. I. Lenin, vol. 39: 347–48. Kyiv: Vydavnytstvo politychnoï literatury Ukraïny, 1974.

———. "Zasedanie vtoroe (30 marta, utrom)." In *Deviatyi s″ezd RKP(b) mart–aprel′ 1920 g.*, edited by N. L. Meshcheriakov, 50–97. Protokoly s″ezdov i konferentsii Vsesoiuznoi Kommunisticheskoi Partii(b). Moscow: Partiinoe izdatel′stvo, 1934.

Lenoe, Matthew E. *The Kirov Murder and Soviet History.* New Haven, Conn.: Yale University Press, 2010.

Liber, George O. *Alexander Dovzhenko: A Life in Soviet Film.* London: BFI, 2002.

———. *Soviet Nationality Policy, Urban Growth, and Identity Change in the Ukrainian SSR, 1923–1934.* Cambridge: Cambridge University Press, 1992.

Liubchenko, P. P. "Vohon′ po natsionalistychnii kontrrevoliutsiï ta po natsionalukhyl′nykakh." *Chervonyi shliakh*, no. 10 (1933): 186–207.

Lozyts′kyi, V. S. "Polityka ukraïnizatsiï v 20–30-kh rokakh: Istoriia, problemy, uroky." *Ukraïns′kyi istorychnyi zhurnal*, 1989, no. 3: 46–55.

Luts′kyi, Iu. *Literaturna polityka v radians′kii Ukraïni, 1917–1934.* Kyiv: Helikon, 2000.

L′vov, V. *Sovetskaia vlast′ v bor′be za russkuiu gosudarstvennost″.* Berlin: n.p., 1922.

Mace, James E. *Communism and the Dilemmas of National Liberation: National Communism in Soviet Ukraine, 1918–1933.* Cambridge, Mass.: Harvard Ukrainian Research Institute, 1983.

Makaryk, Iryna. *Peretvorennia Shekspira: Les′ Kurbas, ukraïns′kyi modernizm i radians′ka kul′turna polityka 1920-kh rokiv.* Kyiv: Nika-tsentr, 2010.

Manilov, V., ed. *1917 god na Kievshchine: Khronika sobytii.* Kyiv: Gosudarstvennoe izdatel′stvo Ukrainy, 1928.

Marples, David R. "Decommunization, Memory Laws, and 'Builders of Ukraine in the 20th Century.'" *Acta Slavica Iaponica* 39 (2018): 1–22.

———. *Heroes and Villains: Creating National History in Contemporary Ukraine.* Budapest: Central European University Press, 2007.

———. "Stalin: Authoritarian Populist or Great Russian Chauvinist?" *Nationalities Papers* 38, no. 5 (2010): 749–56.

Martin, Terry. *The Affirmative Action Empire: Nations and Nationalism in the Soviet Union, 1923–1939.* Ithaca, N.Y.: Cornell University Press, 2001.

———. "The Origins of Soviet Ethnic Cleansing." *Journal of Modern History* 70, no. 4. (December 1998): 813–61.

Masliichuk, Volodymyr. "Marksysts′ki skhemy ukraïns′koï istoriï: Matvii Iavors′kyi, Volodymyr Sukhino-Khomenko, Mykola Horban′." *Ukraïna Moderna* 14, no. 3 (2009): 63–77.

"Materialy fevral′sko-martovskoho plenuma TsK VKP(b) 1937 goda." *Voprosy istorii*, 1995, no. 2: 3-26.

Mazepa, I. P. *Ukraïna v ohni i buri revoliutsiï, 1917–1921*. Dnipropetrovsk: Sich, 2002.

Medvedev, Roi. *Blizhnii krug Stalina. Soratniki Vozhdia*. Moscow: Eksmo-Iauza, 2005.

Meslé, France, and Jacques Vallin, eds. *Mortalité et causes de décès en Ukraine au XXe siècle*. Paris: Institut national d'études démographiques, 2003.

Mialo, Pavlo Ivanovich. "Hromads'ko-politychna diial'nist' V. Ellana-Blakytnoho: Evoliutsiia svitohliadu." PhD diss., Zaporizhzhia National University.

Morozova, A. Iu. "Golodovki politzakliuchennykh v 1920–30-e gody: Mesto v tiuremnom soprotivlenii i opyt klassifikatsii." In *Istoriia stalinizma: Zhizn' v terrore*, edited by A. Sorokin, A. Kobak, and O. L. Kuvaldina, 364–73. Moscow: Rosspen, 2013.

Mozokhin, O. B. *Pravo na repressii: Vnesudebnye polnomochiia organov gosudarstvennoi bezopasnosti*. Moscow: Kuchkovo Pole, 2011.

———. *Repressii v tsifrakh i dokumentakh: Deiatel'nost'' organov VChK-OGPU-NKVD-MGB (1918–1953 gg.)*. Moscow: Veche, 2018.

"Oblastnoi s"ezd RSDRP (b-kov)." *Letopis' revoliutsii*, no. 5(1926): 64–92.

"Ob ukrainskom separatizme: (*Tsirkuliarnoe pis'mo* Gosudarsvennogo politicheskogo upravleniia [Sekretnyi otdel] *ob ukrainskom separatizme)*. Kharkiv: n.p., 1926.

Ocherki istorii Kommunisticheskoi partii Ukrainy: Izdanie chetvertoe, dopolnennoe. Kyiv: Izdatel'stvo politicheskoi literatury, 1977.

Ostannia adresa: Rozstrily solovets'kykh v'iazniv z Ukraïny u 1937–1938 rokakh. 2nd ed. Vol. 1 Kyiv: Sfera, 2003.

"O tak Nazyvaemoi 'Sultan-galievskoi kontrrevoliutsionnoi organizatsii.'" *Izvestiia TsK KPSS*, no. 10 (1990): 75–88.

Panchuk, Mai. *"Bili pliamy" heroïchnoho litopysu: Iz istoriï Komunistychnoï partiï Zakhidnoï Ukraïny*. Kyiv: Politvydav Ukraïny, 1989.

———. "Natsional-ukhyl'nytstvo: Anatomiia problemy." In *Marshrutamy istoriï*, edited by Yurii I. Shapoval, 215–43. Kyiv: Politvydav Ukraïny, 1990.

———. "Zhyttia i smert' Oleksandra Shums'koho." In *Pro mynule—zarady maibutn'oho*, edited by Yurii I. Shapoval, 319–31. Kyiv: Izdatel'stvo pri Kievskom universitete, 1989.

Papkov, S. A. *Obyknovennyi terror: Politika stalinizma v Sibiri*. Moscow: Rosspen, 2012.

Pauly, Matthew D. *Breaking the Tongue: Language, Education, and Power in Soviet Ukraine*. Toronto: University of Toronto Press, 2011.

Petrov, Nikita. *Pervyi predsedatel' KGB Ivan Serov*. Moscow: Materik, 2005.

———. "Shtatnyi gosudarstvennyi ubiitsa (reabilitirovannyi): Dva dnia iz zhizni Pavla Sudoplatova." *Novaia Gazeta*, 7 August 2013.

Petrov, N. V. [Nikita], and K. V. Skorkin. *Kto rukovodil NKVD: 1934–1941*. Moscow: Memorial, 1999.

Pidhainyi, Semen. *Ukraïns'ka inteligentsiia na Solovkakh: Nedostriliani*. Neu Ulm: Prometheus, 1947.

"Pidsumky i naiblyzhchi zavdannia provedennia natsional'noï polityky na Ukraïni." *Chervonyi shliakh*, nos. 8–9 (1933): 261–72.

Pipes, Richard. *The Formation of the Soviet Union*. Rev. ed. Cambridge, Mass.: Harvard University Press, 1964.

Pirog, R. Ia. "Kak pogib predsedatel' Sovnarkoma Ukrainskoi SSR P. P. Liubchenko." *Izvestiia TsK KPSS*, no. 10 (1990): 140–41.

Popovych, M. V. *Narys istoriï kul'tury Ukraïny*. Kyiv: ArtEk, 1998.

Postanovlenie Politbiuro TsK VKP(b) "Ob arestakh, prokurorskom nadzore i vedenii sledstviia," 17 November 1938.

Postyshev, P. P. "Radians'ka Ukraïna—nepokhytnyi forpost velykoho SRSR." *Chervonyi shliakh*, nos. 8–9 (1933): 245–60.

Prusin, Alexander V. *The Lands Between: Conflict in the East European Borderlands, 1870–1992*. Oxford: Oxford University Press, 2010.

Prystaiko, Volodymyr, and Yurii I. Shapoval. *Sprava "Spilky vyzvolennia Ukraïny": Nevidomi dokumenty i fakty*. Kyiv: Intel, 1995.

Radians'ke budivnytstvo na Ukraïni v roky hromadians'koï viiny (1918–1919): Zbirnyk dokumentiv i materialiv. Kyiv: AN USRS, 1962.

Rees, E. A. *Iron Lazar: A Political Biography of Lazar Kaganovich*. London: Anthem Press, 2012.

Rubl'ov, O. S., and Ia. A. Cherchenko. *Stalinshchyna i dolia zakhidnoukraïns'koï intelihentsiï*. Kyiv: Naukova dumka, 1994.

Rudling, Per Anders. "Historical Representation of the Wartime Accounts of the Activities of the OUN–UPA (Organization of Ukrainian Nationalists–Ukrainian Insurgent Army)." *East European Jewish Affairs* 36, no. 2 (2006): 163–89.

———. *The OUN, the UPA and the Holocaust: A Study in the Manufacturing of Historical Myths*. Carl Beck Papers in Russian and East European Studies, no. 2107. Pittsburgh: Center for Russian and East European Studies, University of Pittsburgh, 2011.

Rudnyts'kyi [Rudnytsky], Ivan Lysiak. *Istorychni ese*. 2 vols. Kyiv: Osnovy, 1994.

Rzheshevskii, O. A. "Sekretnye voennye plany U. Cherchillia protiv SSSR v mae 1945 g." *Novaia i noveishaia istoriia*, 1999, no. 3: 98–123.

Semiriaga, M. I. *Kollaboratsionizm: Priroda, tipologiia i proiavleniia v gody Vtoroi mirovoi voiny*. Moscow: Rosspen, 2000.

Shapoval, Yurii I. "Aleksandr Shumskii: Sud'ba narkoma v imperii 'pozitivnogo deistviia.'" In *Sovetskie natsii i natsional'naia politika v 1920–1950-e gody: Materialy VI mezhdunarodnoi nauchnoi konferentsii (Kyiv, 10–12 oktiabria 2013)*, 54–64. Moscow: Rosspen, 2014.

———. "'Buv i zalyshaiet'sia ideinym ukraïns'kym natsionalistom': Povernennia Kyryla Os'maka." *Voienna istoriia* 5, no. 41 (2008).

———. "Ego tainy. Ispolniaetsia 120 let so dnia rozhdeniia Aleksandra Shumskogo." *Den'*, 19 November 2010.

———. "'Ia pomyliavsia, vziavshy na sebe provynu': Do 90-richchia M. S. Volobuieva Artemova." *Z arkhiviv VUChK-HPU-NKVD-KHB*, no. 1 (1994): 104–10.

———. "Klynok ne distav serts´a: Iak kolyshnii narkom osvity Ukrainy boronyv svoie chesne im'ia." *Vitchyzna* 10 (1991): 154–61.

———. *Lazar Kahanovych.* Kyiv: Znannia, 1994.

———. *Liudyna i systema (Shtrykhy do portreta totalitarnoï doby v Ukraïni).* Kyiv: Instytut natsionalnykh vidnosyn i politolohiï NANU, 1994.

———. "L. M. Kahanovych na Ukraïni." *Ukraïns´kyi istorychnyi zhurnal,* 1990, no. 8: 62–74; 1990, no. 10: 117–29.

———. "Nevidomi storinky biohrafiï Iuliana Bachyns´koho." *Istoriia Ukraïny* 14 (2000): 5-7.

———. *Nevyhadani istoriï.* Kyiv: Svitohliad, 2004.

———. "'Ne samohubets´!': Zlochyn, rozsekrechenyi cherez 46 rokiv." *Literaturna Ukraïna,* 25 February 1993.

———. "Oleksandr Shums´kyi: His Last Thirteen Years." *Journal of Ukrainian Studies* 18, nos. 1-2 (1993): 69–84.

———. *Oleksandr Shums´kyi: Zhyttia, dolia, nevidomi dokumenty.* Kyiv: Ukraïna moderna, 2017.

———. "'On Ukrainian Separatism': A GPU Circular of 1926." *Harvard Ukrainian Studies* 18, no. 3/4 (1994): 275–302.

———. "Sprava 'Spilky vyzvolennia Ukraïny': Pohliad iz vidstani 75 rokiv." *Ukraïns´kyi istorychnyi zhurnal,* 2005, no. 3: 132–43.

———. "Tekst iak dolia." *Den´,* 27 February 2003.

———. "The Tragic Faith of Yulian Bachynskyi." *Journal of Ukrainian Studies* 23, no. 1 (1998): 25–39.

———. *Ukraïna 20–50-kh rokiv: Storinky nenapisanoï istoriï.* Kyiv: Naukova dumka, 1993.

———. "The 'Union for the Liberation of Ukraine' ('SVU') Trial: Fabrication, Mechanisms, Consequences." In *Political and Transitional Justice in Germany, Poland and the Soviet Union from the 1930s to the 1950s,* edited by Władysław Bułhak, Jürgen Zarusky, and Magnus Brechtken, 36–53. Göttingen: Wallstein Verlag, 2019.

———. "'Vynnym sebe ne vyznaiu': Nevidomi storinky Iuliiana Bachyns´koho." *Rozbudova derzhavy,* no. 1, 1996, 52–57; no. 2, 1996, 53–55.

Shcherbakova, I. L., ed. *Nakazannyi narod: Repressii protiv rossiiskikh nemtsev.* Moscow: Zven´ia, 1999.

Shearer, David R., and Vladimir Khaustov. *Stalin and the Lubianka: A Documentary History of the Political Police and Security Organs in the Soviet Union, 1922–1953.* New Haven, Conn.: Yale University Press, 2015.

Shemshuchenko, Iu. S., ed. *Zhertvy repressii.* Kyiv: Iurinform, 1993.

Shevchenko, Serhii. "Vypusknyk 'solovets´koï akademiï.'" *Dzerkalo tyzhnia,* 21 February 2014.

Shevel´ov, Iurii. *Vybrani pratsi.* Vol. 1, *Movoznavstvo.* Edited by Larysa Masenko. Kyiv: Kyiv-Mohyla Academy, 2009.

Shkandrij, Myroslav. *Modernists, Marxists and the Nation: The Ukrainian Literary Discussion of the 1920s*. Edmonton: Canadian Institute of Ukrainian Studies Press, 1992.

———. *Ukrainian Nationalism: Politics, Ideology, and Literature, 1929–1956*. New Haven, Conn.: Yale University Press, 2015.

Shlikhter, O. "Posylymo bil′shovyts′ku pyl′nist′ na fronti borot′by za zdiisnennia lenins′koï natsional′noï polityky na Ukraïni." *Bil′shovyk Ukraïny*, nos. 9–10 (1933): 58–79.

Shtendera, Ie., ed. *Litopys Ukraïns′koï Povstans′koï Armiï*. Vol. 8, *Ukraïns′ka Holovna Vyzvol′na Rada, 1944–1945*. Toronto: Litopys UPA, 1992.

Shums′kyi, Oleksandr. "Ideolohichna borot′ba v ukraïns′komu kul′turnomu protsesi." *Bil′shovyk Ukraïny*, no. 2 (1927): 11–25.

———. "Stara i nova Ukraïna." *Chervonyi shliakh*, no. 2 (1923): 91–110.

Skliarenko, Ie. M. "Ostannia forma protestu." In *Reabilitovani istoriieiu*, edited by P. T. Tron′ko, 260–63. Kyiv: Ridnyi krai, 1992.

Slaveski, Filip. *Remaking Ukraine after World War II: The Clash of Local and Central Soviet Power*. Cambridge: Cambridge University Press, 2021.

———. *The Soviet Occupation of Germany: Hunger, Mass Violence and the Struggle for Peace, 1945–1947*. Cambridge: Cambridge University Press, 2016.

Slyvka, Iu. Iu. *Storinky istoriï KPZU*. L′viv: Kameniar, 1989.

Smith, Jeremy. *The Bolsheviks and the National Question, 1917–1923*. London: Macmillan Press, 1999.

———. "The Georgian Affair of 1922: Policy Failure, Personality Clash or Power Struggle?" *Europe-Asia Studies* 50, no. 3 (May 1998): 519–44.

Smolii, V. A., ed. *Politychnyi teror i teroryzm v Ukraïni XIX–XX stolittia. Istorychni narysy*. Kyiv: Naukova dumka, 2002.

———, ed. *Ukraïnizatsiia 1920–30-kh rokiv: Peredumovy, zdobutky, uroky*. Kyiv: Instytut istoriï Ukraïny NAN Ukraïny, 2003.

Snyder, Timothy. *Bloodlands: Europe between Hitler and Stalin*. New York: Basic Books, 2010.

———. "A Fascist Hero in Democratic Kiev." *New York Review of Books*, 24 February 2010.

Soldatenko, V. F. *Nezlamnyi: Zhyttia i smert′ Mykoly Skrypnyka*. Kyiv: Knyha pam′iati Ukraïny, 2002.

Solomon, Peter. *Soviet Criminal Justice under Stalin*. Cambridge: Cambridge University Press, 1996.

Sorokin, A., A. Kobak, and O. Kuvaldina, eds. *Istoriia stalinizma: Zhizn′ v terrore. Sotsial′nye aspekty repressii*. Moscow: Rosspen, 2013.

Stalin, Iosif V [Joseph]. "Ob uklonakh k natsionalizmu." In *Marksism i natsial′no-kolonial′nyi vopros*, 199–200. Moscow: Partizdat TsK VKP(b), 1937.

———. "Pis′mo V. I. Leninu 22 sentiabria 1922 g." *Izvestiia TsK KPSS*, no. 9 (1989): 198–200.

———. "Tov. Kaganovichu i drugim chlenam PB TsK KP(b)U." In *Sochineniia*, by Iosif V. Stalin, 8:149–54. Moscow: Gosudarstvennoe izdatel′stvo politicheskoi literatury, 1948.

———. *Works*. Vol. 8. Moscow: Foreign Languages, 1954.

———. "Za russkii narod." Toast given on 24 May 1945. *Pravda*, 25 May 1945.

Statiev, Alexander. *The Soviet Counterinsurgency in the Western Borderlands*. Cambridge: Cambridge University Press, 2010.

———. "The Strategy of the Organisation of Ukrainian Nationalists in Its Quest for a Sovereign State, 1939–1950." *Journal of Strategic Studies* 43, no. 3 (2020): 443–71.

Storinky istoriï Kompartiï Ukraïny: Zapytannia i vidpovidi. Kyiv: Lybid′, 1990.

Sudoplatov, Pavel. *Razvedka i Kreml′: Zapiski nezhelatel′nogo svidetelia*. Moscow: TOO Geia, 1996.

———. *Spetsoperatsii: Lubianka i Kreml′ 1930–1950 gody*. Moscow: Olma-Press, 1997.

Suny, Ronald Grigor. *The Revenge of the Past: Nationalism, Revolution, and the Collapse of the Soviet Union*. Stanford, Calif.: Stanford University Press, 1993.

Suny, Ronald Grigor, and Terry Martin, eds. *A State of Nations: Empire and Nation-Making in the Age of Lenin and Stalin*. New York: Oxford University Press, 2002.

X z'ïzd KP(b)U. 20–29 lystopada 1927 r. Stenohraf[ichnyi] zvit. Kharkiv: Partiine vidavnytstvo TsK KP(b)U, 1928.

Tepliakov, A. G. "Organy NKVD Zapadnoi Sibiri v 'kulatskoi operatsii.'" In *Stalinizm v sovetskoi provintsii: 1937–1938 gg., Massovaia operatsiia na osnove prikaza no. 00447*, edited by M. Iunge, B. Bonvech, and R. Binner. Moscow: Rosspen, 2009, 536–71.

———. "Portrety sibirskikh chekistov." *Vozvrashchenie Pamiati: Istoriko-arkhivnyi al′manakh*, 1997, no. 3: 68–113.

Trymbach, Serhii. *Oleksandr Dovzhenko: Zahibel′ bohiv*. Vinnytsia: Hlobus-pres, 2007.

Ukraïna: Statystychnyi shchorichnyk na 1928. Kharkiv: Tsentral′ne statystychne upravlinnia USRR, 1928.

Ukraïns′ka tsentral′na rada: Dokumenty i materialy. Vol. 2. Kyiv: Naukova dumka, 1997.

"U Kyievi: Zasidannia Tsentral′noho vykonavchoho komitetu." *Borot′ba*, 7 August 1919.

Ushkalov, Oleksandr, and Leonid Ushkalov, eds. *Arkhiv rozstrilianoho vidrodzhennia: Materialy arkhivno-slidchikh sprav ukraïns′kykh pys′mennykiv 1920–1930-kh rokiv*. Kyiv: Smoloskyp, 2010.

Vasyl′iev, Valerii. *Politychne kerivnytstvo URSR i SRSR: Dynamika vidnosyn tsentr-subtsentr vlady (1917–1938)*. Kyiv: Instytut istoriï Ukraïny NAN Ukraïny, 2014.

Vasiuta, I. B. *Politychna istoriia Zakhidnoï Ukraïny (1918–1939)*. L′viv: Kameniar, 2006.

Vatlin, A. Iu. "Soprotivlenie na etape sledstviia: Po materialam 'nemetskikh del' Moskovskogo upravleniia NKVD 1937–1938 gg." In *Istoriia stalinizma: Zhizn′*

v terrore; Sotsial'nye aspekty repressii, edited by A. Sorokin, A. Kobak, and O. Kuvaldina, 411–17. Moscow: Rosspen, 2013.

"V bahni natsionalizmu." *Bil'shovyk Ukraïny*, no. 4 (1928): 3–11.

Vermenych, Ia. V. "Diial'nist' O. Ia. Shums'koho po zdiisnenniu polityky ukraïnizatsiï." *Istoriia Ukraïny: Malovidomi imena, podiï, fakty*, no. 2 (1997): 89–103.

Verstiuk, V., and T. Ostashko. *Diiachi Ukraïns'koï Tsentral'noï Rady: Biohrafichnyi dovidnyk*. Kyiv: Natsional'na Akademiia Nauk Ukraïny, 1998.

———. "Shums'kyi Oleksandr Iakovych." In *Ukraïns'ka pedahohika v personaliiakh*, edited by O. V. Sukhomlins'ka, 2:58–63. Kyiv: Lybid', 2005.

Viola, Lynne. "New Sources on Soviet Perpetrators of Mass Repression: A Research Note." *Canadian Slavonic Papers* 60, no. 3–4 (2018): 592–604.

———. *Peasant Rebels under Stalin: Collectivization and the Culture of Peasant Resistance*. New York: Oxford University Press, 1996.

———. *Stalinist Perpetrators on Trial: Scenes from the Great Terror in Soviet Ukraine*. Oxford: Oxford University Press, 2017.

"V kolehiï komisariatu Osvity." *Borot'ba*, 3 August 1919.

Vlasenko, Svitlana I. "Lysty Oleksandra Shums'koho iz zaslannia (iz fondiv TsDAHO Ukraïny)." *Publikatsiia arkhivnykh dokumentiv*, 2011, 165–78.

Volin, M. *Istoriia KP(b)U v styslomu narysi*. Kharkiv: Proletar, 1932.

Wheatcroft, Stephen G. "Agency and Terror: Evdokimov and Mass Killing in Stalin's Great Terror." *Australian Journal of Politics and History* 53, no. 1 (2007): 20–43.

———. "The Great Terror in Historical Perspective: The Records of the Statistical Department of the Investigative Organs of the OGPU/NKVD." In *The Anatomy of Terror: Political Violence under Stalin*, edited by James Harris, 287–305. Oxford: Oxford University Press, 2013.

Zaitsev, Oleksandr. *Ukraïns'kyi intehral'nyi natsionalizm (1920–1930-ti roky): Narysy intelektual'noï istoriï*. Kyiv: Krytyka, 2013.

Zberovskaia, E. L. "Spetsposelentsy iz Zapadnoi Ukrainy v Krasnoiarskom krae (1945 g.–nachalo 1960-kh gg.): Protsess sotsiokul'turnoi adaptatsii." *Vestnik KrasGAU*, 2014, no. 5: 250–54.

"Zmazaly." *Proletars'ka borot'ba* (Zhytomyr), 11 November 1919.

Zubkova, Elena. *Russia after the War: Hopes, Illusions, and Disappointments, 1945–1957*. Translated by Hugh Ragsdale. Armonk, N.Y.: M. E. Sharpe, 1998.

INDEX

Harvard Series in Ukrainian Studies

Recently Published

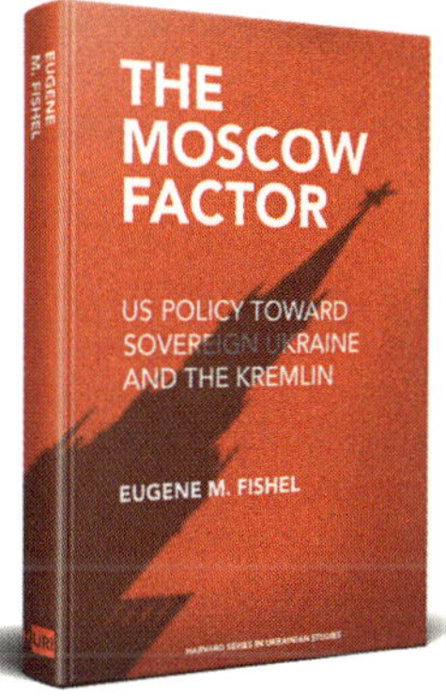

The Moscow Factor: US Policy toward Sovereign Ukraine and the Kremlin

Eugene M. Fishel

This unique study that examines four key Ukraine-related policy decisions across two Republican and two Democratic U.S. administrations. Fishel asks whether, how, and under what circumstances Washington has considered Ukraine's status as a sovereign nation in its decision-making regarding relations with Moscow.

2022 | 324 pp., 2 figs.

ISBN 9780674279179 (hardcover) | $59.95
9780674279186 (paperback) | $29.95
9780674279421 (epub)
9780674279193 (PDF)

Harvard Series in Ukrainian Studies, vol. 82

Read the book online

The Frontline: Essays on Ukraine's Past and Present

Serhii Plokhy

The Frontline presents a selection of essays drawn together for the first time to form a companion volume to Serhii Plokhy's *The Gates of Europe* and *Chernobyl*. Here he expands upon his analysis in earlier works of key events in Ukrainian history.

2021 (HC) / 2023 (PB) | 416 pp. / 420 pp.

10 color photos, 9 color maps

ISBN 9780674268821 (hardcover) | $64.00
9780674268838 (paperback) | $19.95
9780674268845 (epub)
9780674268852 (PDF)

Harvard Series in Ukrainian Studies, vol. 81

Read the book online

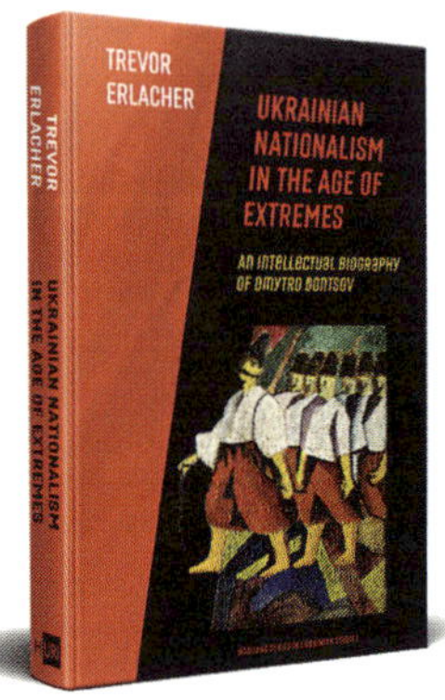

Ukrainian Nationalism in the Age of Extremes: An Intellectual Biography of Dmytro Dontsov

Trevor Erlacher

Ukrainian nationalism made worldwide news after the Euromaidan revolution and the outbreak of the Russo-Ukrainian war in 2014. Invoked by regional actors and international commentators, the "integral" Ukrainian nationalism of the 1930s has moved to the center of debates about Eastern Europe, but the history of this divisive ideology remains poorly understood.

2021 | 658 pp., 34 photos, 5 illustr.

ISBN 9780674250932 (hardcover) | $84.00

9780674250949 (epub)

9780674250956 (Kindle)

9780674250963 (PDF)

Read all chapters online

Harvard Series in Ukrainian Studies, vol. 80

Survival as Victory: Ukrainian Women in the Gulag

Oksana Kis

Translated by Lidia Wolanskyj

Hundreds of thousands of Ukrainian women were sentenced to the GULAG in the 1940s and 1950s. Only about half of them survived. With this book, Oksana Kis has produced the first anthropological study of daily life in the Soviet forced labor camps as experienced by Ukrainian women prisoners.

Based on the written memoirs, autobiographies, and oral histories of over 150 survivors, this book fills a lacuna in the scholarship regarding Ukrainian experience.

2020 | 652 pp., 78 color photos, 10 b/w photos

ISBN 9780674258280 (hardcover) | $94.00

9780674258327 (epub)

9780674258334 (Kindle)

9780674258341 (PDF)

Read all chapters online

Harvard Series in Ukrainian Studies, vol. 79

Harvard Series in Ukrainian Studies
Forthcoming Titles

Omeljan Pritsak and the Intellectual Origins of the Ukrainian "Harvard Miracle"

Andrii Portnov

This is the first English-language intellectual biography of Omeljan Pritsak, the co-founder of the Harvard Ukrainian Research Institute (HURI) and the first professor of Ukrainian history at Harvard. Andrii Portnov places Pritsak's life and legacy in the context of Ukrainian and world historiography and illuminates the development of his scholarly interests from their emergence in interwar Poland, through the Sovietization of Western Ukraine and the perturbations of World War II, to German Oriental Studies in the 1940s and 1950s, North American Slavic studies, and to the international studies of the origins of Rus´.

Breaking the Bonds of Corruption: From Academic Dishonesty to Corrupt Business Practices in post-Soviet Ukraine

Elena Denisova-Schmidt

This study makes an important contribution to the maturing study of informal practices in Ukraine and the region. Elena Denisova-Schmidt takes a broad view of corruption and its prevalence in societies globally and uses the case of Ukraine for examining the practices that are considered corrupt in their historical, social, and economic perspective. The author considers corrupt behavior in higher education internationally and in Ukraine, and examines the reliance on acts of corruption while doing business in Ukraine.

Find out more about these titles at https://books.huri.harvard.edu

The Eye of the Mind: Vision, Memory, and Meditation in Seventeenth-Century Ukrainian Preaching

Maria Grazia Bartolini

This study explores the role of vision, memory, and meditation in the sermons produced in Ukraine during the second half of the seventeenth century. It argues that the cognitive importance that vision and memory enjoyed in medieval and early modern culture informed their centrality in these sermons. *The Eye of the Mind* demonstrates how preachers used verbal and visual images to encourage the meditative re-creation of biblical events in the minds of their audiences. An investigation of the mental furniture of early modern Ukrainian preachers and their audiences, this book recovers a fascinating tradition that merged word and image to build "multimedia machines" for the spiritual elevation of the faithful.

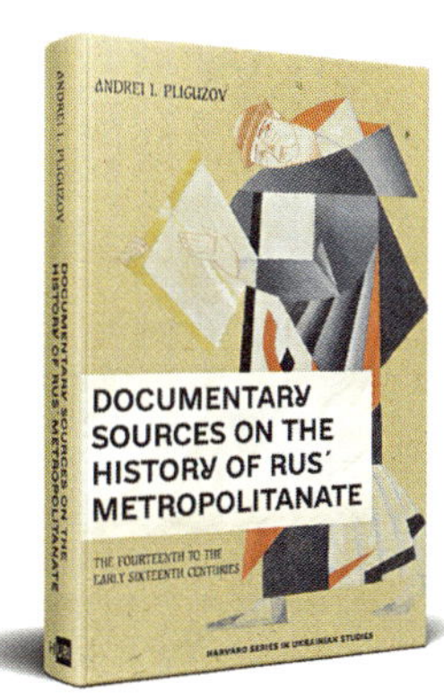

Documentary Sources on the History of Rus´ Metropolitanate: The Fourteenth to the Early Sixteenth Centuries

Andrei I. Pliguzov

This work is an extensive collection of letters and documents relating to the late medieval Orthodox Church, edited and curated by the renowned medievalist Andrei Pliguzov. *Documentary Sources on the History of Rus´ Metropolitanate* is a rich resource for any reader interested in the controversies and preoccupations of the Orthodox hierarchy and the clergy throughout the Rus´ metropolitanate up to the early modern period. For the first time, the volume includes acts, edicts and decrees regarding the lands in the metropolitanate's jurisdiction, reports prepared for the metropolitans by their secretariat, and the letters of the hierarchs themselves

Find out more about these titles at https://books.huri.harvard.edu

Harvard Library of Ukrainian Literature
Recently Published

Forest Song: A Fairy Play in Three Acts

Lesia Ukrainka (Larysa Kosach)

Translated by Virlana Tkacz and Wanda Phipps
Introduced by George G. Grabowicz

This play represents the crowning achievement of Lesia Ukrainka's (Larysa Kosach's) mature period and is a uniquely powerful poetic text. Here, the author presents a symbolist meditation on the interaction of mankind and nature set in a world of primal forces and pure feelings as seen through childhood memories and the re-creation of local Volhynian folklore.

2025 | appr. 240 pp.

ISBN 9780674291874 (cloth)	$29.95
9780674291881 (paperback)	$19.95
9780674291898 (epub)	
9780674291904 (PDF)	

Harvard Library of Ukrainian Literature, vol. 15

Read the book online

Love Life: A Novel

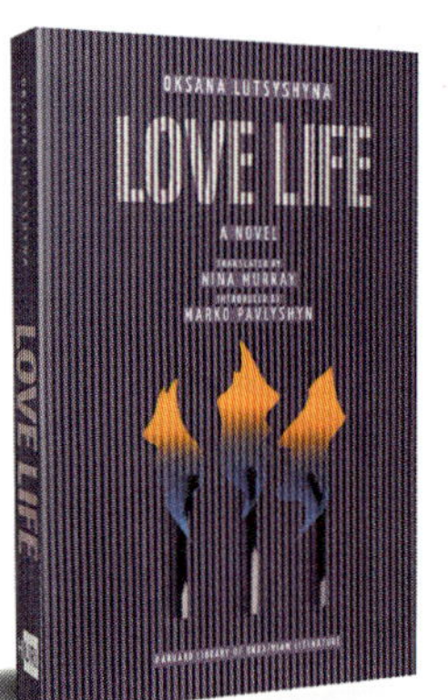

Oksana Lutsyshyna

Translated by Nina Murray
Introduced by Marko Pavlyshyn

The second novel of the award-winning Ukrainian writer and poet Oksana Lutsyshyna writes the story of Yora, an immigrant to the United States from Ukraine. A delicate soul that's finely attuned to the nuances of human relations, Yora becomes enmeshed in a relationship with Sebastian, a seductive acquaintance who seems to be suggesting that they share a deep bond. After a period of despair and complex grief that follows the end of the relationship, Yora is able to emerge stronger, in part thanks to the support from a friendly neighbor who has adapted well to life on the margins of society.

2024 | 276 pp.

ISBN 9780674297159 (cloth)	$39.95
9780674297166 (paperback)	$19.95
9780674297173 (epub)	
9780674297180 (PDF)	

Harvard Library of Ukrainian Literature, vol. 12

Read the book online

Cecil the Lion Had to Die: A Novel

Olena Stiazhkina

Translated by Dominique Hoffman

This novel follows the fate of four families as the world around them undergoes radical transformations when the Soviet Union unexpectedly implodes, independent Ukraine emerges, and neoimperial Russia begins its war by occupying Ukraine's Crimea and parts of the Donbas. A tour de force of stylistic registers and intertwining stories, ironic voices and sincere discoveries, this novel is a must-read for those who seek to deeper understand Ukrainians from the Donbas, and how history and local identity have shaped the current war with Russia.

2024 | 248 pp.

ISBN 9780674291645 (cloth) | $39.95
9780674291669 (paperback) | $19.95
9780674291676 (epub)
9780674291683 (PDF)

Harvard Library of Ukrainian Literature, vol. 11

Read the book online

Earth Gods: Writings from before the War

Taras Prokhasko

Translated by Ali Kinsella, Mark Andryczyk and Uilleam Blacker
Introduced by Mark Andryczyk

This book presents Taras Prokhasko's early writings: genre-bending *Anna's Other Days*, the collection of reflections *FM Galicia*, and *The UnSimple*, an iconoclastic novel that offers an alternative history of the Ukrainian Carpathian mountains of the first half of the twentieth century. Collected here for the first time in one volume, these stylistically and conceptually virtuosic texts testify to the richness of contemporary Ukrainian literature.

2025 | appr. 400 pp.

ISBN 9780674291164 (hardcover) | $39.95
9780674291171 (paperback) | $19.95
9780674291188 (epub)
9780674291195 (PDF)

Harvard Library of Ukrainian Literature, vol. 10

Read the book online

A Harvest Truce: A Play

Serhiy Zhadan

Translated by Nina Murray

Brothers Anton and Tolik reunite at their family home to bury their recently deceased mother. An otherwise natural ritual unfolds under extraordinary circumstances: their house is on the front line of a war ignited by Russian-backed separatists in eastern Ukraine.

Spring 2023

ISBN 9780674291997 (hardcover)	$29.95
9780674292017 (paperback)	$19.95
9780674292024 (epub)	
9780674292031 (PDF)	

Harvard Library of Ukrainian Literature, vol. 9

Read the book online

Cassandra: A Dramatic Poem,

Lesia Ukrainka (Larysa Kosach)

Translated by Nina Murray, introduction by Marko Pavlyshyn

The classic myth of Cassandra turns into much more in Lesia Ukrainka's rendering: Cassandra's prophecies are uttered in highly poetic language—fitting to the genre of the dramatic poem that Ukrainka crafts for this work—and are not believed for that very reason, rather than because of Apollo's curse. Cassandra's being a poet and a woman are therefore the two focal points of the drama.

2024 | 263 pp, bilingual ed. (Ukrainian, English)

ISBN 9780674291775 (hardcover)	$29.95
9780674291782 (paperback)	$19.95
9780674291799 (epub)	
9780674291805 (PDF)	

Harvard Library of Ukrainian Literature, vol. 8

Read the book online

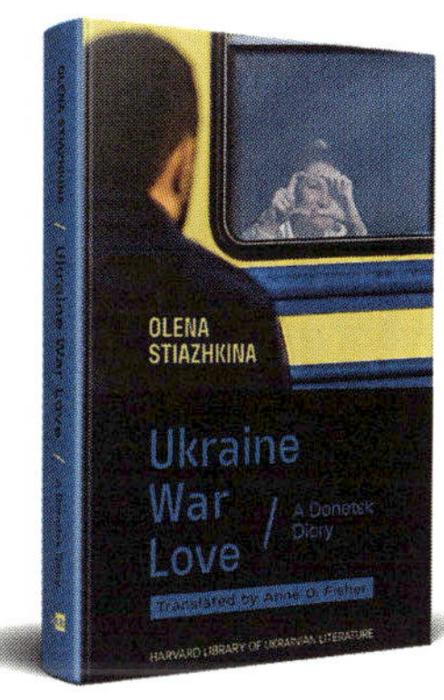

Ukraine, War, Love: A Donetsk Diary

Olena Stiazhkina

Translated by Anne O. Fisher

In this war-time diary, Olena Stiazhkina depicts day-to-day developments in and around her beloved hometown during Russia's 2014 invasion and occupation of the Ukrainian city of Donetsk.

Summer 2023

ISBN 9780674291690 (hardcover)	$39.95
9780674291706 (paperback)	$19.95
9780674291713 (epub)	
9780674291768 (PDF)	

Harvard Library of Ukrainian Literature, vol. 7

Read the book online

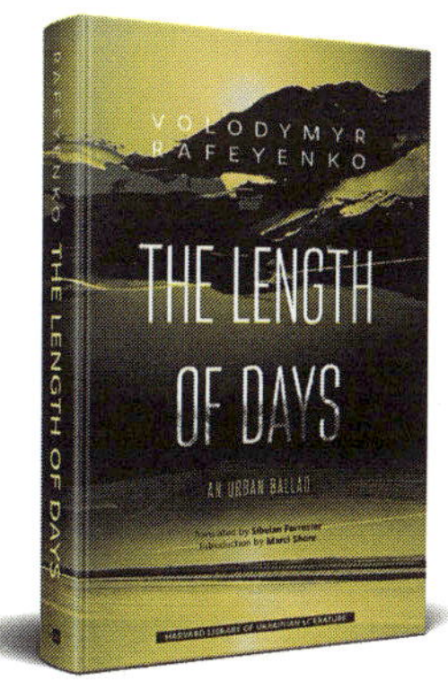

The Length of Days: An Urban Ballad

Volodymyr Rafeyenko

Translated by Sibelan Forrester
Afterword and interview with the author by Marci Shore

This novel is set mostly in the composite Donbas city of Z—an uncanny foretelling of what this letter has come to symbolize since February 24, 2022, when Russia launched a full-scale invasion of Ukraine. Several embedded narratives attributed to an alcoholic chemist-turned-massage therapist give insight into the funny, ironic, or tragic lives of people who remained in the occupied Donbas after Russia's initial aggression in 2014.

2023 | 349 pp.

ISBN 780674291201 (cloth)	$39.95
9780674291218 (paper)	$19.95
9780674291225 (epub)	
9780674291232 (PDF)	

Harvard Library of Ukrainian Literature, vol. 6

Read the book online

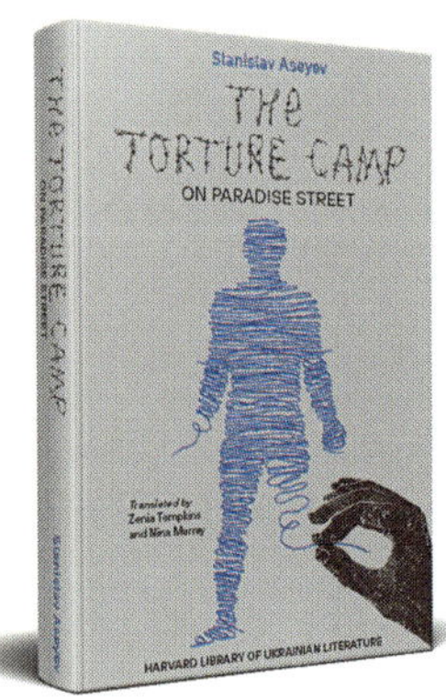

The Torture Camp on Paradise Street

Stanislav Aseyev

Translated by Zenia Tompkins and Nina Murray

Ukrainian journalist and writer Stanislav Aseyev details his experience as a prisoner from 2015 to 2017 in a modern-day concentration camp overseen by the Federal Security Bureau of the Russian Federation (FSB) in the Russian-controlled city of Donetsk. This memoir recounts an endless ordeal of psychological and physical abuse, including torture and rape, inflicted upon the author and his fellow inmates over the course of nearly three years of illegal incarceration spent largely in the prison called Izoliatsiia (Isolation).

2023 | 300 pp., 1 map, 18 ill.

ISBN 9780674291072 (cloth)	$39.95
9780674291089 (paper)	$19.95
9780674291102 (epub)	
9780674291096 (PDF)	

Harvard Library of Ukrainian Literature, vol. 5

Read the book online

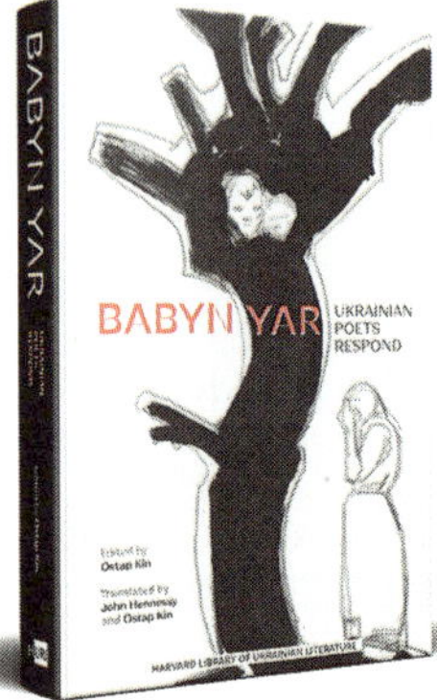

Babyn Yar: Ukrainian Poets Respond

Edited with introduction by Ostap Kin

Translated by John Hennessy and Ostap Kin

In 2021, the world commemorated the 80th anniversary of the massacres of Jews at Babyn Yar. The present collection brings together for the first time the responses to the tragic events of September 1941 by Ukrainian Jewish and non-Jewish poets of the Soviet and post-Soviet periods, presented here in the original and in English translation by Ostap Kin and John Hennessy.

2022 | 282 pp.

ISBN 9780674275591 (hardcover)	$39.95
9780674271692 (paperback)	$16.00
9780674271722 (epub)	
9780674271739 (PDF)	

Harvard Library of Ukrainian Literature, vol. 4

Read the book online

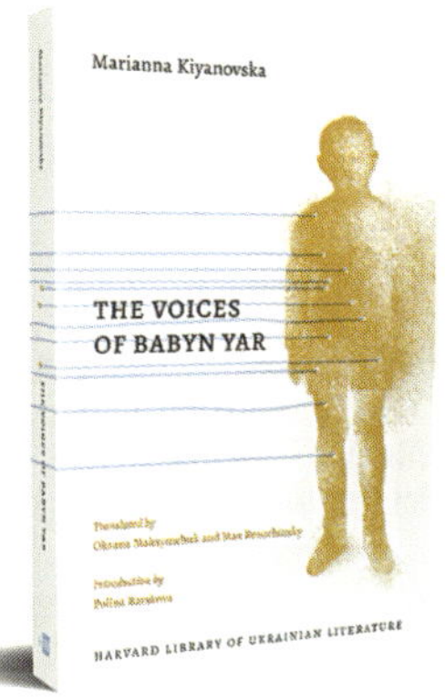

The Voices of Babyn Yar

Marianna Kiyanovska

Translated by Oksana Maksymchuk and Max Rosochinsky
Introduced by Polina Barskova

With this collection of stirring poems, the award-winning Ukrainian poet honors the victims of the Holocaust by writing their stories of horror, death, and survival in their own imagined voices.

2022 | 192 pp.

ISBN 9780674268760 (hardcover)	$39.95
9780674268869 (paperback)	$16.00
9780674268876 (epub)	
9780674268883 (PDF)	

Harvard Library of Ukrainian Literature, vol. 3

Read the book online

Mondegreen: Songs about Death and Love

Volodymyr Rafeyenko

Translated and introduced by Mark Andryczyk

Volodymyr Rafeyenko's novel Mondegreen: Songs about Death and Love explores the ways that memory and language construct our identity, and how we hold on to it no matter what. The novel tells the story of Haba Habinsky, a refugee from Ukraine's Donbas region, who has escaped to the capital city of Kyiv at the onset of the Ukrainian-Russian war.

2022 | 204 pp.

ISBN 9780674275577 (hardcover)	$39.95
9780674271708 (paperback)	$19.95
9780674271746 (epub)	
9780674271760 (PDF)	

Harvard Library of Ukrainian Literature, vol. 2

Read the book online

In Isolation: Dispatches from Occupied Donbas

Stanislav Aseyev

Translated by Lidia Wolanskyj

In this exceptional collection of dispatches from occupied Donbas, writer and journalist Stanislav Aseyev details the internal and external changes observed in the cities of Makiïvka and Donetsk in eastern Ukraine.

2022 | 320 pp., 42 photos, 2 maps

ISBN 9780674268784 (hardcover)	$39.95
9780674268791 (paperback)	$19.95
9780674268814 (epub)	
9780674268807 (PDF)	

Harvard Library of Ukrainian Literature, vol. 1

Read the book online